THE MANSON WOMEN

Also by Clara Livsey

THE MARRIAGE MAINTENANCE MANUAL

THE

MANSON

WOMEN

A "Family" Portrait

Clara Livsey, M.D.

Richard Marek Publishers
New York

Grateful acknowledgment is made for permission to use the following copyrighted material:

From *Sisters in Crime* by Freda Adler. Copyright © 1975 by McGraw-Hill Book Company. Used with permission.

From *Child of Satan, Child of God* by Susan Atkins with Bob Slosser. Copyright © 1977 by Logos International, Plainfield, N.J. Used by permission.

From *Helter Skelter* by Bugliosi/Gentry. Copyright © 1974 by W.W. Norton & Company, Inc. Used with permission.

From *The Criminality of Women* by Otto Pollak. Copyright © 1950 by Otto Pollak. University of Pennsylvania Press. Used by permission of the author.

From letter to Manson's mother by Paul J. Fitzgerald, January 27, 1971. Used by permission of Paul J. Fitzgerald.

Library of Congress Cataloging in Publication Data

Livsey, Clara G
    The Manson Women.

    1. Crime and criminals—California—Case studies.
2. Female offenders—California—Case studies. 3. Murder—California—Case studies. 4. Manson, Charles, 1934–   I. Title.
HV6245.L64   364.1'523'0926   79-26454
ISBN 0-399-90073-X

Printed in the United States of America

To California where some of the worst things in the world happen.
And some of the best.

Acknowledgments

Thanks are due to many people who helped me with this project. To those I can't name here, I want to express my gratitude. I am happy to be able to acknowledge the following by name: The California Department of Corrections, Sacramento. Kathleen Anderson, superintendent of the California Institution for Women, and Robert Borg, associate superintendent. Thomas L. Clanon, M.D., superintendent of the California Medical Facility, and Ed George, staff member at that institution. Carson Markley, former warden of the Federal Correctional Institution at Alderson, W. Va. Warden Charles Turnbo, head of the Federal Correctional Institution for Women at Pleasanton, California. The staff of the Criminal Court Building and the Public Defender's Office of the City of Los Angeles. The staff of the Court of Appeals of the City of Los Angeles, especially Velina Carey. And to Howard J. Schwab, deputy attorney general, for forwarding to me the briefs he wrote (October terms, 1976 and 1977) that were of great help to me. Much of the data referring to my subject's appeals are based on Mr. Schwab's briefs. The staff of the U.S. Eastern District Court of California in Sacramento, and especially Chief U.S. Probation Officer John F. Douville. Jonas R. Rappaport, M.D., chief medical officer, Supreme Bench of Baltimore. Roland Walker, Esq., of Baltimore. Hazen Kniffin, M.D., from the Baltimore Psychoanalytic Institute. Theo Wilson, Los Angeles Bureau Chief of the New York *Daily News*. Seymour Pollack, M.A., M.D., director of the University of Southern California Institute of Psychiatry, Law and Behavioral Science. I am indebted to Dr. Pollack not only for giving me his time but for the volumes he prepared for teaching forensic psychiatrists and lawyers. These volumes, particularly *Forensic Psychiatry in Criminal Law* and *The Defense of Diminished Capacity,* were of great help to me as consultation sources. Pauline and Gregorio Roth who helped and supported me greatly during my stays in Northern California. My husband, Benjamin, and my two teen-age children, Sophie and Alan, who provided me with love and continuous support and who kept our home in shipshape form, thus making it possible for me to concentrate totally on my work.

Contents

Preface

The so-called Manson Family was formed at the end of 1967. When those responsible for the Tate-LaBianca murders were arrested on December 1, 1967, the mansonites—a term I coined for practical purposes to refer to the members of the commune—reiterated that their Family was still alive. And it seemed to be, at least while the culprits were being tried, first for the murder of musician Gary Hinman, then for the Tate-LaBianca murders—a trial that lasted more than nine months—and finally for the murder of Donald Shea. After that the Family probably ceased to be a reality but it continues to be newsworthy to this day. Interest in the group peaked in September of 1975 when Lynette Fromme attempted to assassinate President Gerald Ford.

Reports of the number of people who lived in this commune are at variance—anywhere from twenty to forty at any one time—because not all the people who stayed with the group were bona-fide members. Transient youths stayed for a few days, ex-cons known to the members would visit off and on, cyclers would be around living on the periphery for a while; other people were semiattached to the group without ever actually belonging to it. Some of the mansonites committed crimes and some did not.

The protagonists of this book however were all permanent members of the Family; they had a strong emotional investment in the group which they regarded as their family; all of them have been convicted of crimes identified as being Family "affairs." They are: Susan Atkins (Sadie), Patricia Krenwinkel (Kate), Leslie Van Houten, Charles Watson (Tex), Lynette Fromme (Squeaky), Sandra Good, and, of course, Charles Manson.

Other people are cited in this book. Some of them were also permanent members such as Mary Brunner who was the first to join Manson and who participated in the Hinman murder and in a robbery attempt to steal firearms that were to be used to free Manson from prison; Catherine Share (Gypsy) who also planned and was among those who participated in that attempted burglary. These two women were central figures of the group. Their lives are not discussed in detail in this book because it was not possible for me to obtain information about them beyond what is public knowledge. Both were paroled years ago.

Other names are cited in this book, names of people who participated in some of the murders or who testified in court. Some of them were permanent members of the group, some were not: Robert Beausoleil, indicted for the Hinman murder, was a musician and aspiring actor who traveled around California usually in the company of two or more women and frequently kept in touch with the Family; Bruce Davis, indicted for his part in the Hinman and Shea murders, who was considered a member of the commune although he seemed to have spent more time away from than living with the mansonites; Juan Flynn, a Panamanian Vietnam veteran who usually lived on the same premises but made it clear to Manson that he was not a member of his group; Paul Watkins, at one time Manson's right hand; Brooks Poston, who lived with the group for several months (of all the members he is the only one who seemed to have been quite unhappy at that time, because of personal problems); Paul Crockett, a prospector, and like Manson a student of Scientology, who is credited by Poston and Watkins with "rescuing" them from Manson's influence; Barbara Hoyt who testified for the prosecution in 1970 after she went through a harrowing experience: lured to Honolulu by female mansonites and fed a hamburger laced with

12

LSD to prevent her from testifying (they left her tripping on the street, alone); Ruth Moorehouse (Ouisch) who, like Diane Lake whose testimony was of great value to the prosecutors, was a minor when she joined the group. Her father, Dean Moorehouse, encountered the psychedelic world—and Manson—through his daughter and himself became devoted to the LSD culture; Linda Kasabian who joined the Family about two months before the Tate-LaBianca murders and was a coconspirator in the murders but was given immunity and became the star witness for the prosecution.

I

The Beginning

On the nights of August 9 and 10 of 1969, a group of murderers—one man, Charles "Tex" Watson, and three women, Patricia Krenwinkel, Susan Atkins, and Leslie Van Houten—acting under the erratic supervision of their leader, Charles Manson, brutally killed seven people they had never met. Their mass murders would be known by the entire world as the Tate-LaBianca murders.

On the morning of September 5, 1975, Lynette Fromme, her red cape covering the hand that held her weapon, attempted to assassinate the President of the United States, Gerald R. Ford. Around that same time her close friend, Sandra Collins Good, wrote such virulent letters to industry executives and their wives and made such violent verbal threats that she too was apprehended and then convicted on a federal charge.

All these people were members of a commune they called The Family and had lived together for about two years. Five members of this group have since been convicted for the Tate-LaBianca murders. Three of them are women. Another has the dubious honor of being the first woman ever to attempt to murder a president of the United States.

This book is about these women. It is about their lives and about the

17

motivations that drove them to their criminal behavior. It is about the "family" they chose to form. It is about how they came of age as sinister criminals, a far cry from the destiny envisioned for them by their parents and by society. Much has been written about the Tate-LaBianca murders and about Charles Manson. But this book, although in it I will discuss both, is essentially about the women of the infamous Manson case. I found their lives to be very instructive and I hope that others too can learn and reflect on what I have to say about them.

Charles Manson is regarded by the public to this day as the leader, the somber star of these tragic murders, while the women are perceived as a group in the background, a group that came forward just to follow his commands. I don't share this view.

It can't be denied that the words "leader" and "followers" apply to the mansonites. But in this book I will discuss the elusive quality of the relationship between this leader, Charles Manson, and his followers, his women, and what I perceived when, using my professional experience as a magnifying glass, I looked at these two words not as separate, but as together, defining a process:

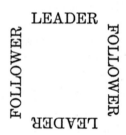

Manson has become a household word that denotes bizarre criminality. Charles Manson is cited as the worst example whenever mass murders are reported in the news and even when murder in general is discussed in print, on television, in films. When people remember young actress Sharon Tate and how she was violently stabbed to death, they don't think of Susan Atkins. They think of Charles Manson who was not even present at the scene of the crime. When people hear about Rosemary LaBianca and how she was stabbed forty-one times, they do not see the faces of Patricia Krenwinkel and

Leslie Van Houten. They see the well-known picture of Manson, his dark magnetic eyes glaring with anger.

Charles Manson is known as the Svengali who seduced naive flower children, all middle-class girls, and infused them with his rage against society, the result of his wretched life, a life spent in and out of prison. People have heard that these women gave up the moral values they grew up with to become Manson's "young loves," after he mesmerized them into submission with his seductive rhetoric and techniques geared at producing fear. I certainly heard that version of the story. Over and over again. And most of what I read researching this book has the same implication: These women committed acts of violence, no doubt about it, but it was Manson who made them act that way. But the more I thought about this, the more I found myself interested not in the leader, but in the followers, in these women whom I regard as being fully responsible for committing deliberate murder. Yet even though jurors who heard all the admissible evidence have found them guilty, I always felt the loneliness of my position because I noticed that most people with whom I talked were either soft on the women or vigorously sympathetic to them. I also sensed that some of the people who condemn them were reluctant to express their feelings openly. No one, I found out, had any reluctance to speak against Manson.

Authors who write about criminals tend to empathize with their subjects, probably because they come to learn what hardships these people went through and what problems motivated their criminal acts. Early in my project I noticed that I didn't feel compassion for the mansonites. There were times, however, when I felt upset by my attitude, about my shift. After all, for many years I have been on the side of the troubled. Now I found myself in the opposite corner. The writer who immerses himself in his subject embarks on a process of self-discovery and thus is likely to encounter aspects of himself that would otherwise lie dormant or be altogether unacceptable. My internal struggle to come to terms with my feelings and with my thinking were, I finally realized, entirely appropriate. I was not engaging in a meaningless debate but in the solitary brainstorming that must precede that thinking that ends up on the printed page as a personal commitment to one's subject. At a certain point I labeled

19

myself as self-righteous and consequently devoid of the objectivity needed to write this book. I am revealing here my internal battle in the matter of my feelings as to the culpability of the female mansonites in order to give a glimpse of how much on the defensive I was in the beginning, how biased, how difficult it was for me to accept that these women committed murder *of their own free will*. Only when I accepted my reactions and my perceptions as valid, as authentic, did I achieve the peace of mind to continue my project. It helped me to empathize with the victims (those killed and their families), to put myself in their place and in the place of those who cared for them.

I must add that I do understand how easily one may fall for the perception of these women as soldiers who acted out their orders. It is so easy to blame only the leader for the deeds of his followers! And so difficult especially to accept that young women can be fully responsible for committing brutal murders. No wonder that for a while a trial of sorts took place within me, counsel for the defense struggling with the prosecutor who was asking for the death penalty for my unborn production. But finally the defense won an acquittal if for no other reason than that in the process I had become hooked on the book to be.

My doubts, my ambivalent feelings, were a necessary part of the "incubation" period. To have mixed feelings about a project is an excellent way to start exploring it because one's doubts are one's devil's advocates.

Preparing this book has been a totally different experience from any I have ever had. I had written before—many papers, another book—but I had always been comfortably alone as I discussed and wrote about ideas born out of my professional experience as a family psychiatrist. For years I had entered other people's lives, but only at their request. Here I found myself involved with a group of people who had not asked me to touch their lives. I was involved with them and yet alone in my involvement; I listened to each of them but also heard voices that came from disparate sources. And unexpectedly these strangers, my subjects, turned out to be celebrated personages sought after by many because of their infamy. Soon enough I realized that those who supported them were eager and free to voice their

20

approval, but that conversely those who condemned them were either gagged by their position or by obeying the truism "If you have nothing good to say, say nothing."

As time went on my subjects ceased to be strangers to me. Talking to many people who knew them, getting to know how they lived (and live), meeting some of them and talking at length with others, all contributed to my familiarity and to my understanding. They started to remind me of others I had known personally and professionally.

Before the subject and the subjects of this book captivated my interest I was planning to write about parenting in our times, about what I had learned during more than twenty years of practicing and teaching family therapy, and particularly in the recent past, about the specific problems parents have to face in trying to help their children integrate rapidly changing social developments. Naturally I had been thinking about some of the issues I eventually turned to in this book, for example, how external circumstances affect the way in which parents raise their children and the way in which the young respond. In this respect, it is important to assess what is cause and effect and what other circumstances besides parental influence affect the development of children.

The culture in which we live, economics, politics, all influence the way in which families function and the way people think about how to raise their children. One need not be an historian to know that western society has undergone many changes in the way youth is perceived and in the way adults see their role as parents or guides to children. Plato in 400 B.C. advised teachers to train children not by compulsion but as if they were playing. Yet centuries later children were to be considered small-sized adults and when they failed to act as adults they were regarded as evil and subjected to cruel punishment. Today we have a more humane way to think about children because we have become interested in their psychological development. Unfortunately there is no way to assess how this interest has affected their mental health. Knowledge, especially that deriving from psychoanalytic theory, raised our hopes for a while that we would get more precise answers about important aspects of child rearing, but people differ in assessing the contributions of psychoanalysis in this regard. Some think that it has made a mark. Others, who recognize the contributions of psychoanalysis think, however, that it has not fulfilled its promise, it has not given us the guidelines about children's emotional development that are sorely needed. Others go one step further. Martin L. Gross, author of *The Psychological Society*, characterizes the influence of psychoanalysis as the psychological crime of the century, an extreme view that assumes that people act as passive recipients who can be manipulated by theories.

One thing is sure: We live in a time of contradictions in regard to child-rearing practices. Should children—and youth too—be better disciplined, more subject to rules? Or have the young of our times changed and should they be allowed more freedoms? Should adolescents, who are people in transition, receive a great deal of appropriate attention from their parents? Or should parents then be free to pursue their own interests? What impact has the two-job, two-career family had on children? Must one parent be home while the children are young? Or should we fight to get more child-care centers? Some of these questions became urgent during the sixties, for the first time. Is it any wonder then that during this period youth problems were blamed on the times?

My subjects were young women during the sixties. The mansonites lived and their crimes occurred in that decade. They were young people who chose to be part of a "family" that challenged all the notions that most people had, even at that time, of what a family should be. The mansonites created their own version of communal life by borrowing from the culture of that time all that was contrary to the models they had grown up with.

In actuality, the sixties provided an atmosphere of freedom to the young (how can we forget!), stimulated in them a wish to explore, to search for new experiences. And we all know the positive strides we made during that decade. Women dared. Blacks and their supporters marched. Young men refused to go to war and left the country. We also remember other things. Many of the young drastically rebelled against their parents and against any form of authority, challenging society's values. Because of their numbers the young became highly visible and strongly supportive of each other. All the forces that until then had acted as controls—parental authority, inhibitions, religion—ceased to be effective. Many adolescents became destructive. Stealing, destruction of property, use of illegal drugs—in other words, breaking the law—were glamorized. The raging, drugged utterances of Janis Joplin, to use just one example, were revered by many as art representing the youth culture, which it did. The young used drugs adults were not familiar with. They ran away in record numbers, secure in the knowledge that a juvenile society existed that would offer them shelter and companionship. Most of these children did not run away from severely adverse family situations; they didn't run *from*, they ran *towards*, searching for a dream world. They despised the material goods that their parents had lavished on them and opted for begging in the streets, for eating and wearing discards. For them being really poor was a novelty. There were no hippies from the ghettos. Not a girl from "the culture of poverty" ever became a Manson follower.

Eventually most of the young, after having had a taste of life in the "Counterculture," left it to go on with their lives. They found work or completed their education, reestablished family ties, accepted adult responsibilities, married. But others who to begin with had little motivation to mature stayed in. Their well-nurtured bodies had grown up (oh, how great it would be if people's bodies and emotions would grow at the same rate!) but their psyches had remained behind because they had found a life-style that accommodated them. The pursuit of thrills, or anomie as a *modus vivendi*, transient camaraderie with transients, drugs to mask fear or discomfort, all served to shape a make-believe world where the unfit could fit. Half-baked adults of all ages, led by the immature and the narcissistic, joined the chorus that proclaimed the emergence of a new era. It is not surprising that trend-setter Manson claimed only a child could lead his Family. Paul Crockett, a witness testifying for the defense during Leslie Van Houten's retrial in 1978, when asked, "Did Charlie ever tell you he was the leader of the Family?" replied, "Charlie never told me he was the leader of the Family. He told me that the youngest one in the group, which was Pooh Bear [Manson and Brunner's child] at that that . . . that the baby was the leader."

The baby was the leader. Seldom has a society been described so accurately in just one sentence.

23

Thus as I began my project, not unexpectedly I asked myself, were the mansonites just a product of the sixties? Were these women swept away into a life of crime by an alien from that other world they were searching for?

It is so tempting to blame most of the problems that affected the young during the sixties on the turbulence of the times, when chaos was readily available and so were drugs that gave an illusion of order and contentment to their users. Many see the female mansonites as casualties of an era that made them vulnerable to Manson's influence. But the extremes of the sixties affected people differently, according to their capacity to cope with its strain; in the very same circumstances some of the young made their choice to mature. Others didn't because they lacked the foundation—and the interest—on which to build a life of their own. Where the first had wrestled with adolescent turmoil during a difficult time, the latter's adolescence had been in body only.

We all know perennial children who see no advantage in attaining maturity, who would go to any extremes to avoid being responsible for themselves. We also know that women have been particularly vulnerable to an existence as eternal little girls. Have been or are? Nobody yet knows for sure how much things have changed in the way we raise our daughters. But no doubt about this: The female mansonites refused to grow up.

I said earlier that my subjects reminded me of others, less extreme in their pursuits, whom I had come in contact with. During the sixties many distressed parents consulted me because of problems with their teen-agers. They brought their youngsters to my office sometimes directly from a hospital emergency room where they had landed after misusing drugs or after a family crisis. They were also referred to me by schools, by juvenile courts, by pediatricians. Most of these youngsters had no interest in negotiating their differences with their parents or in changing their deviant behavior. Some of them were unhappy, others perfectly satisfied with a life that suited them: They wanted to drift, they saw no reason to continue in school, they loved to experiment with drugs. Some who understood their parents' position had no intention however to change theirs. They rejected the idea that there is a need for rules, limits, responsibilities. Some of

24

these youngsters were ambivalent about their new-found life while others were elated by the freedom they experienced once they totally rebelled against their parents. Among the latter were the thrill-seekers, always hungry for new experiences.

I vividly remember a fifteen-year-old girl brought to my office by her parents from a police station. These parents had been greatly worried about their daughter's recklessness and by the company she kept. This time they found out that she had stayed for a few days with a male acquaintance in his apartment. While there, she had witnessed this man killing another during a shoot-out following an argument. Her parents had sounded quite upset on the telephone, concerned about how the incident would affect their daughter. But in my office she looked ecstatic; her eyes shining with excitement, she related the experience to me in full detail, her tale punctuated by exclamations: "Oh boy, what a trip, I can't wait to tell my friends!"

Some of the families who consulted me had severe, long-standing problems that were aggravated by their youngster's behavior. In some cases the child's problems served to keep the parents together. Frequently only one child in the family was troubled, the one most caught in the parents' conflicts. Reasons could be found as to why a particular child was entangled with one or both parents. In some families, for example, this child had or was still having chronic health problems.

Besides their specific problems I observed that these families had a common trait: They were child-focused. These parents seemed obsessed with providing their children opportunities to make them "happy." Or else, and using the same rationale, they had a model of how a "normal" child should be, tried to make the child comply with it, and felt threatened when, as was to be expected, he didn't or couldn't. I also heard a great many complaints from parents who expected a lot from their children, stated in sentences such as, "She is so bright and *we* are doing everything *we* can so she would fulfill her potential. . . . We never had the chances she has . . ." Some of these parents were unhappy with their own lives; unfulfilled, they devoted themselves to their children or to one child.

These children and youngsters, naturally, had lived under the total control of one or both parents. Openly or covertly this parent

25

decided everything about his life and gave him no room to make any decisions on his own. But I don't want to imply that these children were just the recipients of their parents' misguided notions or of their conflicts. On the contrary, once the course was set these children fully participated in keeping the status quo. An overprotected youngster, for example, would usually act helplessly or immaturely and thus stimulate the parent to take over. Some of these youngsters had become charming manipulators; others were constantly angry and dissatisfied with their parents.

I observed much too frequently that the middle-class adolescents I was seeing had a common characteristic: *They were extremely infantile for their age.* The mansonites were immature and similar in other ways to other young people at that time and to many I had known. But how were they different?

For one thing everything about them was excessive; that is they were like others, only more so. This applied to the way in which they expressed their sexuality, the way in which they used drugs, their disdain for society and their submissiveness to the male, an attitude that was to impress people the most and which was misinterpreted, and still is, to mean that these women were sexually exploited.

These were women who wanted absolute freedom to act out their deviant yearnings, their hunger for continuous excitement or power or both. The Orwellian double-speak of Manson suited them well because it did accommodate their own double intent, to yield to their yearnings while at the same time thinking of themselves as superior because they did. These daredevil women had reason to feel much safer within their group than they would have if they wandered alone or with transient companions. They had the ability to assess their situation and consequently realized what the Family and Manson had to offer them.

Not surprisingly to me, these women's traits, their deviant behavior, became apparent during adolescence. I wondered, what happened in their lives as they entered adolescence? And in their families? Why did they join Manson? Why did he join them? As a family therapist, I must find out about the families of the Family.

I set my project in motion by writing to Charles Manson, thinking that he was the one person who surely knew a great deal about the women. As a result we corresponded for a while and then met.

In the summer of 1977 I took the first of many trips to California. I arrived in Los Angeles not knowing really what to expect. I had previously been in California but never in Los Angeles. My initiation into the western fun city took place in the heart of Hollywood, but only by mistake: I had booked a room in the wrong Hyatt! There I was surrounded not by fun-loving tourists or sedate business people but by rock music performers, as colorful in their language as in their attire.

Walking around the hotel I got a taste of the Hollywood scene: seedy shops on Hollywood Boulevard, boutiques that had exquisite merchandise on Sunset Boulevard, a car agency "devoted" to selling Pantheras, well-to-do entrepreneurs, young male and female prostitutes. I was, in fact, staying in the intermediate zone between those who had made it and those who never would.

My first visit, the very next day after my arrival, was to the Criminal Court Building where I was to spend so many hours in the future studying court transcripts. On that occasion I met some of the staff of the Public Defender's Office and had my first encounter with the openness and the friendly attitude that are so characteristic of the Angelenos. This is not to deny that I felt lost in Los Angeles, and confused. How many cities were there? And why didn't Los Angeles have any taxis other than in front of big hotels? I, who for many years had depended on my car for transportation, decided to manage with buses. In Los Angeles, with few exceptions, only the elderly, the poor natives, and the Mexicans travel by bus. I found myself enjoying my bus expeditions. For one thing I had a strong bond with many of my fellow travelers: the Spanish language. Already then I discovered the joys of conversation with strangers, Mexicans and Americans. I will always remember the elderly lady who stood up and passionately urged others to join her and go to City Hall to fight a proposal to increase bus fare; and the debate that followed. I also recall the sorrowful confidence of a woman—we had both been waiting for our bus in the wrong place. She had never made it as a singer but was still taking singing lessons and hoping against all odds. Her husband had left her long ago and she felt terribly alone, unable to make it with men. At the end when we got to the right bus and sat in separate seats we both, I am sure, had arrived at the conclusion that maybe she

27

preferred solitude and didn't want to make it with men; only with strange ladies from the other side of the United States who would sit apart and make no demands.

During that first trip, bent on experiencing my subject's present way of life, I visited the California Institution for Women where Susan Atkins, Patricia Krenwinkel, and Leslie Van Houten reside. At the time of my visit, however, Van Houten had been transferred to Sybil Brand, the women's detention center in Los Angeles, where she stayed during her first retrial. (She was free during her second retrial.)

I talked with Kathleen Anderson, a highly respected prison administrator whose career started at the institution she now directs. I talked mostly with Robert Borg, the associate superintendent, a veteran prison system official. I was to visit the facility two more times but I can't forget my first impressions: the lovely grounds, the rose garden, the beehive of activities, the posters in the entrance hall announcing courses and self-help meetings. I can still see a woman and a young child, both crying; they had just ended a few days' visit with one of the inmates. The institution has the practice of allowing visits of family members for two or three days in their so-called "love cottages." I wondered at the time whether it would be difficult for some of the residents to leave the institution and face the world outside. The recidivism is forty percent but Ms. Anderson does not consider this high in view of the severe problems and the life situation of many of the convicted women. The prison is rather isolated but one can see attempts to bring into it at least part of the world outside.

I informed Robert Borg that I was working on a book about the mansonites. We did not, however, talk specifically about my subjects because prison authorities are not allowed to discuss the inmates. But during this and other visits, I learned a great deal from him that was invaluable as background information. Mr. Borg gave me a lecture on the need for prison security from the point of view of the administration that I will not easily forget because it was so instructive; it helped me to understand some of the limitations the inmates must endure. It hadn't occurred to me, for example, that a typewriter can become a powerful weapon in the hands of an enraged person or that a tightly rolled dollar bill can be used to puncture a person's eyes.

28

As I heard him talking I detected that Mr. Borg's feelings towards female convicts are considerably warmer than towards males.

It was during this first "research" visit to California that I met Manson. My interview with him, which I will discuss in another chapter, was important to my project.

Meanwhile, all the time during my waking hours and even during my sleep the book was shaping up in my mind. And yet I continued to ask myself, why was I undertaking the writing of a book about violent people, focusing on the most unlikely violent people, women? I am not after all an expert on violent behavior; the majority of my patients have not been violent and I had not dealt with jail or prison populations. Yet the more I thought about it, the more I realized that I wasn't so inexperienced. As a child I had known violent people. I had at times lived in the midst of violence. That emotional atmosphere had posed questions in my child mind, questions that I filed away in the recesses of my mind to be reawakened at the proper time, now, when again I was to find myself living in a violent world.

I grew up in a small town in Argentina. When I was eleven we moved to the big city, Buenos Aires, which at the time was lively, cosmopolitan, and peaceful. By my late twenties I was already living in the United States at a time when I could still go for a walk alone after dark. The windows of my home didn't have any bars then.

I have seen the world, literally and figuratively, but thinking back I have to say that I learned all the basics of human nature, including our potential for violence by the time I was nine years old. My hometown was a microcosm of the world, and because of my curiosity about human beings life for me was like a play, with me sitting in the orchestra from which I watched the passions and the tribulations that unfolded before me. Since I was wise enough to keep my eyes and my ears open and my mouth shut, I learned much. In my family children were not expected to know many of the things adults knew. (I wonder why, since my relatives were not prone to hide any skeletons in the closet!)

As a child I led two lives. One was structured by the middle-class values and the Victorian conventions of my family. It called for restraint and a certain degree of pretense. The other was enmeshed in the world of the maids with whom the children were close. Theirs was a world of passionate loves and superstitious fears and hopes.

29

Unbeknownst to my parents I heard confessions of the tribulations of unrequited love and of hate and tales of adulterous affairs, of unspeakable relationships, of young mothers killing their newborn babies, of men killing to defend their honor. I was frightened, relieved, reassured, or mesmerized according to what I heard. And what I saw too because I actually witnessed shoot-outs. People in my hometown usually killed in a fit of passion. During the holidays, particularly during Carnival, our Mardi Gras, violence erupted, incensed by the heat of February, the drinking, the excitement. But I also remember political and other deliberate murders. I was, in fact, published for the first time at the age of eight; the local newspaper printed a poem I wrote in memory of my young piano teacher who had been accidentally killed during a political rally.

My father who himself was born and raised *tierra adentro*, in a small town in the provinces, was an expert in violence. He told stories he remembered from his childhood, stories reminiscent of the American wild west. He "explained" the murders to me and more important, the people who murdered. Towards them he had an understanding and rather patronizing attitude. According to him those who killed or assaulted others were people whose lives were usually run by their passions. They were, he thought, those who had grown up without moral restraints or guidelines, mostly the very poor, occasionally the well-to-do. The implication was that we, the "right," the responsible kind of people were definitely different; we did not kill. There weren't any conversations about death wishes on the fantasy level. Thinking back I believe that it was helpful to me, a child witnessing violence, to be told in no uncertain terms: "Understand those who kill but think of yourself as different from them." I was a spectator of that other world, but I didn't belong there. Violent behavior was presented to me by him as a handicap and violent people as those whom, no matter how benignly, one looked down upon.

Today a child learns of murder, rape, all kinds of destructive behavior mostly through the filtering television screen which has institutionalized violence and packaged it carefully to meet entertainment standards. In our times murderous behavior is explained with a sophistication that was unavailable to my father, although it cannot be denied that his basic understanding was correct. We are told that we all have a potential to commit murder—the unlawful killing of a human being—that the seeds of murderous behavior grow in the fertile soil of rage and intense frustration brought about by interpersonal conflicts or by severe deprivation caused by socioeconomic conditions or a combination of both and there is ongoing research on the organic causes of violent behavior as well. The criminal today is frequently portrayed as a victim, which he sometimes really is. Because of the violent times in which we are living there is a great deal of interest in knowing more about violent behavior, and today we do know more about people who kill than we used to. But we have a long way to go to fully understand, and more important, to use our understanding to prevent violence.

Under the pleasant and sometimes unpleasant surface of my family life lurked, I knew, the forbidden. The surfaces of a life are, however, as real as its deep layers. Surfaces do not mask reality but are part of it, like our skin that covers all the stormy dramas of the anatomy and the physiology of our bodies. As I think of my subjects, the Manson women, I often reflect about the surfaces of their emotional lives as they were growing up, about how rigidly fragile those surfaces must have been, how faultily integrated with what they covered. I wonder how many women have not become violent because their aggressive drives were repressed. If cultural conditions stimulate a lessening of inhibitions, would some women who hitherto repressed their aggressiveness become violent, as frequently violent as their male counterparts?

We don't yet know how to help the violent individual to channel his drives into constructive pursuits before he becomes destructive. But there is one thing we all know and agree about: We don't need more violent people.

When I started this book (only in my mind at first), I thought that the Manson case was dead. I knew, of course, that it would remain in the annals of crime because of its bizarre nature, because of Manson's own impact, and because of the fame and wealth of the victims. Only after my first trip to Los Angeles did I learn that Leslie Van Houten was being tried again. Perhaps her retrial resuscitated the case, but I suspect that I had been wrong or naive in thinking that the Manson

31

tragedy was now past, an almost forgotten affair. To be sure, Prosecutor Vincent Bugliosi and a reporter, Ed Sanders, had written best sellers about the case; but I thought of these books (then) as paperbacks that people would pick up to read while waiting for a plane or on a rainy Sunday afternoon.

I soon realized, however, that the case was still alive in part because *these criminals' actions are not yet fully understood.* The recent concern about cults and their leaders has brought the name of Manson again into the news. Women's violent participation in terrorist activities puzzles and shocks people. And questions that arose during the Manson trial and the Van Houten retrials are as yet unanswered. Can people be influenced by others to an extreme, even to the point of killing? Can certain people be brainwashed into holding beliefs that would otherwise be foreign to their way of thinking? How do hallucinogenic drugs affect people's minds? Can these drugs influence behavior if taken on a long-term basis? What is the relationship between the liberation of women from long-held inhibitions and women's criminality? I had from the start one question of particular interest to me because I think it is crucial: What can we learn about families who harbor individuals capable of committing deliberate acts of violence?

I also realized that my subjects are to this day "famous" and because of that their treatment by different agencies, the law, the press, is not the same as that accorded common criminals. In talking to people I also found that many are still quite interested in this case. To be sure, a few said that they could not care less, but their verbal indifference was betrayed by the interest in their voices. Some are frankly fascinated by the mansonites and others still perplexed by them. Some are still angered by them while others have become their friends and supporters. I was surprised at the humorous attitude that some people have towards the mansonites. One person referred to the women as Charlie's Angels and indeed, the television show where an invisible boss, a man, directs a group of three young women well trained in the use of weapons seems like a parody, albeit benign and inane, of the other Charlie and his women.

I realized quite soon how difficult it would be for me to obtain the data I needed to have an accurate profile of my subjects. I started by reading everything published. As a matter of fact when I first got the idea to write this book, I decided to read *Helter Skelter*; I think I hoped that after reading it I would give up the idea altogether. But it did not happen. That book did not answer my questions because it was a different book from the one that lay dormant in my mind. To my distress many of the serious people I talked with, no matter how motivated they were to help me, were unable because of their position to give me information they had, the opinions they held. But on the other hand they provided me with background material that was invaluable. Because of our legal adversary system the court transcripts were greatly useful to me since I could, like the jury, evaluate the pros and cons of the witnesses' testimony. I spent many hours in offices of the Criminal Court Building in Los Angeles and in the Court of Appeals, hours of exciting work for as I read documents and took notes I added my own questions and observations. What by then I was calling "my" book was taking shape. It was on one of my trips to Los Angeles that on a rainy afternoon I wrote the outline of the book in the Los Angeles public library, a couple of blocks away from the Los Angeles Hilton that became my home away from home. My inspiration came after one of the talks I had had with Paul Fitzgerald who had been Patricia Krenwinkel's attorney during her trial. He was on the staff of the Public Defender's Office at the time of the Manson trial in 1970, and faced with a conflict of interest he decided to leave his job to become part of the defense team. I talked with the youthful-looking attorney, a warm and intelligent person, in his office in Beverly Hills. His office walls are covered with photographs taken during the Manson trial.

After I discussed with him the book I wanted to write, he asked me some questions and posed some issues that deserve to be answered:

"Why not devote your time to writing about the women who populate our prisons?"

"Don't you agree that the Mansons are an extraordinary exception and because of that they are statistically insignificant?"

* * *

33

"Aren't these girls anomalies, freaks, not your ordinary criminals?"

"Everybody has trouble understanding the Manson case. Are they the total metaphor of the sixties?"

I want to try to answer Paul Fitzgerald's questions here briefly although some of them will be discussed more extensively in other chapters.

There can be little doubt that the problems of women who end up in the penal system deserve to be researched and written about, much more than they have been so far. Dr. Rita James Simon, in her monograph *The Contemporary Woman and Crime* published in 1975, called the woman in prison "The Forgotten Offender." She thinks that several factors account for this lack of interest, such as their numbers, which are considerably fewer than those of their male counterparts. There are forty state institutions for women and two hundred fifty for men. Women inmates do not act in a manner that calls attention to themselves. But public and official interest are influenced by the occurrence of major disruptions caused either by the number and the types of crimes felons commit or by riotous inmate behavior. Women seldom cause these upheavals. Women who fill our penal institutions, like their male counterparts, are the very poor and, in most sections of the country, the black.

I fully agree with Mr. Fitzgerald that this population should be the subject of more studies; but he was thinking about a different book from the one I am writing, a book that nevertheless deserves to be written. If I were to write about the more "typical" female offender, I still would opt for selecting a few and would focus on how specifically they ended up as criminals. In my dealings with the very poor I have often wondered about their strengths. I think it would be of significance to learn why some people who are brought up under extremely difficult socioeconomic conditions do not break the law while others do.

Although I do agree that the mansonites are exceptional murderers, I do not agree that they are not deserving of further inquiry. It is possible that I felt challenged because in my readings I found no full

34

explanation for their behavior. To say to myself that they are freaks did not satisfy my curiosity. I was also puzzled because Manson did not have a history of violent behavior and neither did the others. Susan Atkins had a history of antisocial behavior since childhood, which increased during her adolescence, and Leslie Van Houten started to show antisocial traits as an adolescent. But of the women, only Susan Atkins had been arrested prior to joining Manson.

I know that after the mansonites' crimes became known, many people wished that these people could be studied. Others, perhaps the majority, simply concluded that they were mentally ill. We have a tendency today to use mental illness as the basket label for criminal behavior that we don't understand, which just blocks attempts to understand the criminal. The truth is that most people who are mentally disabled do *not* engage in criminal activities. [I am not claiming that I know the full story behind these people's motivations nor that I started with such grand expectations. There are many handicaps on the road to getting data about the characters of a highly notorious case, as I learned while researching this book. All the same, because these people are so anomalous I think that some light should be thrown on their psychological makeup instead of regarding them as a freak show.]

Schizophrenics were once regarded as freaks and relegated to institutions. But the study of schizophrenics has provided a great deal of knowledge about the problems of self, of human relatedness, and today much research is being done in brain chemistry and in genetics that will hopefully be of benefit to us all. In recent years one type of shocking criminal behavior has become the subject of scientific and public scrutiny: the abuse and battering of children. This problem as well as infanticide has been known to exist throughout history. It was not, however, until 1946 that Dr. J. Caffey reported his observations of abnormal findings in the X rays of some of his child patients, and by the late fifties Dr. Henry Kempe at the University of Colorado was investigating this problem and setting up treatment centers for these children and for their parents. Eventually public opinion was stirred into action concerning this problem that affects all social classes. Today radiologists, pediatricians, mental health professionals, the law, and social welfare agencies are trying

35

to do something about this serious outcome of parental behavior. The perpetrators of these crimes are indeed unusual and there has been considerable cover-up about the problem of child abuse. But today we have a profile of the child abuser, an individual who frequently has been abused as a child, who is immature, and whose expectations of the child are totally unrealistic. Although this problem is by no means controlled as yet, abusive and neglectful parents are now offered treatment, so the child can remain with them or be returned to them after they are able to become more caring parents, thus avoiding for the child the added trauma of separation from his family. Self-help groups now exist that offer parents with similar problems a way to express their anguish and to correct their reactions.

Studies of this problem and that of battered wives focus on family transactions. We can offer better help than in the past and prevent some tragedies and that is important enough. But equally important is the fact that because we have explored and are dealing with these crimes with more knowledge, we are learning a great deal about parenting and about intimate human relationships.

Yes, the mansonites' crimes are statistically insignificant when compared with the problem of the abused child. But to explore any aspect of violent behavior, searching for more understanding—the type of understanding geared to action—is worth trying. We can learn much by doing so which can be of help to parents and others to prevent bringing up children who otherwise could turn out to be destructive to others or to themselves.

To continue with Paul Fitzgerald's questions, I am fully aware that people who have tried have trouble understanding the Manson case which is one of the reasons why I became interested in this project. Mental illness, the culture of the sixties, drugs, and above all the influence of Manson himself—evil or sick according to who does the talking—have been blamed for the group's murderous behavior; most frequently a combination of all these factors. And I agree that all these factors played a part, but I cannot dismiss the question of personal responsibility, or more exactly I question why some people abdicate their responsibility for their actions or find ways to mask it.

I also wanted to know more about the process the Family

36

underwent, why and how they went from being a hedonistic group to becoming a violent one.

Does this case represent a metaphor of the sixties? Was this "family" and its crimes a bloody splash, and the pathology it represents unique to its times? I debated with myself a great deal before answering this question. Many believe that indeed the Manson tragedy could have happened only during the sixties, a time when too many youngsters ran loose, supported by a peer society, a time when drugs other than alcohol reached the middle classes. During the sixties gurus became both fashionable and needed. They were sought after by people in need of the spiritual guidance they could no longer accept from religion or from their elders. But gurus were also enthroned by those in search of ready-made answers—as long as these answers were seductively packaged. When Manson came out from the cold the times were ripe for him. The Beatles and Mia Farrow had taken highly publicized trips to India to search for serene truths. It was natural for some to identify with them, to imagine that by finding the right guru they could also achieve on a grand scale, become famous or at least feel important. It was easy for them to ignore that hard work is the sibling of fame and that talented people who find success must cope with strains unknown to others and may need a great deal of emotional support.

Since Hollywood became a make-believe reality, many have been fascinated by stars from the entertainment world. For most people it has always been impossible to attain the symbols of stardom, the legendary mansions, the Rolls-Royces, the unique jewels. Stars and their accoutrements were unreachable. But during the sixties gurus and drugs became equalizers. The boy next door could use the same drugs that Jimi Hendrix took. Tex Watson and Dennis Wilson of the successful Beach Boys rock group could share the same guru. One could search for and find a wise man (I don't recall hearing of any women gurus) and feel in unison with the stars.

I don't believe that things have changed much during the seventies and consequently I dismiss the notion that the mansonites should be placed in the context of the sixties only. Not only did mass murders continue to erupt but nonviolent versions of Manson continue to attract followers. Charles Manson first attracted his women, and a few men, by telling them what they wanted to hear over and over again: "You are beautiful"; "You are perfect"; "There is no wrong." He was, indeed, a harbinger of things to come, beyond the sixties.

Many people who consult me need help in accepting themselves. They need to learn to caress their egos and to perceive the good and the beauty that is already a part of them. The last decades have brought an increasing awareness of the value of taking a loving look at oneself. Not that such ideas are new. The American psychologist William James long ago wrote and spoke extensively about the salutary effects of self-acceptance. But something is happening now in our culture. Somehow the concept of what is "positive" has lost its perspective, merged into a Me philosophy of the seventies, and we find ourselves living in an era of self-massage. Self-acceptance is no longer a "work towards" goal. It has become a product, a label one can peg to his life after purchasing it from any local or regional workshop supermarket. People in search of their private nirvana are encouraged to look at themselves in a mirror and say to their projected image: "I am terrific." Not, mind you, "I wish to be terrific which for me means . . . and I am going to work towards becoming a terrific person." Happiness is being promoted as "total freedom" and "perpetual ecstasy" (to quote the themes of two workshops I recently saw advertised in Marin County, California). Drug abuse continues to be an enormous problem. The poor countries that produce drugs don't seem to be using them. We, the most advanced, the most powerful country in the world, are the biggest consumers. Why hassle with anxiety? Cocaine, the stimulant, has become popular among the wealthy and the highly successful—the only ones who can afford it—who, however, seem unable to get a high or to be satisfied with their accomplishments. To them "average" is "hype" that is excessive. And this is the world in which our children are growing up. Parents today must have both strength of character and the ability to convey the advantages and the joys of being disciplined, of being moral, in a most skillful way because there is such a media explosion of hype advertising. Enormous amounts of money are paid to inane "personalities" or sports figures. Fame galore is lavished on the conveyors of trivia. Violence and sexual perversions are inundating our eyes and our ears, packaged to attract the public's interest.

I think that one of the most powerful motivations that prompted me to undertake the writing of this difficult book was the realization that what brought about the murders on the nights of August 9 and 10, 1969, is still with us. I am not only concerned about physical violence but also about the corrosive destruction of what is humane that is so prevalent today.

We are all curious and uneasy about acts of violence because it is human at times to do violence to others in our fantasies. In our imagination we at times eliminate those who hurt us or who are in the way of our getting what we need or want. But most people do not act out these wishes. Why do others? Why do some people, like the mansonites, wish to and find themselves able to kill deliberately?

Not only the violent aspects of this case puzzled me from the very beginning. The Manson women were (are) an exaggerated version of the helpless, dependent woman, of the submissive sex object, and Manson of the macho man. The family they formed was a caricature of the stereotypes that have so badly damaged the family.

Not long after I started planning this book I realized that I was wrestling with questions I had dealt with for years in my work: Why and how people find each other to form attachments? And above all, how did my subjects become the infamous Susan Atkins, Patricia Krenwinkel, Leslie Van Houten, Lynette Fromme, and Sandra Good?

With Intent to Kill

And then there were none . . .

The mansonites are remembered because of the Tate-LaBianca murders which became a *cause célèbre*. These crimes were perpetrated by permanent members of the so-called Family. Other characters gravitated toward the group, men who visited or stayed for a while at the Spahn Ranch, its central home, but who were too independent to accept Manson as their leader. Robert Beausoleil and Bruce McGregor Davis were two of them. The crimes they committed were related to circumstances that the Manson group faced when its very existence became threatened.

To better understand these women's and Manson's deeds and to have a more accurate picture of them one must keep in mind that the Family's season of violence, actual violence, did not start and did not end with the Tate-LaBianca murders.

It all began in July 1969.

The Gary Hinman Murder

On July 31, 1969, the body of a young man, Gary Hinman, was found at his home in Old Topanga Canyon Road in Los Angeles. It was lying on the floor of the living room, badly decomposed. Blood was splattered all over, on the body, on the furniture, on the walls. Written in blood on one of the walls were the words "Political Piggy." A drawing of a print of a paw was found on another wall.

Near his body were Hinman's Buddhist prayer beads. The coroner's examination revealed that the victim had been stabbed twice in the chest. He also had a nonfatal large cut on his face that went from the left ear to the left lip.

On August 6, 1969, Robert Beausoleil was arrested in the San Luis Obispo area while driving a Fiat car that belonged to Hinman (for which he had ownership papers). Beausoleil was arrested after one of his fingerprints was found in the Hinman home. After a while Susan Atkins and Mary Brunner were also arrested. Brunner was an inner-circle mansonite, the first woman to join Manson. They had met in Berkeley, where she was a librarian, shortly after Manson was released from prison; she had a child by him.

Beausoleil was a handsome itinerant musician who frequently kept in touch with the Family, usually accompanied by his own group of women. Like Manson and his followers, he had ambitions to make it big as a rock musician and this common interest was the basis for his relationship with them. Beausoleil had done maintenance work for Hinman and it was through him that the mansonites met Hinman, a piano teacher and a musician who also had a Ph.D. in political science.

Gary Hinman was a peaceful, gentle man, an active member of the Buddha Society. At one time Manson had asked him to play in the band he was planning to form. Rightly or wrongly, Manson thought that Hinman had money and other assets in his property and decided to ask him to give his possessions to the Family. At that time the mansonites were hard pressed financially and thus unable to pursue their musical ambitions.

During the Hinman trial it was established that on July 25, 1969, around midnight, Robert Beausoleil, Susan Atkins and Mary Brunner were driven to Hinman's home by Bruce Davis who then left. When asked by Beausoleil, Hinman denied that he had any money to give. The two got into a fight during which Beausoleil hit the other with a gun he was carrying. Unable to get results, he called Manson on the telephone. Manson, accompanied by Davis, responded promptly. He came armed with a sword that he used to cut Hinman's face, to further intimidate him. He left, but Beausoleil, Atkins, and Brunner remained in the musician's home for a total of two days and two nights of terrorizing. They searched the home for valuables while taking turns to watch over Hinman who by then was bleeding profusely and in a state of despair. Finally Beausoleil stabbed him. The trio cleaned up the place after writing "revolutionary" messages to disguise the robbery motive; the paw was drawn to implicate the Panthers. Before they left, however, they noticed that Hinman was still breathing, so they took turns in holding a pillow on their victim's face until all signs of life were gone. They took with them Hinman's Volkswagen; Manson had already taken the murdered man's Fiat and the ownership pink slips.

While at Hinman's home the three murderers took precautions to protect themselves. Friends who had called Hinman at the house testified that a woman with a British accent answered the telephone and told them that Hinman had left for Colorado because of a family emergency. The "British" woman was Susan Atkins.

Surprisingly, no connection was made at the time between the Hinman and the Tate-LaBianca murders that were committed a few days after Beausoleil's arrest. The crimes were related only after Susan Atkins, while awaiting trial at the Sybil Brand Institute, as a suspect in the Hinman murder, revealed her participation in the Tate murders to two cellmates. Unable to contain herself, she gleefully gave details of her murderous deeds, obviously to impress the others who at first found it hard to believe what they heard. They thought that Susan was bragging to appear "big." But they decided to report to the police the gruesome tale they had heard from her.

Beausoleil, Manson, Davis and Atkins were convicted of murder in the first degree just before the Tate-LaBianca trial. The ubiquitous Mary Brunner, who had been in and out of courtrooms as a witness, was granted immunity in return for her testimony against the others. The court made it clear that Brunner had a vested interest, to protect herself, in cooperating with the prosecution (Court of Appeals, 1971):

> The facts regarding such grant of immunity were fully
> disclosed to the jury in order that it could evaluate such

testimony in the light of the fact that it was given under bias and prejudice, if any, generated by a grant of immunity.

This woman, who fully participated in two days of debauchery in the deliberate murder of a human being, has never been punished for that murder.

The Tate-LaBianca Murders

During August of 1969, movie director Roman Polanski and his wife, actress Sharon Tate, resided at a luxurious home on 10050 Cielo Drive in Los Angeles. They had sublet the house from music entrepreneur Terry Melcher. The home was owned by Rudi Altobelli who was also in the entertainment business. Mr. Polanski was out of the country at that time and two friends of his wife were staying with her, Abigail Folger and her boyfriend, Wojiciech Frykowski.

On August 9, Winifred Chapman, the Polanskis' housekeeper, came to work as usual in the morning. She discovered a ghastly scene.

A Rambler automobile was near the entry gate and inside it was the body of a young man, Steve Parent. The bodies of Frykowski and Abigail Folger were on the front lawn. In the living room, tied together with a piece of rope, were the bodies of Sharon Tate and her friend Jay Sebring. A towel was wrapped around Sebring's neck and covered his face. Blood was spilled all over the property and had been used to write the word "Pig" on the front door.

The coroner's examination showed the obvious, that the victims had suffered numerous injuries:

Sharon Tate, who was in the eighth month of her pregnancy, had sixteen wounds.

Abigail Folger was stabbed twenty-eight times.

Jay Sebring's body showed seven penetrating stab wounds and one fatal gunshot wound.

Wojiciech Frykowski's body had fifty-one stab wounds, his scalp had thirteen lacerations, and he also had five gunshot wounds.

Steve Parent had five gunshot wounds.

On August 10, 1969, Frank Struthers, fifteen-year-old son of

43

Rosemary LaBianca, returned from a vacation to his home at 3267 Waverly Drive, in the Griffith Park section of Los Angeles. He had stayed one day more after his parents' return from their vacation home. He discovered the body of his stepfather, and after calling his sister the police were summoned to the home.

They found Leno LaBianca's body in the living room. His face was covered with a blood-soaked pillowcase. His hands were tied behind his back with a leather thong. A carving fork was stuck in his abdomen where the word "War" had been scratched. An electric cord was knotted around his neck from where a knife protruded. Rosemary LaBianca's body was found in the front bedroom, her hands tied with an electric cord. A pillowcase covered her face and a cord was wound around her neck.

"Death to the Pigs" was written in blood on a wall of the living room and "Raise" over a door. And, on the refrigerator door, "Helter [sic] Skelter."

Mr. LaBianca had thirteen stab wounds and fourteen puncture wounds made by the tines of the carving fork.

Mrs. LaBianca had forty-one separate stab wounds.

There was no evidence of ransacking in either the Polanski or the LaBianca homes although there were valuables in both. It was later learned that a wallet containing some money and credit cards had been taken from the LaBianca home and some money from the Polanskis'.

These mass murders shocked the world not only because of their bizarre nature but because of the identity of some of the victims. Sharon Tate was a beautiful movie actress. Her husband, Roman Polanski, was a talented movie director whose interest, as fate would have it, was in creating macabre films, and both were members of the international jet set; heiress Abigail Folger was a social worker who devoted a great deal of time to social concerns; Jay Sebring was a well known and successful businessman who operated a chain of beauty shops; he had been Sharon Tate's boyfriend in the past and had continued to have a close friendship with her and with her husband. Eighteen-year-old Steve Parent had gone that particular night to sell a radio to young William Garretson who did maintenance work for the Polanskis and who lived in the caretaker's house. The night of the murders Garretson remained in his quarters, ignorant of the tragedy that was taking place in the main residence.

These murders made national and international news, but it was the Los Angeles community that was most affected. The city was overtaken by a wave of fear. People, especially those residing in affluent neighborhoods, were terrified that the unknown assailants would in the dark of night strike at them. Rumors spread. Were these crimes drug-connected? Had the murders been committed by a well-organized terrorist group? Were these random murders or did the victims have some connection with their murderers?

Finally, on December 1, 1969, Charles Manson, Charles "Tex" Watson, Patricia Krenwinkel, and Susan Atkins were identified as primary suspects and shortly thereafter so was Leslie Van Houten. After the mansonites' arrest, the already massive coverage of the case only increased. The victims' newsworthiness was eclipsed by that of the victimizers, a diabolic guru who had managed (how did he do it? people still ask) to attract and to dominate a harem of young girls *en fleur*, white girls from the middle classes, attractive in spite of their filthy, disheveled appearance at the time of their arrest. Details of the deviant life-style of the Family, of their sexual and drug orgies, became front-page news and the subject of articles in major magazines. Those mansonites who were not arrested, mostly women, tried to enlist public opinion by presenting Manson as an innocent man, the victim of an unfair social system that only he could correct. It became known that some of his followers regarded him as a Christ-like figure. Manson became a star, and realizing that this was his chance for fame, he orchestrated the movements of his friends on the outside and on the inside. He and the others, especially his most daring female follower, Susan Atkins, were sought after by reporters and by lawyers before the trial began, with the jury selection, on June 15, 1970.

By December 14, 1969, the Los Angeles *Times* had already published what actually was the content of Susan Atkins' testimony before the grand jury, essentially the same as her revelations to her cellmates. The expose was headlined EXCLUSIVE DETAILS, SUSAN ATKINS' STORY OF 2 NIGHTS OF MURDER. This article was subsequently enlarged and made into a book, *The Killing of Sharon Tate*.

On December 19, 1969, *Life* magazine featured on the cover a full-face photograph of Charles Manson under the banner THE LOVE AND TERROR CULT—THE MAN WHO WAS THEIR LEADER—THE DARK EDGE OF HIPPIE LIFE. Susan Atkins' and Manson's pictures were spread on the inside.

On March 8, 1970, the entertainment section of the Los Angeles *Times*, and other major newspapers, had an advertisement about a film that was unmistakably an exploitation of the Tate-LaBianca murders and of the Manson Family. And so the public "entertainment" continued.

Because of the enormous publicity, Manson and the other defendants produced several motions for mistrial and for change of venue, arguing that the publicity was so devastating that they could not be tried with fairness in any California court. But these requests were deemed unreasonable by the Court of Appeals simply because the publicity of the case was not limited to California. Furthermore the court made a controversial yet often true statement, that "massive publicity does not automatically translate into prejudice."

Paul Fitzgerald, attorney for Patricia Krenwinkel, admitted that a change of venue or moving for a mistrial would be ineffective:

> Even if you put this case over five years I doubt if the publicity would really abate. Perhaps . . . the publicity would substantially abate in two or three years, but once there was an announcement that the trial was about to take place I think the publicity would be on again in full force and swing and I seriously doubt that it would ever substantially abate to the degree that the defendants could be afforded a fair trial.

The trial was characterized by the disruptive behavior of the defendants who frequently had to be dismissed from the courtroom to follow their own trial on closed circuit television. On top of that, other circumstances further complicated the already charged atmosphere of the courtroom. For example, on August 4, 1970, Manson exhibited, in the presence of the jury, a Los Angeles newspaper carrying the headline NIXON SAYS MANSON GUILTY. The following day his codefendants, the women (Watson was in Texas fighting extradition and was tried separately) chanted, "Why don't you convict us, the President says we're guilty." Judge Older had to interview each juror to learn what effect such publicity had on each one, after which he decided that "the jurors were capable of proceeding without violating their oath and obligations."

When Ronald Hughes, attorney for Leslie Van Houten, disappeared at the end of November 1970, all sorts of speculations flared. Maxwell Keith was appointed as Van Houten's attorney, remained as her lawyer after she was convicted, and was instrumental in getting a new trial for her in 1977. The body of Hughes was found and his death was ruled accidental.

To present just a few of the complications of this trial, Susan Atkins testified to the grand jury on December 5, 1969. Later on, after dismissing her attorney, Richard Caballero, and engaging Daye Shinn, she stated that her testimony had to be invalidated because it had been obtained from her under duress. Consequently it was not introduced at the trial.

The defendants were incriminated by the testimony of an eyewitness, Linda Kasabian. This young woman had been traveling around California before she joined the Family. She had moved from commune to commune, committed to the life-style of the counterculture. She had a child when she joined the mansonites, only two months before Manson asked her to participate in the murderous expeditions. In other words, she joined the Family just as it was becoming violent. She did not participate in the Tate-LaBianca murders directly but was with the defendants and witnessed some of the killings. She helped dispose of the evidence, blood-stained clothes after the Tate murders, a wallet stolen from the LaBiancas, which, following Manson's orders, she placed in a location where a black person was likely to find it.

In her testimony, Kasabian confirmed that Manson was not at the Polanski residence on the night of August 9. According to her, the murderers, Tex Watson, Patricia Krenwinkel, and Susan Atkins, went directly to the Cielo Drive residence which was known to Watson who had visited Terry Melcher while he was living there. Kasabian waited outside while the three killed the victims. The second night Manson drove with the murderers because, Kasabian

47

testified, he complained that the Tate killings "had been too messy and this time he wanted to show them how to do it." This time the group had not planned in advance for a destination; they drove around before deciding on the Griffith Park home of the LaBiancas. Manson went inside alone and returned after a short while; he said to those waiting in the car that he had tied up a man and a woman. According to Kasabian he then spoke directly to Watson, Van Houten, and Krenwinkel, advising them, "Don't let them know you are going to kill them." The three entered the home while the others, Kasabian, Atkins, and Clem Grogan, left to find, following Manson's orders, other victims. (About Grogan: This young man, according to what I have read about him, was either psychotic or retarded or brain injured; or maybe had multiple problems. I was surprised that he was convicted for the Shea murder rather than declared incompetent.) Obviously such orders from their leader did not carry too much weight with them since they returned to the Spahn Ranch instead. Kasabian testified that she averted another murder by purposely taking the group to the wrong apartment rather than to the one occupied by an actor she knew, who was marked as the next victim.

Kasabian made an excellent witness for the prosecution. She was granted immunity in return for her testimony although she was a coconspirator in the murders. She went willingly with the others to the Polanski home, she witnessed the brutal murders, and she went again with the murdering party the following night; and both times she helped conceal evidence. Her testimony started on July 27, 1970, and concluded on August 19, 1970. The immunity order was signed on August 10 and the charges against her were dismissed on August 13, so she had given substantial testimony before she was granted immunity. But she had applied for it—and most likely knew it would be granted—at the very start of her testimony.

Kasabian has testified for the prosecution in most of the mansonites' trials. Today she is one of the minor celebrities who have sprung from the Manson case. To give immunity to a defendant in return for testimony that incriminates others is a regrettable but necessary procedure in our system of justice. All the same I find it hard to accept that this woman who was present and played the role of all-around helping hand during the Tate-LaBianca murders has

48

never been convicted. That she was totally cleared in return for her testimony gives one a glimpse of how doubtful the prosecutors must have been of otherwise getting a conviction for the defendants Manson, Watson, Atkins, Krenwinkel, and Van Houten.

One question that puzzled everybody about these murders was that of motive. The prosecution did not have to present a motive in order to convict the defendants but prosecutor Vincent Bugliosi chose to do so. According to him the Tate-LaBianca murders were motivated by Manson's plan to start a race war. It was learned that Manson and his followers had been developing what I can't help but call a fantasy along these lines: The tensions between blacks and whites would increase; the mansonites would precipitate a crisis by randomly murdering white, affluent people with the intention of blaming the blacks for these murders. This would produce a state of chaos, "helter skelter," a war that the blacks would win. However, because of their inferiority they would be unable to take charge. At this point Manson and his followers, by then numbered in the thousands and living on a spot in Death Valley that they named The Bottomless Pit, would be called to assume power.

This fantasy was started by Manson and added to by other mansonites. It was inspired by recordings of the Beatles' *White Album*, mostly by the songs "Helter Skelter" and "Revolution 9" which the mansonites allegedly interpreted as being prophesies similar to those in the Book of Revelations.

From a distance of ten years both this motive and its acceptance by the prosecution seem absurd. But in fairness I have to say that some "revolutionary" theories and illusions of fringe groups seem laughable or crazy to any sane observer. Furthermore the idea that the solution for society's ills is to destroy it and then build a new and just world has been adopted by violent groups from time to time. Their proponents, of course, assume that they will eventually be the ones in power.

In another chapter, "From Love to Violence," I will discuss the dynamics behind the helter-skelter fabrication. Here I want only to say that it lacks credibility as a motive. I doubt that this fantasy was held as a reality by any of the mansonites consistently, least of all by Manson. It did, however, fit these people's megalomania, their wish

49

to play at being revolutionaries with a grand design, and it is likely that at times some of them believed their own creation. From what I know of my subjects, I am convinced that these killers had, each one, his own hidden agenda to be served by their criminal actions. If one were to accept that they truly believed the helter-skelter fantasy and that it really motivated these murderers, one would have to conclude that they were psychotic (a hole in the desert, where thousands of people would live?). But they were not psychotic, clinically or legally.

The defendants, some of them to this day, claimed that the Tate-LaBianca murders were "copycat" killings planned so Beausoleil would be exonerated in the Hinman murder. The idea was to give the impression that other politically inspired murders were being committed by the same persons who murdered Hinman at the time when Beausoleil was already under arrest. I find the "copycat" motive credible. The Tate-LaBianca murders were perpetrated only a few days after Beausoleil's arrest; and the mansonites probably feared that his relationship to the Family would be traced thus implicating Susan Atkins, Mary Brunner, and Manson.

It is noteworthy that Manson insisted that other people be murdered immediately after the Tate murders. I think he feared that he and his group could otherwise be suspected because their connection with Terry Melcher, former occupant of the Cielo Drive residence, was known. Many also knew that Melcher had refused to sponsor the group's musical career and that Manson had been enraged by his rejection. I speculate that the LaBianca murders could have been intended by Manson as a red herring, to give the impression that a revolutionary group was committing random murders. This "political-revolutionary" smoke screen had already been used in the Hinman murder, the motive for which was robbery perpetrated by criminals who didn't care to have a witness testify against them.

There can be no doubt that Manson selected the Polanski residents as the victims and that in doing so his motive was revenge. He could not kill Melcher without implicating himself but symbolically he chose those who were living in Melcher's home. In murdering those who were wealthy and successful the mansonites also expressed their rage at those who had what they so much wanted for themselves.

50

After the Tate-LaBianca murders the mansonites had plenty of problems to face. Their days of wine and roses were over.

Much has been said and written about their preparations for a utopian life in the desert as they awaited the day when they would be called to take power. They did start to move and they were indeed concerned and fearful. But they did not fear Armageddon and the chaos that would come before their ultimate triumph. Instead, they were afraid of the police, worried that they would be suspected since probably others inside the Family or who were close to it knew that some of its members were responsible for the Tate-LaBianca murders. And they did not move to Death Valley following an idealistic, Christian design, but out of necessity because they were forced to leave the Spahn Ranch.

The Donald Shea Murder

The living quarters of the Family for most of its short-lived existence was the Spahn Ranch in Chatsworth, near Los Angeles. A Mr. Frank Retz had been buying land around it and also part of the ranch. By July 1969 he had purchased the entire property. He had noticed before that the mansonites had practically taken over the ranch and had complained about it, and ordered Manson off the property several times. The mansonites, indeed, had hopes to persuade George Spahn to give the property to them and to that effect Lynette Fromme took care of this old blind man. She cleaned and cooked for him and gave him good dosages of t.l.c., hoping that he would be seduced into deeding his property to the commune.

Once Mr. Retz became sole owner of the ranch, he decided to take action. He told George Spahn, in the presence of Lyn, that he intended to get the group to move out and that he wanted to hire a guard to keep it permanently off his property. Spahn suggested that he hire Donald Shea.

Shorty Shea had lived at the ranch for several years, working as a cowhand and as a handyman. Occasionally he would leave to work somewhere else or to stay with friends, always informing someone of his whereabouts. At the time of these events, he was separated from

51

his wife, a black chorus girl who worked in Las Vegas, but the two kept in touch. Shea's ambitions were to become an actor and a stunt man, ambitions that he was about to fulfill. In the summer of 1969 he was promised a small part in a movie to be filmed several months in the future. When Retz early in August offered him the job of guard, he accepted.

On August 16, 1969, the police raided the Spahn Ranch because of complaints about the Manson commune. Manson was arrested, admonished, and then released, an action that was later to embarrass the police no end! After he returned to the ranch, Manson, in the presence of various people (some of whom later testified in court), angrily claimed that Shea was responsible for the raid, that he was trying to get the Family kicked out. By the end of August, according to witnesses, Shea seemed to be anxious and preoccupied. Chances are he knew his life was in danger. One, Pearl Ruby, testified that one evening in the latter part of August she saw Shea getting into a car with Manson, Davis, and Grogan. Shorty Shea was never seen again.

During the Shea trial, former Family members testified that Manson freely admitted killing Shea with the aid of Davis and Grogan. He repeatedly made statements such as (in the words of one witness), "You remember Shorty, don't you? We had to do him in. He was bad-mouthing the ranch and calling the Man on us, and scheming with Frank Retz to get the ranch. . . . So we hit him on the head, took him for a ride. And when he started to come to Now [sic], we stuck him with knives . . . he was really hard to kill. . . . So Clem had to cut his head off."

Manson, in effect, bragged, as though he wanted to show that he, too, had come of age, that he, too, could kill. He aimed at presenting himself as "big," as capable of murdering a traitor who threatened his Family. It is likely that he also wanted to instill fear among those who knew about the Tate-LaBianca murders and who could be tempted to denounce the murderers.

The trial of Manson, Davis, and Grogan for the Shea murder took place about six months after the original Manson trial had ended; the three were convicted of murder in the first degree. At the time of the trial the body of Shea had not been found. (A body, allegedly his, was found a few years later.) The defendants were convicted on strong circumstantial evidence. On appeal Manson claimed that he could not be tried because there was no corpus delicti but, with a touch of irony, the court ruled against him:

> Here Manson places great emphasis on the fact that Shea's body was never recovered. The fact that Shea's body was never recovered would justify an inference by the jury that death was caused by a criminal agency. It is highly unlikely that a person who dies from natural causes will successfully dispose of his own body.
> . . . The fact that a murderer may successfully dispose of the body of the victim does not entitle him to an acquittal. That is one form of success for which society has no reward.

The prosecution proved that Shea was not alive by contacting hospitals, jails, credit organizations, relatives, friends, and persons throughout the country with whom Shea had any previous contacts.

It was while Manson was being tried for the Shea murder that a group of his followers robbed a gun shop to obtain weapons to rescue him. Their plan was to take the judge and the prosecutor as hostages and thus get Manson released. The robbery attempt failed after a gun battle between the police and the burglars. Apprehended, besides two male ex-convicts, were two hardcore mansonites, Mary Brunner and Catherine Share, who were indicted and served time at the California Institution for Women. Mansonites are suspected of having committed other murders that had never been solved. One is that of John Philip Haught, an acquaintance of the mansonites known as Zero to them. He was found dead on November 5, 1969, when the police were summoned to a house in Venice, a suburb of Los Angeles. He was living there with a group of Manson sympathizers, mostly women. They stated that he had shot himself in the right temple while playing Russian roulette. But the gun had been fully loaded and there were no fingerprints on it.

Some violent groups similar to the Manson Family, noticeably motorcycle gangs, also started as deviant groups that shouted their pride in their unconventional life-style; some of these gangs developed into criminal organizations usually dealing in drugs. It is likely that Manson, who unsuccessfully sought the support of bikers, also had in mind a family closer in purpose to the Mafia than to a revolutionary outfit. Had he been successful in forming such a crime organization, he might however have had problems with two of his closest friends, Lynette Fromme and Sandra Collins Good, whose designs for the Family were more impressive.

To Kill a President

On September 5, 1975, Lynette Fromme pointed a .45 caliber automatic pistol at President Gerald Ford as he was walking from the Hotel Senator to the Capitol in the city of Sacramento. A special agent grabbed the weapon and pushed the President away, as Lyn uttered, "It didn't go off. Can you believe it? It didn't go off. . . ." and, to the Secret Service men, "Why are you protecting him, he's not a public servant!"

It was found that the gun was loaded with four live rounds in the clip and none in the chambers. Because the live ammunition was not in the chambers when she pulled the trigger, some people speculate that Lyn had not really planned to kill the President. (Even if the jury would have accepted this she still would have been charged with intent to murder.) Others think that she simply knew nothing about how to use a firearm. Lynette had stolen the gun from a male acquaintance while visiting him shortly before the attempt.

Lyn stated that her action was motivated by her wish to call attention to the fact that the world was being destroyed by pollutants. She felt that her purpose, to save the world, could only be accomplished by killing those who pollute the environment and those in high power who permit such destruction.

The trial of Fromme was characterized by her attempts to disrupt the judicial process. As I read the court transcripts, I marveled at the patience of Judge Thomas J. McBride and the defense and prosecution lawyers. E. Richard Walker, Head Federal Defender, was appointed first to defend her. Lynette promptly became dissatisfied with him so another attorney was added to assist him. Again she expressed her discontent with this arrangement, which prompted the judge to say, "Mr. Walker brought him (Holley) along as his assistant. Now you want to reverse it to make the Public Defender the assistant to the assistant," to which Fromme replied, "Yes, just like making the child the parent. I want to reverse it."

The difficulties continued. Finally, against the court recommendation, Lynette Fromme acted as her own counsel and attorney. John E. Virga was appointed as co-counsel. Lyn tried to persuade the court to let Manson testify on her behalf:

> Charles Manson is the only human being who knows me well and could, if so decided, give testimony as to my character leading to my intent. Charles Manson is the only one who can save me the hell he has been through his entire life, and I add, the only one who can in truth save my physical life.

The court, of course, denied her request. Fromme, however, had the right to call President Ford to testify as a witness for the defense. The President testified *in camera* from Washington on November 14, 1975. He was asked questions about his perception of the defendant at the time of her attempt on his life, but he could not contribute much because of the rapid and emotionally charged nature of the event:

> . . . I noticed this lady in a brightly colored dress [Lyn was wearing her red robe] who wanted to apparently move closer to me, and I assumed to shake hands, and so I hesitated instead of keeping . . . moving as I normally do, and as I stopped I saw a hand come through the crowd in the first row . . . in the hand there was a weapon . . . The weapon was large. It covered all or most of her hand as far as I could see, and I only saw it instantaneously because almost automatically one of the Secret Service Agents lunged, grabbed the hand and the weapon, and then I was pushed off by the other members of the Secret Service detail.

President Ford estimated that the gun had been pointed somewhere between his waist and his knee and was about two feet away from him.

55

The possibility of an insanity defense was contemplated by the court but Lynette refused to undergo a psychiatric examination. She was examined only as to her competency to stand trial and was declared competent. Evidently the court and Fromme were working at cross-purposes. The court regarded her as a defendant who was being tried for a major crime and it offered her all the help usually accorded to anyone in her situation. Fromme, however, didn't accept that she was a defendant on trial. For instance, she stated at one point, "Your Honor, what I am arguing is that I came to the court specifically to give him [Manson] a voice." She really attempted to use her trial to get her "messages" publicized. Her verbal and written statements reveal her violent nature. Here is a sample:

"Your Honor, Manson and that family is my own heartbeat and if they're not allowed to put on a fair trial, lives will be lost all over the country."

". . . It's going to get bloody if they're not allowed to speak."

"Would you or I give our lives to stop the world from burning? Charles Manson, Bruce Davis, Steve Grogan, Robert Beausoleil, Charles Watson, Patricia Krenwinkel, Leslie Van Houten, Susan Atkins did."

". . . If not allowed to explain, there will be many more young murderers, beginning with the person typing this letter."

Some of her statements show the cunning and the duplicity of Lynette Fromme. She knew that the motive for the Hinman murder was robbery and certainly knew the motive for the Shea murder. Neither of these two murders, she well knew, were socially motivated.

Lyn's attempt on the President's life was probably precipitated by his visit to Sacramento. It is likely that her act was the culmination of hers and Sandra's increased frustration and anger, their feeling that life was passing them by, the realization that nobody really needed them, that the chances for them to realize their dreams of glory were nil. They had been trying constantly and unsuccessfully to obtain permission to visit Manson or to correspond with him, hoping, as they still do today, that he would provide them with a blueprint for success in their endeavors.

The night before her attempt Lynette was restless; feverishly, she had been making threatening telephone calls to some men hunters, who were about to go on an antelope hunt. Lyn and Sandra had been making violent threats for a while and had tried to persuade others to inflict violence on those they felt were responsible for destroying natural resources. Lyn corresponded for instance with a young man from Pennsylvania who had previously become interested in Manson and had corresponded with him. The two women tried to use him as their arm to commit violent acts. I don't know whether this man, Edward Vandervort, volunteered to testify or whether he was asked to. His letters in response to those of the women were not presented in evidence during the trial. (I have no evidence that he went along with their requests.) In one of her letters to him Lynette wrote,

If Nixon's reality is wearing a Ford's face we're going to have bedrooms again like the Tate and the LaBianca's and Mai Lai."

To Edward Vandervort she gave instructions by letter (neither woman ever met him). In one she wrote:

Go to your library and find a Corporate Directory. The Corporate Directory tells of the names of all the heads of the big corporations. Get the phone number of these corporations' heads on the East Coast. Call the corporation if necessary (and if it is long distance call person-to-person, collect to the corporate head and give another name . . .) Be a good detective and find out where you can reach the person. What we really want to know is where the wives congregate. Get as close to the head of the corporation as you can. Preferably to his wife. . . .

. . . Next when you find a phone number of the wives's meeting place or the husband's secretary even, muster up your meanest voice, think of your dying world, and call, speak slowly and precisely and clearly and as mean and frightening as you can, tell the following, 'your product or activity . . . is killing, poisoning the world. There is no excuse for it.' Now, say this very slowly: 'If you do not stop killing us, Manson will send for your heart. If the company pollutes the air close the shops. Flee the country. Or watch

57

your own blood spell out your crime on the wall. Remember Sharon Tate.

In this letter she recommends that Manson be used as the bugaboo. In another, written later, she gave more urgent instructions:

I just sent you a list of corporations to call. This one is to take care of NOW. William Roesch, President of Kaiser Company, makers of more forms of pollution than I can count . . . Do not threaten him first. Kill him. Destroy him. Here is how, 1. Case it out. Check for kids. We want to avoid hurting any kids. But get him and the wife however you can. Use gloves. Be careful and sly. Could wear paint clothes. Take with you an aerosol can of Ban deodorant. Take also a can of pink paint and a large paint brush. When bodies are dead, paint as much as you can of them with PINK paint. Put the aerosol can in the man's mouth . . . Do not write anything about Helter/Skelter. Or anything about Manson. Do as we say.
. . . If you do two good ones back there, we'll send for you to come here. Can you get the silencers?

Fromme and Good had no other interest but their "cause." They had lived in Sacramento since 1972 and, according to Sandra, they had supported themselves by having an "ecology enterprise," Good and Fromme, Inc., but I doubt that such business ever existed. It is likely that they supported themselves with small contributions they asked for and received from people scattered around the country with whom they corresponded. Vandervort (who learned of their whereabouts from Manson) testified that he himself had included money in one of his letters to them. He also sent them a knife they had requested. Until 1975 Sandra received a $200 monthly allowance from a trust fund. For a while a like soul, Susan Kathryn Murphy, lived with them. (She was arrested and tried with Sandra Good.) They managed to survive financially because they led a frugal life but there was nothing frugal about their aspirations. And even their trials have not hampered these aspirations.

On November 26, 1975, the jury in the Fromme trial after deliberating for two days returned a verdict of guilty to the charge of "knowingly and willfully attempting to kill the President of the United States of America, Gerald R. Ford." She was sentenced for the term of her natural life. The judge, in pronouncing that sentence, explained his reason for giving her the maximum penalty: "Frankly, I don't think that any amount of rehabilitation, rehabilitative effort will change you and I think that you agreed to this yourself." Shortly after Lynette Fromme's trial ended, on December 17, 1975, Sandra Good was indicted on a charge "of conspiring to commit offenses against the United States by causing to be delivered by the Postal Service according to the directions thereon, letters addressed to persons, containing threats to injure the person, addressee, and others." To put it in less florid terms, she threatened to inflict violence on others verbally and by letter.

It was learned that on September 5, 1975, the same day of the assassination attempt, she and Susan Murphy gave a man, Michael Davies, 171 letters to mail for them. Davies had met Lyn and Sandra through a casual acquaintance early in August 1975. At that time Sandra had talked with him at great length, explaining that she and Lyn "were into programs that they thought would bring awareness to others about the environment." Sandra asked Davies to compile a list of executives or members of boards of directors of organizations involved with power plants, particularly nuclear power plants. Later on Sandra told him that she wanted the letters to be sent to the wives. The letters she gave him to mail were enclosed in stamped (franked) pink envelopes that had as a return address the name of a Catholic organization in Berkeley. The envelopes had been stolen from that institution. I have no evidence whatever that Davies knew the contents of the letters he mailed.

On September 10, 1975, Sandra Good called Robert Ruby, a radio personality, at WWL radio in New Orleans and made threats against executives of chemical industries and their wives. On September 11 she called Denny Bixler who owned a radio station in Altoona, Pennsylvania, and again made similar threats. Other calls followed in which she continued to attempt to use the media (she called reporters too) to transmit her threats to the public. After Fromme was indicted, Sandra Good again showed her violent nature. She told reporters that her friend had not received a fair trial, that "once

59

again you have judged yourselves; your children will raise up and kill you . . . Los Angeles will burn to the ground."

During her trial, which was also presided over by Judge McBride, Sandra made verbal and written statements to the effect that she could not get a fair trial. Her statements contain veiled and open threats. She wrote, "I believe that Judge McBride is afraid that if I am allowed to go free I will physically harm him." Sandra became so vicious that bodyguards had to be assigned to the judge. It was reported that the jurors in the Fromme and Good trials feared for their safety. Nothing could have pleased Sandra more.

Sandra Good, like her friend, insisted on acting as her own attorney. During her trial she kept referring to an International People's Court, which from her description was a group of assassins. She stated that the group "approached us in 1969 when we were kneeling on the corner (during the Manson trial). The IPC knew we were real enough to go to the gas chamber, that we weren't bullshitting like Abbie Hoffman or Jerry Rubin or other phony revolutionaries or people who express concern and do nothing."

Of this organization she said that it was a group of approximately a thousand strong who were scattered throughout the country and that they would bring "justice to these people who were in the position to do something and didn't." Sandra explained how the IPC operates: "Accidents, unexplained accidents happen every day!" She went on to say that "Manson is the head of the IPC and only his hands, only his move can call them home." Affirming her belief in the effectiveness of violence, she stated, "There is a saying that the only thing you could prove to a fool . . . is his own death."

I believe that the IPC, which Sandra presented as a well-organized group working with her, Fromme, and Manson, was a figment of her imagination that she created to give the impression that she and her friends belonged to a group. To be sure, it is likely that a few persons had corresponded with these women, that they shared their beliefs and got satisfaction out of being involved in violent ruminations. And others had and do contact them out of curiosity. But in reality, Sandra and Lyn are not part of any group. Instead the two for years had lived wrapped in their loneliness, unable to relate to others, their

60

narrow world populated by the images created to satisfy their illusions of grandeur.

Sandra was sentenced to fifteen years in prison. Judge McBride in giving her the maximum penalty said that he "was disturbed most of all . . . because of the violent extremes to which you have committed yourself to correct what you consider to be our environmental problems, and incidentally to help Charles Manson."

Sandra Good had her day in court. No matter how she broke the law, she had the right to use the judicial process to benefit herself. Sandra did not use that right. She was too engrossed in gratifying her need to feel important. How did she go about accomplishing this? By trying to frighten people, on a grand scale. Only when she succeeds or thinks she does, can Sandra attain the feeling of being powerful that is so dear to her. So dear that for many years she has devoted all her emotional and intellectual energies pursuing the illusion of power. I can imagine how greatly satisfied she must have felt after the Tate-LaBianca murders when for a while the Los Angeles community lived in fear.

It is also true that once the only person who provided her with emotional support was imprisoned, she had little motivation to stay on the outside. Sandra was sincere for a change when, after she was convicted, she told the judge: "I've already stated how I wish to proceed. I wish to proceed directly to prison. I want to be inside with my family . . . It is my desire to go to prison."

I carefully read the court transcripts and other reports about these two trials to get information. As I was doing so, however, my imagination took me away from the "facts," beyond the carefully worded legal and reportorial documents I was examining. In my mind I saw a scene, I envisioned two willful little girls, their faces stained by tears, their eyes darkened by fury, their fists raised against large figures that looked at them disconcertedly, both sides rendered helpless by their inability to speak a common emotional language. I wondered, was this just a fantasy of mine? No, I don't think it was. These two women's rage at executives and at their wives—not at their children who they predicted would rise against their parents—that rage and their violent ruminations were directed at their own parents. The events that led Lyn and Sandra to be defendants in a court of law had started many years before. And the courtroom drama I was reading about was a repeat performance.

Violence is all around us. It has many causes. It has many faces. Some people *react* violently when they are intensely fearful or hurt. People do kill to defend themselves or in a fit of passion. Some people are vulnerable and more likely to react violently because they have poor control of their impulses. Others because they had grown up with so many deficits, so little nurturing, that their rage is always within them; they are like walking bombs ready to explode at any provocation. But some people's violence is not an impulsive response to an attack, real or imagined. Instead, their destructiveness is carefully thought out. They *act* out their wishes to destroy rather than react to a stimulus.

The violence of the mansonites, like everything else about them, was deliberate. Their savage attacks on their victims made them appear like people who went berserk. But their murders were planned. While they were stabbing their victims, as one of them has said, their "adrenaline went up"; but before and after their murderous actions they were careful to avoid being suspected and did their best to cover their tracks. Their crimes were deliberate and premeditated.

In the public's mind the Family is associated mostly with the Tate-LaBianca murders. As I look today at these murders I can see that once the culprits were apprehended their wealthy and famous victims were almost forgotten. The mansonites took the limelight away from them. But the suffering of the victims' relatives did not end with the death of their loved ones. The greatly advertised trial with its carnival atmosphere was a long one. These relatives and friends had to undergo the trauma of hearing "revelations," some true, some false, none ever intended for public consumption. In some circles some of the victims' life-style was equated with that of their murderers so there were those who rationalized, "Could it be that they had been asking for what they got?"

Of the relatives only Colonel Paul Tate, Sharon's father, made his presence felt. A former intelligence officer, he tried to use his skills to find the culprits. No other voices were heard in protest. The victims' relatives and friends have chosen to remain silent. Susan Struthers, Mrs. LaBianca's daughter, had a nervous breakdown after her mother's murder. Her brother, young Frank Struthers, was so traumatized that he became a recluse. Stevie Parent's family moved to another state.

The two friends, Abigail Folger and Sharon Tate, rest in the same cemetery, Holy Cross in Los Angeles. Other cemeteries in the same area, where they once lived, are now the final dwellings of Leno LaBianca and Steven Parent. Someone somewhere has kept the ashes of Rosemary LaBianca. Jay Sebring's body is back in Southfield, Michigan, where his father was born. Frykowski's ashes are back in his native Lodz, Poland.

Gary Hinman never got to go to Japan, as he had planned. Shorty Shea never lived his dream, to have a part in a movie. Wojiciech Frykowski did not have a chance to write a book. Abigail Folger never completed her work, based on her concerns for social welfare. Sharon Tate never got to be a mother. Steve Parent never reached his full manhood. The LaBiancas never lived to see their children full grown and with their own families.

The lives of these people were crossed out, their chances voided by a group who wanted to escalate to a peak their fun and games, people driven by their basest passions obscenely camouflaged as love.

Diminished Capacity

When I began planning this book I did not intend to get involved with the legal aspects of the Manson case. I've always had a lay person's interest in the workings of the law but like most psychiatrists I had been reluctant to get professionally active with the legal side of human affairs. Although I had testified in divorce and child custody cases, my interest in the forensic had remained peripheral and consequently when I started this project I lacked the knowledge and the experience to evaluate the legal aspects of my subject. Eventually, however, I changed my mind and delved into the legal issues of the Manson case because I realized that one cannot fully explore a criminal case and the criminals involved in it without understanding how the law works.

Many psychiatrists testified as expert witnesses for the defense and a few for the prosecution in the mansonites' trials. Psychiatrists figured prominently although only two defendants pleaded the types of defenses that are based on psychiatric testimony: Charles Watson, who pleaded non-guilty by reason of insanity in 1971 and Leslie Van Houten who won an appeal and was tried again in 1977 and 1978 and who pleaded diminished capacity "because of being under the influence of Manson who was mentally ill." Even though only two

64

pleaded psychiatric impairment, because of the bizarre nature of the crimes, the alleged control of Manson over his followers, and the mansonites' extensive use of hallucinogenic drugs, psychiatrists were asked to give their opinions in court on behalf of all of Manson's followers during 1970 and 1971, opinions that the defendants were not interested in hearing.

As expected, many people, on learning about the life-style of the mansonites and about their crimes, concluded that these criminals were insane. How else, they wondered, could one explain their "philosophical" ruminations and their complete disregard for human life that led them to kill for an esoteric "cause," to provoke a race war that would put them in power? Or for no cause at all but simply out of loyalty to Robert Beausoleil?

Not only did the defendants (with the exception of Watson) not plead insanity during the original trial, but on the contrary they made clear that they were sane and that the society that was judging them was in the wrong. Nevertheless it was the opinion of one psychiatrist, Joel Hochman, who testified for the defense in the original trial, that created the rationale behind the appeal made by lawyer Maxwell Keith on behalf of his client, Leslie Van Houten, in 1977. In Dr. Hochman's opinion, the Family's murderous actions were the result of their psychopathology, a case of *folie en famille,* a rare syndrome in which a dominant, mentally ill person controls the actions of one or more submissive partners who are much less affected.

Watson, whose attorney was also Maxwell Keith, and later on Van Houten were found guilty of first degree murder in spite of the impressive group of psychiatrists their lawyer called to testify as expert witnesses.

The issue in these trials—and in any in which psychiatric testimony is required—is the personal responsibility of a defendant for his crimes; thus the role that psychiatrists play in the judicial process is a subject of increasing controversy. Public opinion is stirred when a legal defense based on mental grounds wins an acquittal for a defendant or lessens his charge. The marriage of psychiatry and the law is a stormy one and yet the two disciplines must live together out of necessity. In the words of psychiatrist Seymour Pollack, director of

65

the Institute of Psychiatry, Law and Behavioral Sciences at the University of Southern California:

No topic in American psychiatry is more controversial than the relationship of psychiatry and law, and none more emotionally freighted when discussed. Ranging from heated arguments on the merits and demerits of the M'Naghten Rule of criminal insanity to more recent concerns about psychiatry as an agent of social control, issues in psychiatry and law have been aired in both the professional literature and lay press.

And yet, according to him:

During the past 20 years mutual interest in this relationship [psychiatry and law] has increased markedly and interdisciplinary involvement is growing. Today more legalists are concerned about mental health law and more psychiatrists are involved with legal issues than ever before. In the U.S. every year there are probably over a million psychiatric evaluations for legal purposes.

Both the insanity (which I will define shortly) and the diminished-capacity defenses are a thorn in the side of the legal and mental health professions. The latter, diminished capacity, is much used— some think abused—in California, probably because of dissatisfaction with the harshness of the M'Naghten Rule, the one accepted in that state to determine legal insanity. I wonder about the consequences, had Leslie Van Houten's conviction of first degree murder been changed to a lesser one, as almost happened in 1977. A precedent would have been set, that a person who commits a serious crime can be less guilty if it can be proved that he acted under another person's influence. The leader of the criminal group could conceivably then be held to be primarily responsible for his followers' crimes and they would be convicted of a lesser charge. The allegedly dominant partner in a relationship between adults could be legally accountable for the other's actions, while the submissive one would be subjected to a lesser punishment. This linear hierarchy of responsibility could

66

incorporate brainwashing and mind control into the legal process although as yet we really know little about these processes. One just has to keep in mind that a defendant's mental capacity *is* admitted as evidence even though we still have a nebulous understanding of the relationship between mental illness and personal responsibility. No norm exists because people are different, even mentally ill people. Yet the law provides that the legally insane should not be accountable for their crimes. Does this really benefit the mentally ill and society?

Part of the problem is that the public, which in the end has the last word, lacks information about what is involved in these issues. People have a tendency to label defendants who commit "senseless" crimes as "crazy." But increasingly most people are feeling uncomfortable about accepting the fact that a person can literally get away with murder because he is mentally ill or that he can be convicted of a lesser charge and be out of prison after a few years. Interestingly, only when the defendants are women does the public's protests seem to be absent. The public's response to criminals and to their crimes naturally also depends on who the defendant is and on the circumstances in which he committed his crime. Some crimes of passion evoke compassionate feelings in all of us. People can also be manipulated by lawyers, the press, and advocates to feel sympathy towards the accused.

Some jurists and mental health professionals question defenses based on the mental state of defendants. They point out that the mentally ill defendant can be convicted for his crime and then offered treatment for his problems; they assert that a defendant can be considered "bad and mad," to use a phrase coined in recent years in forensic circles. But others ask, how can a person who was severely mentally ill when he committed a crime be found guilty if he didn't know what he was doing or that what he was doing was wrong? But even they must admit that in many cases to determine the mental state of a defendant at the time he committed a crime is not that simple. Different psychiatrists may have different opinions about the same defendant, and how, precisely, a mental disturbance affected his ability to plan a murder, for example; or whether a person who has a drinking problem should or should not be held responsible for his destructive behavior because he was under the influence when he

67

harmed or killed another human being. In all probability such a person had been asked to do something about his problem many times. He might have been unwilling or unable to stop drinking. But, again, should he be considered less responsible and have a lesser punishment for his violent actions? There are a number of reasons why both lay and professionals want to do away with these types of defenses and find other solutions to deal with defendants who are mentally ill or incapacitated. Psychiatrist Abraham Halpern, for example, thinks that the insanity defense should be abolished to "extricate the criminal justice system from its present confusion and abuse." He notes that the sensationalism of a trial involving the insanity plea makes the public conclude that mental illness and dangerousness are synonymous, thus blurring the difference between antisocial behavior and psychotic behavior.

Before I go any further I want to define briefly the different charges in the case of murder.

Murder is the unlawful killing of a human being. When it is proven without a reasonable doubt that the murder was premeditated and deliberate with malice aforethought, the charge is murder in the first degree. If premeditation cannot be proved and the killing was intentional but occurred under certain circumstances, for example during an argument, or in the heat of passion, or while the accused was intoxicated, the charge may be of murder in the second degree or of voluntary manslaughter; in California and in other American jurisdictions the defense may plead diminished capacity in these cases so a defendant can be convicted on either of these two charges.

Legal insanity and insanity from a psychiatric point of view are not necessarily interchangeable concepts. Although the designations "non-guilty by reason of insanity" and "diminished capacity" seem to be self-explanatory there are specific legal guidelines that apply to these defenses. California's judicial system abides by the M'Naghten insanity rule that states that a person is considered legally insane if at the time of the commission of the crime "he is laboring under a defect of reason from a disease of the mind as not to know the nature and quality of his act; or, if he did know it, that he did not know what he was doing was wrong." A person whose contact with reality is greatly impaired may, for example, kill someone because he falsely

68

believes that his own life is endangered by his victim. Or he may hear voices that tell him to attack or to kill someone. Or he may suffer from both delusions and hallucinations.

The M'Naghten Rule originated in England during the trial of David M'Naghten in 1843. The defendant felt compelled to assassinate Queen Victoria's Prime Minister Robert Peel but by mistake killed his secretary. During the trial it became evident that the accused was suffering from delusions of persecution and that he considered Robert Peel to be his persecutor. M'Naghten's counsel relied on the ideas of the humanitarian American physician Isaac Ray who had written a treatise on insanity. M'Naghten was found non-guilty by reason of insanity. The Queen was upset by the results of this trial, quite concerned about the consequences that the insanity defense could have in the administration of justice. She summoned the fifteen chief justices of the common law courts and asked them to formulate rules of criminal responsibility, to specifically limit the scope of this defense. And thus this rule was born out of humanitarian concerns. But it opened up a Pandora's box whose contents the legal and the psychiatric professions and the public at large have been unable to come to terms with to this day.

Because of the inconsistencies and the difficulties in interpreting this rule, other rules have been developed that are today used in different American jurisdictions. But the complications, if anything, seem only to have increased. For example, a defendant may be found legally insane in one jurisdiction that abides by one rule and legally sane in another that abides by a different rule.

To complicate matters more, the public is confused about the insanity and other defenses based on the defendant's mental state. These defenses are not seen by the public for what they are, legal defenses, but are thought of as being psychiatric defenses. *There is no such thing as a psychiatric defense since psychiatrists do not write laws.* The public, however, reacts emotionally and holds psychiatrists responsible for court decisions, although a psychiatrist's job is just to examine a defendant and present his findings when he is called to do so. As I have said, in many cases this is not a routine or a simple matter. The legal and the psychiatric disciplines are different and have a different language. Legal rights and legal responsibilities are based

69

on a set of rules subject to interpretation; they can be vastly different from rights and responsibilities as psychiatrists see them. The law expects a person to be responsible for his actions but leaves the door open for questions and for negotiating these questions. Thus the defense may argue that the mental condition of a defendant was severely impaired at the time he committed a crime and call expert witnesses to testify to this assertion; or that the defendant's actions were the result of a powerful emotion such as fear, that he, for example, mistakenly or rightly thought that his victim intended to attack him. Or that the accused hurt or killed someone in the course of a heated family argument. The defense may also prove that all the evidence is circumstantial, and that in spite of appearances to the contrary it cannot be proved beyond a reasonable doubt that the accused committed the crime for which he is being tried.

A person on trial, although considered innocent until proven guilty, is in the eyes of the law a defendant. Forensic psychiatrists are frequently thought of as regarding defendants as patients and as being mostly concerned with psychopathology. In some circles psychiatrists are perceived as sob sisters easily manipulated by criminals and by their lawyers. Because of this kind of criticism an increasing number of forensic psychiatrists are becoming much more skillful in evaluating defendants, more systematic, and also better prepared to present their findings in court. But psychiatry is a discipline, the study of man's behavior and emotions, not a science. Psychiatrists can evaluate the mental and the emotional state of a person and elaborate on how they may affect his behavior. But their evaluations can be and are subject to different interpretations, particularly regarding a person's legal responsibility. One must also remember that psychiatrists examine defendants after they had conferred with their lawyers. Furthermore, psychiatrists are human; at times they exhibit the same competitive attitudes that the lawyers on each side have; they may use rationalizations to defend their opinions, mostly because they believe that their opinions should prevail. The results of psychiatric evaluations about the same defendant can be, from a legal or clinical point of view, significantly different. For example, the behavior of the mansonites—their ideas, their "convictions," their speech punctuated by idiosyncratic words—was regarded by some as proof that these defendants, particularly Manson, were highly disturbed people. Others expressed their opinion that the same or similar behavior, unconventional philosophy, and unusual speech are part of the life-style of certain types of people who definitely cannot be considered mentally ill.

In our adversary system of justice the twelve people of the jury hear evidence from witnesses called by the defense and by the prosecution. They also hear these witnesses' testimony challenged by the other side, and they hear the judges' instructions. Many people fail to realize that the jury is instructed to consider the testimony of psychiatrists as they would that of any other witness. A psychiatrist cannot give an opinion as to the culpability or the innocence of a defendant. All he can do, all he is allowed to do, is to present, and validate his evaluation, of the mental state of a defendant at the time he committed his crime and to answer pertinent questions asked by the lawyers and by the judge. A psychiatrist's image and his credibility, like those of any witness, can be enhanced or discredited by the defense and prosecution lawyers. Only the jury has the last word as to the innocence or guilt of the accused, and in the latter case to what degree.

The degree of guilt makes all the difference for a defendant. For example if the jurors had decided that Leslie Van Houten was guilty of second degree murder or of voluntary manslaughter she would have been set free immediately because she had already served enough time. Equally important, in the public eye she would not be regarded as being fully responsible for her part in the LaBianca murders since the jury would have concluded that she acted under Manson's influence.

The defense of diminished capacity is a "Yes, but . . ." type of defense since the accused admits to his crime but at the same time tries to justify himself on mental grounds to reduce the charge and the punishment. This defense probably originated in 1915 when the Supreme Court of Utah reduced a conviction of murder from first to second degree on the basis that there was no evidence to support premeditation. In this case, *State* v. *Anselmo,* the defense doctors testified that the defendant, an epileptic, had an abnormal sensitivity to alcohol and had been incapable of premeditating and deliberating

71

upon his intent to kill because he was intoxicated at the time he committed his crime.

The defense of diminished capacity, in use in about eighteen states, is also called diminished reponsibility, a denomination objected to by some jurists because this defense actually refers to defendants whose *mental capacity* renders them unable to premeditate a crime. If a defendant's diminished mental capacity cannot be disproved by the prosecution, he is considered less responsible for his crime, thus justifying the less accepted name of this defense. As in the case of the insanity defense, the interpretation and the application of the defense of diminished capacity is not the same in all jurisdictions that use it. Furthermore, this defense has been and continues to be refined and expanded by other cases on trial.

As in the case of the pioneer *Anselmo* opinion, the role that intoxication and abuse of drugs had in incapacitating the mansonites was argued over and over again during their trials.

The life-style of the mansonites included the use of hallucinogenic drugs, mainly LSD and marijuana. During the trials psychiatrists testifying for the defense said that the accused's behavior had been in part determined by the effects of drugs. But others expressed the more accepted view that hallucinogenic drugs affect people differently, that some have bad reactions while others don't. Many people have used these drugs occasionally, others for quite a while before stopping their use, with no discernible ill effects. In spite of the claims of some of the defendants there was no evidence that they were under the influence at the time of the murders. These drugs are not physiologically addictive; they were being used less frequently by the defendants at the time of the murders, probably because they were no longer achieving the intense pleasurable enhancement of the senses the mansonites sought from their use.

Hallucinogenic drugs are dangerous. Their long-term effects, how they affect the genetic structure, are not yet known. Some people have ended in a mental hospital in an acute state of panic after using them; others have died while being under their influence because their distorted perceptions led them to put themselves in dangerous situations. There is no evidence, however, that people are more prone to act violently because of chronic use of these drugs or while they are

72

experiencing their effects. Prolonged use of hallucinogenic drugs did not make the mansonites into killers. They used the drugs because they had the emotional makeup of those inclined to use hallucinogenics. They used them to enhance their sensations, to search for "peaks," for a spectrum of visual and sensual experiences not usually available without these drugs' effects. The use of drugs in the Family was careful and supervised, a group activity they made into a ritual. The mansonites knew the effects of drugs and also knew how to take care of themselves. Only once did they have as a group a panicky reaction after ingesting LSD. Highly dangerous addictive drugs such as barbiturates and heroin were not used by the members of the Family.

Reflecting on the defense pleaded by Leslie Van Houten in 1977, diminished capacity, I realized how exactly it defines the attitude of the Manson followers, beyond its legal implications. In essence all of them are saying that they were not fully responsible for their criminal actions.

A convicted felon, of course, tends to rationalize his motivations for breaking the law and tries to put the blame somewhere else. Some of these people, in spite of the help they could have, keep repeating their offenses and never admit that it is ultimately up to them to change the course of their lives, while the rest of us have to suffer the consequences of their behavior. We all know that sociopaths do exist, habitual criminals whose actions bring them repeatedly in conflict with society, who seem unable to feel guilt or to learn from experience. Charles Manson is a classic example. Some psychiatrists think that these people are very sick. I fail to see how they arrive at such a conclusion. These people are morally disturbed or altogether amoral, not sick. The mansonites' major area of disturbance is also moral. Their real philosophy, devoid of their ornate philosophy, can be contained in one sentence: "Do as you please, and don't give a damn!" They felt that they had the right to indulge their whims even at the expense of others. The pain they caused to their families, even before they became killers, meant nothing to them. An easy way out for them was (and is) to put the blame on others when things didn't work out for them.

Charles Manson is the product of a troubled and deprived upbringing, but nevertheless he had a choice of becoming other than what he is. To this day his conversation is plagued by his comments blaming society, the system, for his misfortunes. His close Family associates came from the middle class and grew up with a modicum of family stability. But when the time came for them to assume adult reponsibilities they chose to avoid them and blamed society or their families for their unrest that was due to their lack of interest in adjusting. The lingo of the sixties provided them with the term Establishment to kick around. They still live wrapped in their own world, hearing only what suits them. At times they pay some tepid lip service to their own responsibility for their crimes; it sounds good, it is the clever thing to do, but they have (as I will discuss later) internalized the conviction of their diminished responsibility.

Although only Van Houten had tried to make it legal, other convicted mansonites are using the "Yes, but . . ." idea in one form or another. The culprit or the master, according to who is talking, is Charles Manson. It is he and he alone who made them commit their crimes. They are pleading their own version of diminished capacity to justify themselves and to get themselves out of prison, if possible in a cloud of glory and admiration.

The mansonites and their supporters continue to try to convey the idea that a great injustice has been inflicted on them, that they really have gotten an unfair deal from the judicial system. Their idiom is cautious, but listening to them one gets the impression that they believe society is the loser because they are in prison instead of being free, leading normal and constructive lives (Van Houten), or accomplishing their mission to help humanity (Watson, Atkins, Fromme, and Good).

The subtitle of Charles Watson's book is *The Man Who Killed for Charles Manson;* it says it all. Susan Atkins is more indirect in blaming Manson. She describes her liaison with him (that led her to crime) as the work of the devil. The way in which these two prostitute religion is shocking, yet it has served them well in attaining a great deal of publicity and good connections. Each has written books that tell their own self-serving account of their lives and their criminal activities. The pair, who have no qualms in proclaiming that Jesus is

74

their attorney, work assiduously towards being paroled not just—they claim—to enjoy a free life, but because humanity is awaiting their ministrations. Leslie Van Houten has presented herself, carefully prepared by her able attorney but also by using her own remarkable salesmanship skills, as an all-American girl who at one time became the victim of Manson's sick and sickening influence, and as a person who has struggled courageously to overcome it. For which the world, it seems, should reward her.

Patricia Krenwinkel has blamed her life as a mansonite and her crimes on the peer pressure of the others in the group.

Lynette Fromme and Susan Good are more subtle in making Manson responsible for their deeds, and I don't think they are aware of doing so. They reacted with surprise and some irritation when I discussed my views about this with them. Their intense involvement with Manson, which continues to this day, is based on their expectation that Charles Manson will someday give them the "word" that will guide them towards a great destiny. Since they proclaim their submissiveness to him, he has and would have the ultimate responsibility for their actions.

Charles Manson, while cleverly trying to keep himself safe from any implication that he was primarily responsible for the group's criminal actions, enjoys the feeling of importance given him by his former associates, although as years go by that feeling has been dimmed by the stark reality of his life in the maximum security unit in which he is likely to remain for years to come.

It is appropriate to discuss here the attitude of a former mansonite, Paul Watkins, who also blames Manson for having unduly influenced others. Paul, a runaway since age sixteen, joined Manson two years later and became second in command and one of the group's few male permanent members. It is likely that he stayed because being Manson's right hand gave him status and a feeling of importance. Probably Manson, who found it difficult to recruit men, saw to that. When the group's talk turned to violence Watkins left it. I met him during Van Houten's second retrial where for the first time he testified for the defense; in all previous trials, including Van Houten's first retrial a few months earlier, he had testified for the prosecution. He explained his decision to change sides by saying that he realized that Van Houten, like him, had successfully struggled "to rid her mind" of Manson's influence. Because of his former ties with Manson, Paul has attained some renown. He has been on television with Vincent Bugliosi when the latter promoted his book and has given talks to law enforcement groups on the subject of drug abuse. When I met him he had finished writing a book about his experiences as a mansonite and his subsequent change.

I asked Watkins how was he different from other mansonites who stayed with the group and became violent, but unfortunately he was unable or unwilling to give me an answer. According to him he had been capable of leaving Manson physically and mentally because of the help of Paul Crockett, a miner who was at the time prospecting in Death Valley. When Paul joined him Crockett was already helping young Brooks Poston who had left the Family after a frightening experience which might have been in part due to the effect of drugs he took; he had been unconscious for a few days, perhaps in a deep sleep or perhaps catatonic. I had heard much about these rescue operations, implying that Crockett literally took away these two young men who allegedly could not otherwise have left Manson. It is true that this man gave considerable emotional support to Brooks and Watkins but only after they had decided to leave the Family, as he himself testified in court under cross-examination by the head prosecutor Dino Fulgoni:

> Q: Mr. Crockett, you said that Poston approached you about helping him get free of Manson?
> A: Yes.
> Q: That's definite in your mind? You did not approach him?
> A: (Nods head.)
> Q: So he approached you and asked you to help him get rid of Manson's influence, is that correct?
> A: Yes.

Poston and Watkins obviously felt perfectly safe to leave Manson once they decided to do so and once they found a supportive parental figure.

Paul Crockett, a man in his forties at that time, was like Manson a

76

former Scientology student. While testifying on behalf of Van Houten he tried to expose his philosophy and above all his superiority over Manson, with whom he had a few upmanship encounters when the two were neighbors in the desert. His descriptions of those feats were labeled by a member of the court as "the battle of the gurus." Watkins, however, denied that Crockett with whom he worked "to rid his mind of Manson" for seven years, considers himself a guru. Seven seems to be a magic number in the world of Scientology, but all the same I can imagine Manson's satisfaction on learning that it took his former ally so many years to feel free of him. Chances are that Watkins was not the kind of person who would engage in or condone violence, and that at a certain point he felt capable of defying Manson and decided to leave. I suspect that Watkins, who is fond of his mentor who gave him support when he needed it, was when I met him trying to promote Crockett as a deprogrammer at least of people who had fallen under the alleged extraordinary power of Manson.

"Powerful" Manson and his "weak, submissive" women, all one and the same. I can describe them best by borrowing from the poetic language of the law, saying of them that "the circumstances attending their killings showed an abandoned and malignant heart."

Making the News

February, 1971. Susan Atkins is testifying :

> That is what I understood. In other words, out of a hundred percent, Mr. Schiller would get 25 percent off the top. 60 percent out of the 75 percent would come to me. And then 40 percent out of the 75 percent would go to Mr. Caballero.

This is how this supposedly "confused" girl described the hard financial facts concerning the book *The Killing of Sharon Tate* written by Lawrence Schiller and a Los Angeles *Times* reporter, Jerry Cohen, and based on the notes taken by attorney Richard Caballero while he interviewed Susan. I hasten to say that I don't know that there was anything illegal in their enterprise. Big news is big news regardless of what it conveys or of who is making it. Already then Susan had become receptive to exploiting her news value, and so had others.

From the day they were arrested the mansonites became a hot press event. It had everything going for it, celebrities among the victims, bizarre violence, sex, a guru. The trial was heavily advertised and became a daily source of ghoulish news. The jurors had to be sequestered to avoid any chance that they would learn anything to bias their judgment.

78

The criminals were well aware of their position center stage and tried to capitalize on it. Manson via his couriers on the outside ran the show, and attorneys for the defendants were accepted or dismissed according to his whims. His women—those who had not been arrested—kept vigil outside the courtroom, camped on the street, and made news themselves. Inside the courtroom the attention-getting maneuvers of the defendants became so disruptive, which of itself made news, that finally they had to be removed from court. The court had to deal not only with the unruly defendants but with the problems arising from their communications with each other, with members of the press, and with a shifting array of attorneys. Rumors and facts ran interlaced. Did some attorneys provide drugs to the women while they visited them at Sybil Brand where they were detained? Was there too much fraternizing between the reporters and the defense attorneys? Or, on the contrary, was the press condemning the defendants already? Were randomly selected people still in danger of being killed by the Family?

Bill Farr, then a reporter for the *Herald Examiner,* wrote an article in which he disclosed that threats had been made to celebrities such as Elizabeth Taylor and Frank Sinatra. According to him he had received the information from one of the attorneys. Each of them, and the prosecutors, denied under oath that he was the culprit. Mr. Farr refused to reveal his source and he was within his rights in doing so. But a few months later when Farr was no longer working as a reporter, Judge Older ordered him to disclose his source. Since Farr still refused, he was found to be in contempt and was jailed for forty-eight days. We still have no answer to the dilemma that both Mr. Farr and the court had to cope with, when the making of the news interferes with the process of law. A reporter's job, his bread and butter, lies in finding and reporting newsworthy events. Particularly in the case of controversial or "famous" cases he has to use any sources available but in some cases he will be sworn to secrecy about revealing these sources. What I am personally concerned with in this particular instance is the motivation of the source. If it was important to disclose that some people were being threatened by members of the Family, why didn't this source go through legal channels and inform the court and the other attorneys in the case?

79

The blame for the conflicting results of what is published and how it is published is too frequently and unfairly laid on reporters. Surely it was not a reporter's decision to put Squeaky Fromme on the cover of *Time* magazine. Sometimes, however, as I will discuss later on, I wonder if management really knows how its reporters operate and what their motivations are.

When crime becomes big news it also becomes important business of the day for attorneys, reporters, witnesses, and others involved. The words of Meursault, the narrator-murderer in Camus' *The Stranger,* kept coming to my mind as I reflected on the trial I was concerned with:

> Just then I noticed that almost all the people in the courtroom were greeting each other, exchanging remarks and forming groups—behaving, in fact, as in a club where the company of others of one's tastes and standing makes one feel at ease. That, no doubt, explained the odd impression I had of being de trop here, a sort of gate crasher.

No such introspective ruminations bothered the mansonites who did not feel like outsiders in the drama they had created but, on the contrary, like stars enjoying the limelight. Their trial was a landmark. It became clear then that the big criminal had become a product to be used and to be sold by different interests including those of the defendants. The communications explosion had created a dilemma since we can't selectively cut it off. Television, the press reports, and other written matter have acquired extraordinary importance and have become social instruments that no longer just inform the public but influence public opinion. Governments "leak" news to reporters; criminals communicate with them directly. Lynette Fromme and Sandra Good revealed their threats to newspeople before they acted them out. Much that is positive has in fact resulted from this awareness. Today we know more, and more rapidly than in the past, about problems and situations that otherwise would remain hidden; the public today is informed about the political process, about business, about issues that concern us even more directly: health, interpersonal relationships, morality. Everything is discussed on the screen and the printed page with less prejudice than in the past.

Increasingly, however, we have been concerned about the influence that dramas that portray violence have on the young, particularly in the case of television, which has become a part of our home life. For example, what happens in the minds of the viewers when they witness the characters of a drama as they kill casually; and worse, when the scene is followed by a commercial, a smiling young girl recommending a deodorant, a dignified man, a certain car as the best? Fictional violence has become part of our everyday life at just the time when real violence is a matter of great concern to us. And yet a notorious criminal, because of the power of the communications industry, can achieve fame—and other rewards tied to being famous—as a result of his crimes or by resorting to attention-getting devices while in prison. Bremer, who shot and crippled Governor Wallace, candidly, too candidly to achieve his aim, reported that he wanted to kill an important political figure in order to become famous and write a book!

We all want freedom of the press. No civilized society could survive without it. It is the gray area between reporting and exploiting the news that should concern us. Defendants, especially those who commit deliberate crimes, if they play their cards right can have an eager audience. Those whose crimes make the headlines either become celebrated figures or acquire certain privileges not accorded to others. The infamous Los Angeles trash-bag murderer, who for thirteen years sexually abused and killed young males, was able to make a deal with an attorney of his choosing by giving him all copyrights. The well-informed defendant of today, the one who has claim to "fame," need not be concerned about his criminal acts but about what legal technicalities he can use in his favor. One who commits horrible crimes automatically acquires a lobby.

Attorneys for the female defendants of the Tate-LaBianca murders have bitterly complained that these women were kept for years in the maximum security ward of the California Institution for Women. As Paul Fitzgerald puts it, "We [he and attorney Maxwell Keith] saw them encased and entombed in what could only be referred to as a concrete pillbox." According to Fitzgerald the CIW administrators did so for fear of public opinion, because the defendants were Manson people. I visited the maximum security unit at the institution and I certainly wouldn't like to live there or indeed in any section of a prison. These "Manson people," however, did not altogether lack privileges. Leslie Van Houten took college courses, participated in other activities, was regularly visited by family and friends, and so were the others. Susan Atkins was allowed to tell her story for publication while living in that "concrete pillbox" and subsequently permitted to give interviews for television and the press.

It is not where a prison inmate lives but who he or she is that makes the difference. Many convicted for lesser crimes never get a break; their crimes are not controversial or do not have enough news appeal. Defendants of important crimes have become more articulate about their plea because they have a support network. The more horrendous their crimes the larger the coverage they get. They can also be selective and choose to talk with those who will print or produce a favorable interview; or they can talk with those who can provide wide coverage and an aura of glamor because of the importance of the reporter. Susan Atkins gets many requests to appear on television. In a letter to me, Tex Watson said he was "swamped" by requests for interviews. He was, at least to my knowledge, on two national television programs, *The Good News,* a religious program, and *A.M. America.* Van Houten was interviewed by Barbara Walters, she who talks with heads of state and stars. And it doesn't matter if the reporter challenges the views of those interviewed. The truth is, challenged or no, these public interviews add to their celebrity status.

Television exposure, being written about, and getting published are after all coveted rewards. An unseen audience of thousands, and in the case of television millions, receive propaganda that even if critical turns out to benefit the criminal who has become, on a grand scale, news fit to print, people fit to be seen and heard. Too much is at stake for society when this happens. The trivialization and romanticizing of murderers and of murder, real murder, when done for mass consumption, has the effect of numbing people's moral sense and this in turn is another incentive to crime. I do believe that our society is becoming increasingly accepting of sociopathy perhaps because we only hear from those who either condone criminal behavior or who report it in a manner that shows the criminal in a favorable light. Most people are reluctant to take a stand for moral values and to speak up against specific criminals publicly. Many fear to be put in the "law and order" corner. It is a sign of our times that today the phrase has negative connotations.

We seldom hear accounts of the victims and their friends' predicament. Relatives are doubly hurt by the consequences of criminal acts as their wounds are constantly opened by the judicial process which may disclose facts about them they would rather keep private. Many remain frightened and traumatized for years. Meanwhile an assorted number of people publicly commiserates with the troubled criminals and wonders what can be done to help them.

To be sure, in the public mind the villain, the bad guy, has always been more interesting than his victims. When the victim is dead we frequently hear that after all he cannot be brought back to life and that we should be concerned with the living, with finding ways to rehabilitate the killer. Not much is done, one notices however, for the poor and the lobby-less who continue to fill our prisons, often, particularly in the case of males, under terrible conditions. But if one who has been convicted is in the public eye he immediately attains a privileged status even without such being the intention of the administrators who, however, know that *they* are being watched. They and their institutions are then under scrutiny because of the interest groups that are attracted by the notorious criminal. A felon convicted of bank robbery may be slapped by a guard and nobody on the outside would be the wiser. One can imagine what would happen, if, for example, such an incident would involve Emily Harris! Inmates attack each other frequently and seldom does this make the news. But when Lynette Fromme hit another inmate at the Federal Institution in Pleasanton, California, the incident was reported in all major newspapers. (As a result she was transferred back to the Federal Prison in Alderson, West Virginia.)

As I researched this book I had occasion to ask myself why some people are so attracted to, so supportive of criminals, especially the notorious ones. The most common answer to this question is that some people have themselves a dark side, impulses that they keep at bay or sublimate instead of acting out and are therefore strongly drawn to those who do. I believe that there are other reasons equally valid. For example, some persons cannot accept that a human being is evil. Among many of the religious, evil is simply a negation of God and people are regarded as being essentially good. Some of these people set themselves to help the criminal to uncover his basic goodness. Religious people who work in prisons and jails help anyone who asks for their help without setting any conditions or prior demands. A few use their work "on behalf" of notorious criminals to seek the limelight for themselves, perhaps to obtain money for their foundations. They diligently set themselves to make public figures out of vicious criminals, arguing that they bear witness to the triumph of good over evil and consequently their lives should be publicized.

Some people are attracted by criminals who commit bizarre crimes simply because they are fascinated by the mysteries of the bizarre. They want to know them for the same reasons that others go to see freak shows at carnivals and in doing so financially sponsor such pathetic spectacles. Still others are stimulated by those who are highly deviant because it is their hope that they can change them. A criminal, after all, has the potential of becoming a prodigal son. Thus he can be saved or persuaded to accept society's mores, consequently providing rewards for the savers and the persuaders. Susan Atkins reports in her book that immediately after she was imprisoned she started to receive offers of support. The more deviant a criminal is, the more challenging he is, and if saved the higher the glory that would reward the savior. But even criminals who do not repent at all attract followers; witness Gary Gilmore's saga, a murderer asking, albeit in a sensationalistic way, to be put to death. Those who "felt" for him completely obliterated from their consciousness the fact that Gilmore had culminated his criminal life by executing a young man in cold blood after a robbery. Gilmore went to his death in a grand manner. A fallen angel has a great deal of appeal, this we can't deny. A prison inmate who obtains a college degree is interviewed on television. Yet a student who makes sacrifices to obtain that same degree but who did not break the law and consequently is not in prison would never be newsworthy.

Naturally the mansonites who have repudiated their relationship with Manson are the ones who elicit sympathy since in doing so they are implicitly disapproving of their way of life when they were members of the Family. They and their verbal supporters ask that they be forgiven, presenting themselves as confused youth who fell prey to Manson and killed for him. These convicts, however, were not children when they committed their crimes; they were all over nineteen years old. They and their friends seem to be saying that our judicial system should turn the page and give them another chance; they point out that nothing is to be gained by keeping them in prison. I agree that in the case of some criminals everybody *is* better off if they are freed or paroled. The circumstances under which they broke the law, the type of crime they committed, and myriad other factors should be and in fact are increasingly considered. On the other hand, what are the moral consequences of making general rules about this issue? Must we accept that people at a certain period in their lives can kill just because they are "doing their thing," sure in the knowledge that if caught they will be freed in a few years because of their assertions that they will not kill again?

Some people who commit serious crimes are punished for life even if eventually they are out of prison. They lack the resources, the support to make something of themselves. For them their crime and their imprisonment are destructive. It has been said of the mansonites who participated in the Tate-LaBianca murders that they have suffered enough, that they will bear a stigma for the rest of their lives. In other words they are thus presented as the victims of their own actions. I don't share this view. I don't see these women as victims. Were they to be paroled they would have—they have already—people who support them, a network to belong to. They could easily turn deaf ears to those who still condemn them. They keep requesting parole hearings because they *know* that they can have a satisfying life on the outside and rewards not usually available to other criminals who did not achieve their "fame."

These women don't have to talk with anyone who is impartial. Instead, as I said before, they can select members of the media who either provide wide coverage for them to state their views or those who are biased in their favor. This was blatant in the case of Leslie Van Houten (and is better known in her case because she was retried).

Before her new trial she gave interviews to two reporters, Bill Farr (whom I mentioned earlier) of the Los Angeles *Times* and Judith Frutig of the *Christian Science Monitor*.

On February 17, 1977, Farr wrote an article whose title already suggests a positive view of the defendant and leads the reader to feel compassion for her, "Two Murders Still Haunt Former Manson Cultist." (Even though reporters are not usually responsible for headlines, whoever prepared this one was reflecting the content of the article.) In the first paragraphs the attempt to elicit sympathy continues as he quotes Van Houten:

> I know that I did something horrible . . . I don't expect people to forgive me but I hope eventually they will give me a chance.

The article states that "Leslie Van Houten says she still has nightmares about the murders of Leno and Rosemary LaBianca." We have only Leslie's word about what her dreams are like. At no time does the article mention anything negative about Leslie, for example, that she knew of the Tate murders before she embarked on her own murderous adventure. Instead Mr. Farr elaborates on how Manson, via LSD, dominated her. It also reports on Leslie's plans for the future including her plans for a writing career. Obviously readers of this article did not get an impartial account since it seems to have been written by a friend on Leslie Van Houten's behalf.

The titles of Frutig's articles published on March 16 and 17, 1977, give some hope of unbiased reporting. One, "Leslie Van Houten, Completely Rehabilitated? New Trial May Set Manson 'Family' Member Free"; the other, "Van Houten Six Years Later." In fact, Ms. Frutig chose to embark on a discussion of rehabilitation of convicts, ignoring the fact that Van Houten was not about to go to a parole hearing but about to be tried again for first degree murder (a probation phase did come later after she was indicted again in 1978). In her article Ms. Frutig presents Leslie as a model of a rehabilitated person. Again we read of Manson's—and drugs'—influence on Leslie. Here is a sample of the carefully worded—for such purposes—report:

Leslie Van Houten says she isn't afraid of Charles Manson

anymore. She says she has shaken off his chilling domina-
tion and severed her ties with the Manson Family. And
this time, she says, she will tell the jury the truth.

Ms. Frutig is not bothered by the fact that Leslie was never afraid of
Manson. Commenting on Leslie's remarkable change of attitude as
compared with that during her first trial she states:

And those same officers [prison psychiatrists and correc-
tion officials] who once considered her an incorrigible
threat, are saying privately [after this article no longer so!]
that they hope she wins it.

In these articles Leslie narrates how she rehabilitated herself and
gives credit to her mother for her help and continuous support. She
also says:

I don't give the Corrections Department of California
much credit for what I am today. I had to look inside
myself. I had to change me. I have been exploited in a lot of
ways.

Of interest is that between her two retrials, for several months while
free on bail, Leslie Van Houten lived with Ms. Frutig. So much for
the dignities of unbiased reporting.

There is something obscenely dishonest about using one's profession, that of a reporter, to present one's personal views without saying
so. The reading public has the right to expect that journalists report,
not slant the news according to their wishes and then pass it off as the
real thing. An even more glaring example of the misuse of journalism
occurred during the probation and sentencing phase of the Van
Houten retrial, after she had been convicted. Leslie was eligible for
parole; the discussion centered on whether she was a suitable
candidate. The defense presented witnesses who attested to Leslie's
character today. One of them was Daniel Blackburn, a reporter
employed by NBC as a radio correspondent. He was assigned to cover
the Van Houten retrials and did, although on March 1978 he met
Leslie Van Houten through his friend, Ms. Frutig, and saw her
frequently after that, two or three times a week, usually in the

company of Ms. Frutig. He became a good friend of the defendant whom he described with respect and admiration. He had been with her at parties, dinners, picnics, and found her to have correct social behavior at all times. Mr. Blackburn went so far as to ask a few colleagues to send Judge Ringer letters in support of Leslie; according to him, most agreed to do so but the judge found no letters from them among the case's correspondence. Mr. Blackburn also "managed" to present his positive views about his friend to John Van de Camp, the district attorney! And even asked him what options were open to Leslie after she was charged again. Judge Ringer became incensed by this reporter's unethical behavior:

> Did your superiors at NBC know that you were, in effect, socializing with Miss Van Houten while covering the trial before you advised them that you had been served with a subpoena to testify here?

Mr. Blackburn answered in the affirmative. The subpoena, by the way, had been his idea. (To be subpoenaed meant that he was ordered to testify.) He stated that his ability to report the facts was not impaired, since "The facts are still the facts. They don't change. But I'm not asked to do opinion." To which the judge exclaimed, "I'm about to explode!" and added, refusing to go into chambers because he wanted to be on record:

> The bias of this witness is so obvious, his misconception of his private and civic functions, together with his duties, obligations and rights under the First Amendment of the Constitution of the United States is so blatant, that I think it would be a service to the cause of justice in this state if this witness were allowed simply to quietly slip off the witness stand. . . .

And later,

> I am outraged as a citizen that this kind of thing can occur and that it can occur with, as he says, the approval, or at least the tacit consent of his superiors.

88

Judge Ringer made it clear that his anger was not directed at the defendant or at her lawyers but at the witness. Some of the mistakes that her lawyer Mr. Keith made in selecting and in discussing the case with his witnesses simply amaze me. As for Mr. Blackburn's testimony, Mr. Keith stated that in his opinion anybody who knows Leslie is biased in her favor.

I want to discuss here some of the books that have been written about this case. Their authors "were there" at the time of the trials and, in the case of writer-criminals, at the time of the crimes. Some of these books aim at being factual reports and are and will continue to be useful to the investigator searching for information about the Manson case. Others, written by the culprits, are totally biased creations but nevertheless are useful because they throw light on the writers' characters.

George Bishop's *Witness to Evil* was published in 1971. It has a preface written by Art Linkletter, whose daughter had met her death while tripping on LSD, and in it Mr. Linkletter stressed the deleterious effects that drugs are having on our children. Bishop's book is a diary, from pretrial to the final verdict; it is a serious account of the famous trial with information on and insights into what also went on behind the court stage. Mr. Bishop's opinions about some aspects of the trial are interesting. For instance, on Bugliosi presenting the Helter-Skelter motive in spite of the opposition of his colleagues who thought it was too implausible, Bishop comments, "Ironically it was quite possible that Bugliosi believed in Helter Skelter more than did Manson!" According to this author, Manson was not capable of putting such "demented" theory together and it was Bugliosi who "supplied that organized, reasoning mind."

Helter Skelter, published in 1974 and authored by the prosecutor, Vincent Bugliosi, and Curt Gentry is also written in a diary form. This best seller is a fascinating account not only of the trial but of the prosecutor trying to get his man in spite of great odds, which the book discusses in detail. The book reads like a Simenon story, Inspector Maigret doggedly bent on achieving his purpose. Only at the end, like an afterthought, does Bugliosi concern himself with the culpability of the women. The book discusses the women's responsibility for their criminal actions but fails to be convincing, because Bugliosi seems to accept the "explanation" offered by the psychiatrist I mentioned, Dr. Joel Hochman, who thought that the Manson group suffered from a case of *folie en famille,* in which Manson's mental illness was transferred to other members of the Family.

In *The Family,* published in 1971, reporter Ed Sanders traces the life of the Manson group up to the point of their arrest. He deals, to a great extent, with the occult scene in Los Angeles. His book is a vivid picture of the sleazy side of that city and is a good document in spite of the author's superficial interpretations and a breezy style which almost conveys the impression that the author did not take himself seriously.

Two books were coauthored by the convicted murderers themselves. Susan Atkins' *Child of Satan, Child of God,* written with Bob Slosser, was published in 1977. This is, as is to be expected, a self-serving account of Susan's life and her eventual conversion in 1974, when she became a Born Again Christian. It was coauthored by another writer and like all books was edited by yet another professional. Yet it is amazing how it presents Susan today as the same exhibitionistic woman she was at the time when she revealed herself after the Hinman murder. In her book Susan states that the Tate-LaBianca murders were intended as copycat murders, an attempt to show that Bobby Beausoleil was not guilty of killing Hinman, but that someone else still at large was the culprit. Her book acccomplished Susan's purpose: It put her back on center stage.

Charles "Tex" Watson's book, *Will You Die for Me?* as told to Chaplain Ray Hoekstra, is a biography which emphasizes the changes Watson underwent while under Manson's influence. According to him there were various motives for the Tate-LaBianca murders, to provoke Helter Skelter, to clear Beausoleil of the Hinman slaying, and robbery. Tex makes no bones about relinquishing responsibility for the crimes he committed: Manson and drugs made him do it too:

> One of the many effects of speed is to make the intention or thought of an action and that action itself almost insepar-
> able, as if you leap ahead in time and experience your next

90

move before you actually make it. There is that living room on the hill, with Charlie's instructions ticking through my brain, it was as if time telescoped, until one act tripped over the next in sudden bursts of blinding color and motion.

He presents himself, while brutally slaying his victims, as an automaton with "Charlie's tapes inside my head" ordering him to kill. Naturally he completely dismisses prosecutor Bugliosi's assertion that a mental collapse he says he suffered during his trial was a fake. Like Susan, he ends his book with an account of his religious conversion and involvement. This continues to be used commercially. There is a current mail order offering of tape cassettes, *Powerful Sermons by Charles "Tex" Watson, Former Member of the Manson Family, Now A Servant of Christ in Prison!*

We hear from and read about people who have won their battles against mental illness and alcoholism, from those who are severely handicapped and yet are making it. Our spirit is uplifted by their stories which tell of man's capacity for surviving against great odds. I do not put self-serving stories written by criminals in the same category, although their writers and their supporters want to do so. And I question the wisdom of permitting these stories to be published. I know that my opinion in this respect will raise serious questions. I think, however, that the First Amendment is stretched too far when it protects the right of the criminal to profit from his crimes. In our country we have witnessed a remarkable example of a democracy at work. When the most powerful people in the United States, the President and his aides, broke the law, they were expelled from office and with the exception of Nixon they were convicted and served time. But because of their unlawful behavior they have become hot property for major publishers and television producers, and as a result today they are wealthy and sought after, although there are plenty of people who have written about the Watergate scandal, people who had no personal part in it and are qualified to tell the story. What is the use of living in a democracy, or working to maintain it, if those who blatantly break the law can profit from their crimes? Why should convicted criminals who committed deliberate crimes have the same rights that noncriminals have? The

91

right, for example, to use the printed page and television to tell their self-serving stories?

The idea that censorship by any other name is still censorship is legitimate. I can understand why some people want to prevent *Hustler* magazine from being published; I find it reprehensible that a periodical such as *High Times,* devoted to instruct people on the use of all kinds of drugs, sees the light. But I wouldn't favor censoring either; we can't spoon-feed adults on what material to read. And the publishers of these and other similar material so far have broken no laws.

Of course some people have been convicted of "crimes" that actually were an expression of their moral or political convictions. I fail to see, however, why in cases of clear criminality, such as that of the mansonites, we should be concerned about the dangers of censorship. I do think that some criminal's self-serving creations should be censored. For, what is the implication of not doing so? Are we to continue to send utterly confusing messages in the name of "rights"? Should, for example, members of the Nazi party be allowed to parade when we all know that by definition they stand for a criminal, perverted way of life? The argument that if they are not permitted to express themselves in public other groups may lose their right to do so sickens me. Such argument has a black or white, all or nothing implication. To me it represents the "criminal chic" absurd misreading of the democratic process.

There is one type of crime literature that is very popular and because it is I have hopes that human beings, after all, are interested in seeing that justice be done. I am referring to the detective and mystery genre. Millions read these stories in which the criminal is always caught, proof is offered of his guilt, and the assumption is that he will be convicted. The Chinese, who were writing detective stories one thousand years ago, give in theirs detailed accounts of the punishment finally meted out to the criminal. People who write these tales and those who read them want the criminal caught and punished. Whether he is Conan Doyle or Agatha Christie or Dee Goong or Bao Goong we realize that these writers are anticrime, not pro-crime. To be sure in some cases disclosure of violence and sex exploitation help sales. But what people buy by the millions all over the world is the fictionalization of a reassuring statement: Crime does not pay.

Real-life murders are considerably more sordid than their fictionalized counterparts. Many a time I felt dejected while reading the transcripts of the Manson trials. Many lives are touched when a crime of any sort is committed, not only bizarre, mass murders. One is acutely aware of the pain of the victims, relatives, and friends, and of the families of the criminals on whom the murderers inflict great psychological injury. Particularly, they leave their parents with a question carved in their hearts, no matter what they say for public consumption: *Where did I go wrong?*

II

From Love to Violence

> ". . . And they all lived together
> in a little crooked house."

I want to answer a question that arose in my own mind when I first thought about the Manson case. Why did this group that started as a love-in experience turn to violence? This question, in fact, comes to mind whenever a communal group whose members are intensively involved with each other hit the news because of their violent activities. We as a society have become increasingly concerned about violent groups, few of which are violent at their inception.

I am referring here to groups that evolve a system of beliefs centered on religion or mysticism or a style of life or politics. No matter what type, these groups come to revolve around a "cause" that is embraced first by a leader who has personal magnetism and who can seduce large or small numbers of people who themselves have specific characteristics. The leader develops into a savior or a prophet or a political extremist, self-proclaimed as such at first. Some, like Jim Jones, start by using their capacity for personal influence for a good cause, to help the poor, to encourage racial integration, all within a religious framework. Subversive political groups of this type

97

which become violent also start by sponsoring humanitarian concerns about the poor and the powerless. The Berkeley white women who befriended and sponsored black inmates at the California Medical Facility sought—or so they proclaimed—to correct injustice. They were allowed to attend and to participate in the meetings held by inmates of the institution, meetings intended to raise the morale of the prisoners. One of these inmates was Donald DeFreeze who eventually was chosen as the leader of the Symbionese Liberation Army. After being released from prison, DeFreeze kept in touch with some of these women. (This man had such a history of violent behavior that some people, unable to understand why he was paroled, suspected that he might have been paroled so he could act as a police undercover agent.)

Andreas Baader also declared his idealistic concerns when he first became an activist; he started by demonstrating against the Vietnam War and against the totalitarian regime of the Shah of Iran. It was at that early period that he and Ulrike Meinhof met, while she was preparing his defense after he had been arrested. Thus the destructive Baader-Meinhof gang was born. Shortly thereafter they started to attract "educated," well-to-do members and formed what was to become an extremely violent political terrorist group.

The rhetoric used by these people is always the same: Nothing can be achieved by negotiating, by establishing a dialogue between opposing parties. The only thing that works is destroying the enemy and instilling fear by destruction and murder. An arsonist enjoys a great feeling of power when he learns of or looks at the disasters he has caused. The terrorists I am discussing here mask their appetite for notoriety and power with claims about their "idealistic" concerns.

Some of these groups become violent within a relatively short span, like the Manson commune. Some others, like the People's Temple, evolve into violence only after many years. Some go underground, usually the politically subversive, and some, on the contrary, operate as frankly "different," quite aboveground like the mansonites. Some remain allegedly idealistic and rationalize their violence as the means that justify the end. Others, notably the motorcycle gangs that started by asserting their right to a different life-style, became frankly criminal and formed private crime organizations. No matter what their differences are, these groups, once they have become cohesive, have important similarities:

1. Their leaders are charismatic figures.

2. The members are rebels with a "cause" which becomes the group's bond, the justification for staying together, allied in their violence.

3. Their cause is born out of an irrational philosophy based on the alleged need to protect and to lobby for the underdog; but even on superficial scrutiny this cause fails to explain how the members' actions—all sorts of antisocial activities, destruction, and murder— would improve the human condition and how their naive conceptions of how to reorganize the world can be put into operation. It is likely that some of the members of these groups deceive themselves into believing their own rationalizations because only a grand scheme, for example, to suddenly bring about radical changes in society, would satisfy their megalomania and at the same time cover up other personal conflicts.

4. Their "movements" lack the authenticity of, for example, the Russian, the Chinese, and the Cuban revolutions, and the Anti-Vietnam movement. The Bolsheviks, after all, were rebelling against a caste system that completely ignored the needs of the vast majority of the Russian population. In China before the revolution children were dying of hunger while the power structure was corrupt and vicious. Fidel Castro and his followers sought to overthrow the corrupt government of Fulgencio Batista. The Israeli terrorists wanted their Promised Land, a country of their own to protect themselves from cruel persecution; the Palestinians want their land returned to them. No matter how bloody these movements have been or whether one agrees or not with their political philosophy, their causes can be easily understood.

5. Most of the members of the groups I am discussing are middle class and white. The exception was the People's Temple because it was founded—by a white—to pursue racial equality and integration.

6. Violence in these groups is deliberate, not random or accidental but purposeful; the impulsive, the poorly controlled individual is either not accepted or does not carry out important activities, destructive or otherwise.

99

7. Women's participation in the acts of violence has been on the increase. Women are also having a more important role in the power structure. For example it is reported that the leader of the Japanese Red Army is a woman. The Weathermen and the S.L.A. had very active women members. Latin-American guerillas have many women in their ranks. Lynette Fromme, of course, broke tradition by becoming the first woman to attempt to assassinate a president of the United States.

8. The people who form these groups are rigid and immature; the emotional, conflictual motivations that drive these people to these groups are rationalized by them as convictions, as a commitment to their "cause." This cause is the nucleus that serves the individual's conflicts. Being part of the group is seen by the members as the ultimate solution, the ultimate answer which actually becomes their main problem since it supports and thus perpetuates their pathological deviance.

9. These groups are a joint venture. Followers and leader(s) choose each other; their roles are synchronized.

10. The leaders of these groups and the followers have certain characteristics. The leaders are seductive, "feeling"-oriented as opposed to "thinking"-oriented. They convey the sense that they already have or that they have the potential to achieve great power. They also convey to their followers that they are all of them, leader and followers, on the same level. This is an exhilarating experience for these followers since in our society (and in most) there are marked rituals which govern distance and closeness between those in power and the powerless.

In these groups "following" is as active as "leading." I find no substantiation to the claim that followers are snapped or hypnotized into these groups. Followers most probably are people searching for their place under the sun in a magical way. Some of them are people with serious identity problems. Others simply do not fit into the larger society and are either unable or unwilling to learn to adapt. To belong is not enough for them; otherwise belonging would be a powerful motivation to form their own family like everybody else or to join other conventional groups. It is said, however, that these people are rejects, ostracized by their families and other established

100

groups. If this is the case for some of them, I would question why they are rejected. The overwhelming majority of the poor and the oppressed and the seriously troubled do not join these groups. Chicano farm workers, for example, joined Cesar Chavez. Many hopeless alcoholics join the Alcoholics Anonymous or a religious group and become constructive individuals. Many drug addicts who joined Synanon when it was really a self-help group left when it became antisocial. I believe that the people who become followers of the types of groups I am discussing here have a common characteristic: They are grandiose. They are attracted by the possibility of becoming highly important. Their leader acts out his followers' megalomania which in turn reinforces his. The group invests its members with an aura, the feeling that they are special, people destined to make a mark in the world. These reawakened feelings of omnipotence are part of the emotional makeup of people in whom some personality aspects have remained fixated at an early age. Thus, the notion that we must protect young people from the danger of being emotionally seques-tered by cult leaders and their lieutenants is based on a false premise; in actuality these leaders and their followers cannot be contrasted as being the powerful and the powerless, the active and the passive. They attract each other and fit each other at a certain point in their lives because they speak the same psychological language. Although later on I will expand on this, I want to say here that the emotional pathways that lead them to their encounter are traced in their past; they emerge from the interchanges that occur in their families. The family is the architect, so to speak, that ultimately designs whether a person stays on the road once paved or whether he is free to become his own, unique architect. To explore only the psychological themes of these leaders—and I must say that this is being done rather superficially because of the emotionalism of the issue—is to obscure our perception of what these groups represent, of who are the people who form them, of why their utterances are housed in the idiom of violence.

The Manson group was popularly known as "The Family." But even Ed Sanders, author of the book by that name, at times referred to the group as "the alleged family." The label was emphasized by the press during the trial but I don't think that it was just a media

101

creation as some mansonites claim. Off and on they referred to their group as "their family." My question is, was this group a family?

The concept of "family" is continuously being expanded; how to define a family has become as much a subject of controversy as the institution of the family itself. The sixties were characterized by a strong antifamily bias which was in fact exactly that of the mansonites. Yet off and on they themselves, as I said, referred to their group as their family.

A number of mansonites became the permanents of the group and were strongly bonded to Manson and to each other, and some still are. For them, whether they remained attached to Manson or indeed changed into his detractors, "the Manson affair" continues to be the most important period of their lives. It gave them notoriety, even fame, whether they are within prisons or have never been imprisoned. One can well understand that even those who did not participate in the crimes have had an extraordinary experience by having been at some time part of the Family. At this writing, Paul Watkins, Juan Flynn, and Barbara Hoyt, for example, are neighbors. The three seemed quite attached to Leslie Van Houten by the time of her second retrial; so probably is Ruth Moorehouse who testified on her behalf. Leslie and Patricia Krenwinkel kept up their friendship during their imprisonment even though Pat refused to testify in her defense, probably because Pat is still emotionally involved with Manson. Sandra and Lyn continue to be very close and try to perpetuate the Manson mystique.

Women members and sympathizers staged fanatic demonstrations and kept vigil during the original Manson trial. This fanaticism, however, bears little resemblance to the loyalty that exists among members of most families, no matter how close they are. The mansonites' actions at the time of the trial were cultish demonstrations geared at showing that their group was right and the world that condemned their crimes was wrong. They continued to support their group and their leader because they wanted support for their hedonistic life-style and their grandiose yearnings. Their alleged concern for the environment, their tired verbosity on behalf of pure air and clean water never materialized into any constructive action; it was empty. Their secondhand speeches were devoid of significance, their words divorced from their meaning.

102

The mansonites were not just a group of people who met and stayed together by chance, and their activities within their commune were not scattered hither and thither, the result of a moment's fancy. On the contrary, as I said earlier, it was a closely related group that banded together because of the emotional makeup of its individuals, and as such, during its short existence it was similar to a family or rather to an extended family network. I doubt that any of the members that time could relate on a heterosexual or a homosexual level as individual couples. For all their emotional fusion, these people were unable to form one-to-one relationships and were incapable of emotional intimacy. They, however, formed liaisons within the group; Pat and Leslie's relationship, for example, was of a different quality than each woman's relationship to others. But all the same, because of the primitive level on which these people functioned, their coupling lacked the characteristics we usually associate with mature interpersonal relationships, and it is doubtful that they could have sustained them outside this unusual group or any other controlled environment (such as a prison). I will discuss later Sandra and Lyn's bond, its unreal quality speaking of the make-believe world in which they exist.

I speculate that these people had serious deficits in their sense of self and that the group became a self for each one, each contributing a fragment. This type of joining characterizes "closed" human systems, which I will describe shortly.

In an "open" system, that of healthy families and groups, the members have their individual sense of identity; they are aware of their self boundaries, of being separate from others, while at the same time they are able to identify with their group and to feel loyalty towards their relatives or co-members. In the case of a family, the growing child knows that he has choices, he perceives that his emotional stability and his security would not be greatly endangered if, for example, he disagrees with his parents. The behavior of members of healthy groups or families can be spontaneous and creative; the opportunity and the wish exist for both intimacy and space. These groups and their members have the capacity to change and to adapt. A couple without children, for example, functions differently once they become parents. Individuals make certain changes to adapt to life's demands, and there is overt as well as unspoken support in effecting these changes. Most people, to different degrees, adapt to expanding or changing roles within the family, at work, in society. Most people are able, stimulated from early life, to learn to accept frustration, to cope with failure, with criticism, and with a certain amount of rejection from others. And many who do find it difficult eventually pull themselves together and evolve some way to adapt. People who are part of open family systems, no matter what problems they may have, tend to be flexible and in essence grow up emotionally. They are able to face and at times to enjoy adult responsibilities.

As a group the mansonites developed into a "closed" system. Closed groups and families become increasingly rigid; inquiry or criticism of the group's myths by any member threatens the group's emotional balance and consequently that of its members since they are dependent on the group's self. Each member acts as only a part of the whole. The mansonites became, in a manner of speaking, their true, undifferentiated, all-joined self. I believe that Manson's assertion to me, when I spoke with him, that to belong to his family a person had to have his or her self was not only self-serving—to avoid legal responsibility for the others' actions—but it probably was also his perception at the time, based on his intense fear of having any human being emotionally dependent on him. These people felt safe and protected as a group while the going was good. In fact they avoided the discomfort that other people suffer who feel insecure and who have self problems (many, because of their very discomfort, are thus motivated to deal with their problems). A group of this type is highly vulnerable to anxiety in any member, particularly in the designated leader. When he is under strain, unable to function in his usual way, the group trembles. It is well known that in any group or family when those in a position of leadership are under stress, this stress is transmitted to the rest. But healthy groups and families are formed by individuals who have their own resources and consequently have the ability to ameliorate their difficulties, to find solutions. Such was not the case in the Manson group. The leader, as is always the case in this type of group, was as self-defective as the followers but his position made him even more vulnerable. It is indeed stressful to "play" the role of the leader when having to face adversity. At a

104

certain point life for the mansonites became a matter of survival, of trying to maintain the status quo, in their case on an exaggerated, hype level. Closed groups or families as a matter of fact do not just exist or grow; they survive and all the emotional and intellectual energies of its members are invested in keeping a rigid pseudobalance. When external pressures overwhelm this "as if" unreal atmosphere of pretending, there is a breakdown of sorts. For example, families where the motto is that all members love each other all the time do not, of course, allow the expression of anger from one member to another of the family. Instead, anger is projected to the world outside. People on the outside (or society at large) are "wrong" or "inadequate." One step further and the outside becomes "them" against "us." There was a remarkable lack of squabbles, and criticism was nonexistent within the Family. Manson and others disapproved of Susan Atkins' penchant for picking up undesirables but this disapproval was low-keyed. Lynette Fromme told me that after all Susan originated a great deal of "energy" (excitement). Leslie became too interested in and promiscuous with bikers and had to be restrained, but after all these actions did not challenge the group's life-style.

The mansonites truly believed that they did not need the world outside because they were fully satisfied with one another. They saw themselves as a self-contained and self-sufficient group. For the sake of clarity I want to say that the Family became a closed emotional system but this does not mean that the group was literally closed. Anyone was free to go. This, being an important legal point, was emphasized during the trials. The members had the choice of leaving, emotionally and physically. Brooks Poston, for example, left after going through a harrowing experience of pseudodeath (he was either asleep or unconscious for two or three days). Paul Watkins also eventually left. Both did transfer their dependency needs to another available guru, Paul Crockett, who was not a violent man. Juan Flynn, the handsome Pan-American ranch hand, was allowed to remain peripheral to the group. A Vietnam veteran who had been emotionally damaged by his war experience, he was wary of being part of such a rigid group. He was also threatened by Manson's bisexuality and feared venereal disease; at one point he rejected Leslie's advances because she had skin lesions which he thought could be syphilitic. The permanent members of the group remained close to each other voluntarily. In forming such a relationship they were just following their personal emotional maps. Under Manson's and each other's umbrellas they felt comfortably satisfied because they felt free to be who they were. No one, until the advent of their violent period when Paul left, even conceived of exploring other ways to live. They did not want to question because doing so would call for getting on with life and the acceptance of adult responsibilities which, of course, involved much more than their version of self-realization.

To repeat, the Manson group was not a haphazard collection of people whose behavior was errant and unpredictable. On the contrary, its evolution followed a logical process. Many groups and families, to a different degree, go through a similar process. Here I want to trace the evolution of this group. In my discussion I am not concerned with the actual comings and goings of the Family unless they are pertinent; their chronology has been reported already. I will focus instead on the internal processes, the inner movements of this group which inexorably drove them to violence.

Birth of the Family

Berkeley today doesn't look much different from the way it did in 1967 when Manson wandered around Telegraph Avenue. Telegraph is a dirty, ugly street but it also has expensive shops and good restaurants. Pathetic-looking young women dressed as peasants walk next to necklaced middle-aged men. Street vendors abound, selling jewelry, food, posters. Some people have the healthy, tanned California look; others look drugged or psychotic. Berkeley today, as it was yesterday, has the mixture of people that makes for the best and the worst: the transients, the weirdos, and the conservative and the highly disciplined. Berkeley continues to harbor the nucleus of the antiestablishment and the revolutionary from all over the world, both the real and the phony. But Berkeley also has a university that has produced the largest number of Nobel prizes of any American university. On Telegraph Avenue the Center for Independent Living is located, the most exciting experiment in the world in providing a

106

decent life and opportunities for the severely disabled. One can get the most scholarly and "literati" publication in its bookstores—and also the most deviant. In Berkeley today as in the sixties the underground is well aboveground. The hills that circle the town and the waters of the bay are like a basket containing anything one may want to pick as long as it is an extreme.

I can imagine how puzzled Manson might have felt when, fresh out of prison—again—he found himself in Berkeley (which is next door to San Francisco) among myriad young people who eagerly *accepted* him. Here he was, a con, ready to live it up while it lasted, waiting for the moment to pull up his usual tricks from his survival kit, just on another vacation before going back home to some California prison. What a surprise awaited him! He was not despised and rejected by the majority as in the past; on the contrary, he was given flowers and instant friendship. In this world, he soon found out, the deviant was the norm. All his life he had been an outsider, but now he belonged. The Counterculture had grown; it was, in Berkeley, much more visible than the Establishment and its amorphous walls could accommodate even him.

Promptly Manson, always a lady's man, made a liaison with the first woman in his new life, Mary Brunner, a homely twenty-three-year-old librarian who provided him with housing—among other things—first for himself and after that for other girls who joined Manson. Next to nothing is known about this first romance that was to produce a child, Michael aka Pooh Hoo. Mary is an elusive figure; she lied her way in and out of courtrooms. She spent some time in the California Institution for Women charged, with other Family members, in the robbery of a Western Supply Store in Hawthorne, a suburb of Los Angeles. The gang had a grand plan to collect guns to free Manson. While at the California Institution for Women Mary and Catherine (Gypsy) Share made two attempts to escape prison and join Catherine's revolutionary boyfriend. In spite of her criminal activities Mary was paroled, and after residing and working for some time in Los Angeles she is back in Wisconsin with her family and her child. She could tell much about the beginnings of the group but probably she has decided that her best course of action is to remain silent at least for the time being. I wrote to her but got no reply. I have been told that Michael has a strong physical resemblance to Manson. I can't help but wonder what life has in store for him. Catherine, the oldest of the group, was also among its first members. She has also disappeared into anonymity and is reportedly living in Represa, California, where Folsom Prison is located, because her boyfriend is an inmate there.

Soon Manson found himself surrounded by adoring females, including Patricia Krenwinkel and Lyn Fromme; after he took his group to the Haight-Ashbury another of his "permanents" was to join him. This is how Susan Atkins describes the encounter:

> I was breathless as I shut the door of the old brown house behind me and stood for several minutes listening to the music—a man's voice—coming from the big room upstairs. I climbed the stairs slowly and stepped into the dusky room. Seated on the couch in front of the bay window was Charlie Manson, playing a beat-up old guitar remarkably well and singing in a clear, but soft voice, "The shadow of your smile when you are gone will color all my dreams and light the dawn."
>
> After listening to Charlie sing and talk, after dancing with him and making love, after singing and seeing the power of his mind, I knew I would go with him if he asked me. I felt fully responsible for my actions, but at the same time I was attracted to something inside me that was attracted to something inside him. I knew I had never encountered this before, and I knew I had to have what he had.

The group, which also included a few young men, was soon to leave the Haight-Ashbury district of San Francisco that had become a dangerous place because of the extensive abuse of drugs and the drug trafficking. They fixed an old school bus and headed for Los Angeles. They actually traveled not only all along the California coast but got as far as Texas. This was an exhilarating period. All these young people felt a sense of unity and professed love to and for each other and above all, acceptance, which wasn't difficult since they were images of each other. They were indeed investing their emotions in themselves, following their narcissism. They could openly express their disdain for established society and act it out by their use of drugs and by their sexual promiscuity. There was a free-for-all, an elated atmosphere. They all basked in their reciprocal support. For Manson this was an entirely new experience. Not only was he accepted but he was admired by real people, not just by the creations of his mind. His Walter Mitty daydreams had become real.

The bond was crystallizing and the group balance evolved into a hype level. Manson, by then in his early thirties, was increasingly idealized by the rest who had a need to belong to someone who was somebody, one who made a statement, as a way to feel themselves important. And Manson, in turn, lavished praise on his followers who were only too eager to hear him say that they were perfect. He made love to the women, he danced, he sang his own songs, he played his guitar and encouraged the others to sing and dance. I have a vision of the group, each member actually completely self-involved, the pioneers of today's discotheque dwellers.

The Beatles, already a legend, provided the musical background for their life-style. They were fresh and sophisticated. Above all they were superstars and Manson and his acolytes started to wonder, "Why couldn't we too become superstars?"

By the summer of 1968 all the major characters of this drama were part of the Family. Some strong relationships were being established already: that of Sandra and Lyn and Pat and Leslie; and the very special love between Lyn and Manson. Juan Flynn told me that Manson encouraged some of these relationships to strengthen the group.

Regression

During the spring of 1968 Manson, through one of his admirers, Dean Moorehouse—the father of Ruth, a member of the Family—became acquainted with Dennis Wilson, a member of the highly successful singing group The Beach Boys, and with Gregg Jakobson, a promoter. Both became quite enthusiastic about Manson's love philosophy and the life-style of the group. Soon Manson, his girls, and Moorehouse's protégé Tex Watson were practically living in the luxurious Sunset Boulevard mansion that Wilson was renting. Life was sweet and exciting. Sex and hallucinogenic drugs were there for the taking. Hedonism was at its peak. The women cooked for the men, everybody made love. Life was an uninterrupted party and the mansonites rubbed shoulders with the children of the famous and the rich. Here it was, a youthful American version of *La Dolce Vita!* But the aristocratic Romans have generations of experience with decadence. It is theirs, they know how to manage it and how to live it. Manson the jailbird and his middle-class followers were ill prepared for this life; for them fantasy and reality became confused. Manson basked in the adulation of Wilson, Jakobson, and others. He felt increasingly reassured that his ambitions to form his own successful rock group would be realized because of the connections he was making with people in the entertainment business. The mansonites' feelings of omnipotence, their narcissism, were continuously stimulated. Fame, power, great riches were just a dream away.

Wilson, as a member of the Beach Boys, was already a good product in the entertainment business and as such he belonged to a protective network. He also had work to do, rehearsals, publicity, tours. In spite of his life-style he was part of the working force. For him, Manson and his girls were probably just another source of excitement, a new and unusual toy to play with. Obviously he was also generous and willing to share his riches and his good fortune. He believed, at least for some time, that Manson had something that could be marketable and he and Jakobson tried to help Manson to attain the glories he craved. I don't know if Wilson knows the part that his ill-directed generosity played in the tragedy that was to follow. For contact with the rich and the successful produced a heightening of expectations in the mansonites. Before Sunset Boulevard life for them was a love-in albeit on a hype level. By now they had tasted what success meant and they wanted to sit at their own table in their own mansion. Manson wanted his group to make it big in the world of rock music.

The mansonites' life-style proved to be too much even for fun-loving Wilson who finally, unable to tolerate it, decided to move out from his own home and terminate his rental contract. Manson had to find permanent quarters for the group. He did, in a ranch in Topanga

110

Canyon that was used frequently as temporary shelter by hippies. The Spahn Ranch owned by an old, almost-blind man, George Spahn, became home. Lynette provided for George Spahn's needs in exchange.

It was quite a change from a Sunset Boulevard mansion to a dilapidated movie ranch hardly used anymore other than to rent horses. A life of fantasy was needed more than ever to compensate for the difference. Wilson and Jakobson, however, continued both their relationship with Manson and their promises. The Beach Boys, after all, had recorded one of Manson's songs, "Cease to Exist," which they changed first into "Cease to Resist" and eventually to "Never Learn Not to Love."

It is interesting that Susan Atkins reports that shortly after the group moved to Spahn, Manson became depressed and suggested that the group should split. Some of the women left, rented a house up north, and tried to duplicate their life in the Family. But when they were threatened by local boys, the police intervened, found drugs in the house, and the girls were sentenced to three months in the Mendocino County Jail.

Was Manson already aware of the pressures inherent in being a leader? Was he depressed by his eviction from the Wilson mansion? Unfortunately he was not able to escape easily. His followers proved incapable of making it on their own and eventually everybody returned to the Spahn Ranch where he had stayed. The group reassumed their life together, more "together" than ever after having experienced the dangers of the world outside. Of course no one had tried to go back to the straight life.

Under a facade of adult sophistication regarding sex, drugs, values, the group continued to literally regress. Games were played that were actually the acting out of early childhood fantasies. The participants dressed up and pretended to change identities to fit the characters they portrayed. Manson would "become" a fearless pirate, the girls would be witches or ladies-in-waiting or princesses or pirates themselves. I have read that these games were deliberate attempts made by the members to rid themselves of their former identities, part of achieving "ego death." I do not think that such was the case; this was just another of Manson's pseudo-philosophical "packages" to allow

111

everyone to save face, to pretend they were adults while they acted out their infantilism.

The group became organized. The mansonites got along well with George Spahn and with the cowhands. A division of labor was established. Paul Watkins became the procurer of girls who were, albeit, only too willing. He became Manson's right arm. Tex Watson, a good mechanic, fixed up vehicles and was all around to help as needed. Bruce Davis took care of stolen credit cards and fake identifications. The women cooked and sewed and embroidered for the men and for themselves. They hunted for food in the garbage cans of supermarkets. They shared garments and even underwear. Everything was communal. They dressed and undressed and dressed again, in blue jeans or dingy dresses or shorts and a profusion of multicolored beads. Even the children were considered communal.

The women gladly served as magnets to attract males but were also protected from being attacked or raped. Thus they could be promiscuous without threatening their safety as would have been the case if they were on their own.

Lyn had a position of authority; she was clearly a senior in the group, as she had been in her family of origin, the oldest of three. It is likely that it was she who took reckless Sandy, the youngest of three in her family, under her wing.

The use of drugs and sex were not, however, a free-for-all. Hardcore drugs such as heroin or the extremely dangerous barbiturates were not part of the Family's drug scene. Only hallucinogenics and to a much lesser degree stimulants were used. The group orgies were carefully planned and took place once a week or every two weeks (drugs, like food and clothing, were stashed as communal property). At the designated day the women engaged in all-day preparations of food and bedding. The participating males were those who could offer proof of their capacity for erections. Those who could not were advised not to participate. Dramatic orgasms were highly admired in these orgiastic performances. I was told, for example, that only Manson could stop the seizurelike sexuality of Lyn. Food, music, drugs, and sex were shared by all but to a different degree. Sandra was not particularly interested in sex and Barbara Hoyt did not take drugs. Next to nothing is known for certain about the potency of the

112

drugs used and other than in the case of Brooks Poston there are no accounts of bad trips. Otherwise the group joined every evening at suppertime, Manson at the center singing and playing his guitar as joints were passed around. The Beatles' album *Magical Mystery Tour*, released in December 1967, was the musical fairy-tale background for these infants in paradise. The setting was fittingly a movie ranch of yesterday where films for a more innocent generation had actually been made.

Transition and Unrest

Most of the mansonites were thrill-seekers. As I said before, their perception of life did not include stability, routines, and that certain degree of boredom that is a realistic part of our existence. Contact with the rich and the successful produced in them a heightening of their expectations. But great success in the world of rock music no longer seemed to be waiting around the corner. For one thing, Manson was ignorant of the realities of the industry and he simply did not know the steps necessary to take to achieve success. He resented it when his songs were edited. He wasted expensive recording time by all of a sudden deciding to improvise instead of recording what was planned for. He wanted to be accepted only on his own terms and like his followers he expected unconditional support. Before, during his life in prison, he had to negotiate his way around in order to survive. But now he had had a taste of living out his childhood fantasies, and it became extremely difficult for him to stop being an undisputed master. Worse, he was caught in his role, for now he had obligations, responsibilities. His obligation now was primarily to the Family's image of him. He could no longer engage in petty crime and get himself back into prison. It is likely that Manson and Watson tried to make it big in that other get-rich-quick industry, drug traffic. But Manson had never been able to make it big as a criminal. After all, criminals who make the big time, like their counterparts in the straight world, are people geared to success. Big crime is a business which requires work, knowledge, and important family or friendship connections among other things.

Manson, emotionally, was no longer in a position to puncture his

113

scene. For the first time in his life he had something to lose. He had become vulnerable because he had dared to hope.

At some point, entrepreneur Terry Melcher had entered the mansonites' lives and they hoped that he would sponsor their careers. But it seems that Melcher, who had grown up in the industry, did not quite share the enthusiasm that Wilson and Jakobson had for Manson's possibilities. On one occasion, when he went to Spahn to see the Family *in situ* to evaluate its commercial value, he handed Manson fifty dollars before leaving, thinking that he owed them something for their time. Manson felt terribly affronted; if anything he regarded himself as above Melcher. And yet he realized that this man who so casually had deeply injured his self-esteem could be his only chance, his ticket to glories that were proving to be more and more elusive.

The mansonites became restless. By October 1968 some were traveling back and forth to Death Valley, to the Myers Ranch and to the Barker Ranch in the Golar Wash. They traveled by bus and by foot through some almost impassable roads in remote, isolated areas, allegedly to be close to nature. Again there was at this time some scattering of the Family; some traveled up north, others around the Panamint Mountains. Now there were doubts that they could really claim Spahn Ranch. For a while Susan Atkins lived not with the group but with a man in Topanga Canyon.

Attempt at Restitution

By February 1969 Manson's hopes for a big career for himself and the group were finally crushed. He was again a have-not, and this after almost making it. I speculate that by then the mansonites had become intensely resentful and envious of those who made it. They were angry because their wants were not being satisfied, because forces outside their power were in the way, which made them feel powerless. They felt that something important, something they were entitled to had been taken away from them. One must remember that the mansonites were an antisocial group of people by the time they joined Manson or gladly became antisocial after they joined the Family. The murderous behavior of some of them should not hide the

114

fact that they were already a gang of delinquents who burglarized homes, used stolen credit cards, robbed, and used illegal drugs. A career in crime was a natural to them. They were takers with an infantile sense of omnipotence and the belief that it was their right to avail themselves of anything they wished to have, a kind of magic thinking appropriate in the very young child. And the social atmosphere at the time, at least the aspects of it that the mansonites were tuned in to, stimulated their narcissistic thinking. Since most of Manson's followers were women, it is obvious that they must have completely deafened their ears to anything related to women's new awareness. I can only assume that these women invested all their emotional and intellectual energies in their infantile dependency needs. Much has been said about Manson making his followers do his bidding, and not enough about these women making him do theirs. I cannot help but wonder about what would have happened if Manson's biology had been different. Suppose, for example, that he had had a coronary or a stroke at that time. Many men do succumb to illness when under the type of stress he was experiencing then. And some of them profit from the experience and manage to use their illness to get themselves out of the superman position. But Manson had no way out. He felt rejected, demoted. His self-esteem was almost destroyed. He feared losing face with his followers or worse, losing them altogether.

By February of 1969 the group had reassembled in a house on Gresham Street in Topanga Canyon. It was at this house that the songs of the Beatles' *White Album* that had been released in December 1968 became invested with special meanings by the mansonites. The album contains twenty-nine songs and some of them actually do convey an ambiguous impression as to their meaning. A love ballad, for example, is titled "Happiness Is a Warm Gun;" "Piggies" describes little piggies playing in the dirt but implies that straight people are the really big piggies who "always have clean shirts." The big attractions for the mansonites were the songs "Revolution 1," "Revolution 9," and the ill-famed "Helter Skelter." They interpreted "Revolution 9" as being related to the biblical Revelations 9. According to Paul Watkins he suggested the connection between the two. The "lyrics" of "Revolution 9" are the only ones not printed in a

115

sheet included in the album perhaps because they consist of a repetition of the words "Number 9" mixed with noises of gunfire and screams. Yet "Revolution 1 actually exhorts the listener to change himself, to "free his mind" instead of expecting the world, "the institution," to change.

As to the now ill-famed "Helter Skelter," for me it has a sexual rather than a revolutionary, violent connotation; in it the narrator asks a female if she wants him "to make" her and helter skelter seems to be a description of her "coming down fast." It seems that the mansonites chose to interpret "she" to mean revolution.

Another song, "Blackbird," refers to the awakening of the Blacks' yearnings for liberation. The mansonites interpreted this song as prophesying a race war. At times playfully, at times seriously, they created their own melange and evolved their alleged predictions of an imminent Armaggedon by combining their interpretation of the Beatles' songs and fragments of the Book of Revelations.

During the Leslie Van Houten retrial, Maxwell Keith, her attorney, introduced the record as evidence. It was played in the courtroom for what seemed to me (I was there) an interminable period of time. He wanted to impress on the jury the overwhelming influence that such music would have on listeners when played over and over again, particularly if they identified with their interpretation (or, according to Keith, Manson's interpretation of it). The truth is that more than record listening and "interpreting" was going on at the Gresham Street house. According to Beausoleil's testimony during his trial, a room was set aside and used for rehearsals since at that time Manson and others still had some hope of forming their rock group. There was even talk of building a performing center in the desert. So it seems that the mansonites were at that time preparing themselves for two eventualities; either to make it as entertainers or to make it as revolutionaries!

The biblical fantasy caught the fancy of the mansonites because it flattered them. It was great for them to compare themselves with the persecuted early Christians who would triumph at the end. Furthermore nothing unites people more than a common enemy; it was reassuring to these people to think of themselves as together against "them" as the Christians had been when cruelly persecuted during the reign of Domitian. I believe that the mansonites were quite aware

116

that the similarities were symbolic. Comparing themselves with the early Christians, however, reinforced their megalomania. It is no wonder to me that they were willing to hear the record continuously. At the risk of sounding cynical I also want to suggest that the mansonites perceived the Bible as an all-time best seller and relished the opportunity of making themselves into biblical characters. Here again we see another example of a situation where their solution was the problem; that is, they felt better when they reinforced their basic problems. Nothing could quench better these people's arrogance than to compare Manson with Christ who symbolizes the Revelations, since according to the New Testament Christ embodied in His very being God's message. Added to that, in the trivia of their arid souls the Beatles were the intermediaries, the Beatles who embodied the superfame and the superriches the mansonites craved so much.

I can envision these people, who surely talked among themselves about their "interpretations" and about their comparisons and about their ultimate success. I can hear their empty language, their banal "truths" masquerading as wisdom, their ignorance wrapped up in their meaningless philosophizing. I can see them sitting in that Gresham Street house, barefooted, stoned, listening to their record, a masturbatory experience in self-aggrandizement, wondering, were they the chosen ones who could perceive the hidden, divine reality?

John L. McKenzie, S.J., a biblical scholar, states that some kind of "revelation" is found in all religions. In his *Dictionary of the Bible* he has this to say:

> In naturalistic polytheism the divine usually manifests itself first of all in nature, particularly in the more unusual and violent aspects of natural phenomena. These are conceived as personal actions and interpreted as revealing the personal attitude of the being or beings who produce the phenomena. This experience is really more the foundation of revelation than revelation itself; the exact interpretation of the events requires the revealing speech of a charismatic interpreter.

I don't know whether the mansonites had or hadn't information about polytheist cults. But the magic thinking which they attached to Revelations 9 so it would fit their yearnings and their situation as they perceived it make the words of Father McKenzie pertinent to them. Many years after she sat at the Gresham Street house, Lynette Fromme, this time sitting in a room in a maximum security unit of a prison, was to tell me how she was still waiting for Manson to give her—and the world—his interpretation of The Word.

Appeased and reassured at least for a while, the Family left or were asked to leave the Gresham Street house and started to move back and forth between Spahn Ranch and Death Valley. There were some feeble attempts at show business ventures, places, for example, for the girls to work as topless dancers, or plans to open a nightclub in the ranch's saloon.

In March 1969 an incident occurred that was significant because on that occasion Manson felt rejected by people in a position of power; this must have fueled his anger, making him feel how powerless he really was. He had gone to the Cielo Drive residence owned by Rudi Altobelli, a well-known show business promoter who was living in the guest house. At that time Terry Melcher had already sublet the home to the Polanskis. This is how Bugliosi describes the episode:

> The incident had occurred about eight or nine on the evening of Sunday, March 23, 1969—Rudi remembered the date because he and Sharon had flown to Rome together the next day, Rudi on business, Sharon to rejoin her husband and to make a movie there. Rudi was alone in the guest house, taking a shower, when Christopher started barking. Grabbing a robe, he went to the door and saw Manson on the porch. While it was possible that Manson had knocked and the shower had muffled the sound, Rudi was irritated that he had opened the outside door and walked onto the porch uninvited.
>
> Manson started to introduce himself, but Rudi, somewhat brusquely, without opening the screen door said, "I know who you are, Charlie, what do you want?"
>
> Manson said he was looking for Terry Melcher. Altobelli said Terry had moved to Malibu. When Manson asked for his address, Altobelli said he didn't know it, which was not true.
>
> Prolonging the conversation, Manson asked him what business he was in. Though Altobelli felt sure Manson

118

already knew the answer, he replied, "The entertainment business." He added, "I'd like to talk with you longer, Charlie, but I am leaving the country tomorrow and have to pack."

Before Manson left, Rudi asked him why he had come back to the guest house. Manson replied that the people at the main house had sent him back. Altobelli said that he didn't like to have his tenants disturbed, and he would appreciate it if he wouldn't do so in the future. With that Manson left.

I can see Manson, the has-been, the nonbelonger, standing in the shadows begging for help. In this home up in the hills were people who were happy, successful, who belonged together. People who had arrived, people who wanted nothing to do with the likes of Charlie who was completely out of place in Cielo Drive. Cielo is the Spanish word for heaven.

By early June 1969 it became obvious not only that Melcher definitely would not sponsor the Family—by then Manson had guessed it—but that the relationship with important people in the business had cooled off considerably. Manson's attempts at getting the Straight Satans and other bikers to join his group had also failed. And yet another threat emerged in Death Valley: Another guru was competing with Manson. Paul Crockett was prospecting in the vicinity. He attracted Brooks Poston first, today a charming young singer but then a wreck of a youngster in search of paternal support that Crockett quite wisely provided for him. Crockett and Manson had marathon talks. Crockett could use the lingo of Scientology much better than his opponent. Paul Watkins, anxious about the increased talk of violence, defected from the Family and also joined Crockett. This must have been a severe blow to Manson and it greatly increased the group's anxiety.

Manson realized that he had to do something to restore the morale of his followers so they would not fall apart or leave him. I believe that at this point he also dreaded the vacuum of a life without his women. His women were, after all, the signature of the only success he had ever experienced. Males had been interested in him, but not for long. But males envied him because of his harem. His female

119

companions nurtured him and were eager to offer him complete support. But he knew that he had to keep them busy doing something important, otherwise another guru full of grandiose plans could seduce them away from him.

Manson decided to make the fantasy of Helter Skelter more realistic. After Armageddon, at the end of the Rainbow, the Bottomless Pit would again be the nurturing womb where all of them would live happily ever after, masters of the world which found them so unacceptable. The group planned and prepared and these activities were grabbed by Manson's demoralized and scared followers. What he did, essentially, was to provide all, including himself, with the best medicine to combat anxiety and frustration: He gave his group a goal and set them to work towards attaining it. Knowing his territory, he had to give them a grandiose goal, more grandiose than conquering the world of rock music. Their goal became to conquer the world. Or rather, playing the game of attaining supreme power.

The mansonites had been living in a world of fun and games and I think that most of them used the fantasy of finding the Hole that would take them to the Bottomless Pit as the ultimate retreat. This game was far more exciting than their previous ones and more intensively embraced by all because underneath everything they all had a feeling of despair, a fear of losing the only security they had. One must always remember that these were people who had severe problems about leaving childhood. For them, magical thrilling experiences were probably their only way to feel alive. They must have had thoughts at the time of how unbearably boring life would be without experiencing new sensations, of how helpless and powerless they would feel were they to be left alone, each with only her real life to be lived.

Thus everybody was eager to turn a new leaf in the life of the Family. Provisions were accumulated, vehicles for the almost impassable roads carefully prepared, and weapons stored. Money now became a problem.

After Robert Beausoleil, in July 1969, killed Gary Hinman to get the money he allegedly had in his home, the door was open for the Tate-LaBianca murders. Most of the mansonites probably knew about the Hinman murder. Manson realized that the idea of killing did not

120

upset some of his people, that on the contrary they were thrilled at the possibility of committing murder. Power-hungry Lyn, Sandra, and Gypsy reveled at the idea of scaring the daylights out of the rich inhabitants of Los Angeles—to begin with. Susan, Pat, and Leslie yearned for the ultimate thrill, to be able to cancel out human lives. And Tex was there, ready to help where he was needed and to have fun too.

Much has been written and spoken about the mansonites' "alienation." Some of the psychiatrists who testified in court were of the opinion that when these people killed they did so as a result of their extreme alienation; that they did not perceive their victims as human beings but as inanimate objects. I don't agree with this opinion. I think that, on the contrary, *the thrill for them was to kill people.* The mansonite murderers and others like them would not have a feeling of excitement and of power if they really thought that they were destroying a piece of furniture. Young vandals substitute inanimate objects for the real thing to give vent to their rage. Some of them end up killing people but many don't.

Manson plotted the murders for revenge. But he understood his companions' yearnings. There was something for everybody in the commission of the Tate-LaBianca murders.

The Family Attempts to Survive

It is not possible to know exactly how Manson, the actual murderers and the other mansonites who "knew," felt after the murders had been committed. One thing is certain: No one was overcome by guilt or suffered a severe emotional breakdown. If Susan Atkins' relish and uncontrollable pleasure in revealing how she and the others had killed are an indication, the murderers accomplished what they sought. While Susan was in jail, suspected of being implicated in the Hinman murder, the rest of the gang were cautiously covering their tracks.

When the mansonites were finally apprehended and brought to trial they again had reason to feel their importance because they were on center stage. The women—Tex Watson had escaped to his hometown in Texas—presented a united front in support of Manson.

121

They set themselves to prove to the world that he was grand, and consequently so were they, his followers.

The Manson mystique was in full swing during the trials and thereafter—his women saw to it—helped on by a too eager press. Rumors spread about threats and other murders. Later on, female mansonites were arrested and convicted as they were preparing to free Manson. In September 1975 Lynette put herself and her adoptive family again back into the world news.

The workings of the machinery of alienation are being perfected. People are learning with more precision how not to care, as well as why not to. Self-sufficiency and the need for self-satisfaction are increasingly well engineered so as to be integrated into our emotional life—or even take it over, as we hear more and more about how bothersome significant human relationships really are. Why, after all, not be responsible just for oneself? Why not invest everything on the pleasures of the moment? We have for sure only one life to live and perhaps most people would learn to enjoy superficial relationships if labeled as love, and trivial concerns if properly worded as "meaningful," that fashionable word that can so easily be simply meaningless. It is much easier to love without responsibility and to think without reflection. No hassle in doing so, no pressure, no anxieties.

In expressing these thoughts I am not being sarcastic. There is truth in what I've said, which is being perceived by an increasing number of people as what they want for themselves. The mansonites may have been among the first who acted out this way of thinking. Why not experience murdering people? some of them asked themselves. They lived, geographically, in California. But their true country was their cherished land of Now. They made a big production of their success in kicking out their past, oblivious of the fact that they were just playing a disguised version of it. At certain points, just to perpetuate their "now," they planned for the future since no group can exist without a certain feeling of continuity. Their plans were colored by their fractured and grandiose reality. Like many other people today, they could believe in anything that would make them feel comfortable or comfortably thrilled.

122

In our times the land of Now has an increasing number of visitors and some of them decide to stay there. No longer is a Manson needed to guide them through unknown jungles. Well-prepared, well-learned guides are available and good roads have been built. Package tours are available almost anywhere which provide literature on what illusions to use to feel happy. The mansonites' illusion was that they cared a great deal for each other and that they could relax sure in the knowledge that their leader had the formula for their happiness. Each actually had a secret agenda that said: "Here I can get without having to give. Here I can feel powerful and excited and satisfied *all the time.*" Not one of them really had to postpone any gratification or make any but minor sacrifices to be part of the Family. And from the world outside they took and took. The world was theirs for the taking either because they felt it owed them everything or just for the thrill of getting away with robbing and killing.

Under the disguise of love the mansonites' bond was their total mutual acceptance. Their interpersonal aridity has come of age as more people's definition of happiness and fulfillment has come to be anyone's version of "what's in it for me?" Human beings have always been selfishly concerned, but society made it worthwhile for us to explore other aspects of being human. I think the opposite is happening today. People are reluctant, for example, to give of themselves because to do so may mean to become highly vulnerable. The main concern has become not to have a feeling of mastery, of freedom to be, but to have a feeling of power over others as a defense against feeling powerless. What became central to the life of the mansonites, how to achieve great success, how to manipulate oneself—no matter the means used—into that corner office, has become central to many people's lives. It is also a source of despair for the many who can't. To be unsuccessful or meek or powerless is to be a failure, and worse, it carries the risk of being abandoned, rejected by the human family. Or of being just tolerated, another form of being rejected. Some people unable to cope with the possibility or the reality of not being "good enough" are chronically unhappy. Others, unwilling to continue climbing a never-ending staircase, give up the struggle. They radically change their life-style, abandon businesses and professions in which they have invested a great deal. But the most vulnerable are those who aim at the top but are totally ignorant of what it takes to get there. Some of them are crushed when their hopes wane; some recover and learn from their experience. Some become dangerous, their frustration exploding into violence.

The mansonites had "given up" but not just to search for peace of mind by lowering their expectations. On the contrary, they were searchers of a place high above everybody else. For a while during the summer of their content they felt they could live together an ecstatic life of sensations. They came to believe that success, the big time, was just around the corner ready for them to take from the world they actually despised. It shouldn't surprise us because they were not that unrealistic. Their quarters were next door to the entertainment capital of the world, where enormous fortunes are made by the most incredible feats of ugliness or trivia. It is probable that they failed only because Manson was such an individualist and so utterly devoid of the shrewdness that works in attaining success. Otherwise he could have gotten the right agent for the Family who could have fabricated the appropriate deal for their corruption and their amorality. It is being done all the time.

Manson

"All The King's horses,
and all
The King's men . . ."

This sign was found at the Spahn Ranch at the time of the trial. It was written above a poster of Christ:

REWARD for information leading to the apprehension of
Jesus Christ
Wanted—for Sedition, Criminal
Anarchy—Vagrancy, and Conspiring to
Overthrow the Established Government
Dresses poorly. Said to be a carpenter by trade, illnourished, has visionary ideas, associates with common working people, the unemployed and bums. Alien—believed to be a Jew. Alias: Prince of Peace, Son of Man, Light of the World, &c. Professional agitator. Red beard, marks on hands and feet, the result of injuries inflicted by an angry mob led by respectable citizens and legal authorities.
The Young

From the moment he was arrested Manson acquired a place in history among other charismatic leaders. Only a handful of people at one time, however, compared him with Christ. Many more place him in the gallery of the infamous next to the Devil or with a personification of evil, Hitler, with whom he is frequently compared. Every time the public is shocked by the outcome of cultish groups such as the People's Temple or Synanon, the name of Manson surfaces. Any mention of a dangerous group, in fact, brings to mind this leader of mass murderers. Four people were indicted as being directly responsible for the Tate-LaBianca murders and so was Manson although he himself did not murder any of the victims. Nevertheless he remains the central figure of that tragedy. Some people even speculate that Lynette Fromme also acted under his influence. Less remembered is his implication in the Gary Hinman murder and his participation in the killing of Donald Shea. Above all, Manson has left an imprint as a charismatic leader of a group of women and a few men whom he allegedly led to violence. Because of him—and more recently others share this somber distinction—the word "charisma" has become a negative term loaded with dangerous implications.

People tend now to forget that religious leaders—Moses, Christ, Mohammed—were charismatic and so were political and spiritual figures of more recent times such as Gandhi, Roosevelt, and Martin Luther King who are millions of miles removed from Manson's persona; and the types of followers they attracted are also totally different from Manson's acolytes. The type of person who responds to a Reverend Moon, for example, is quite different from the type which would join a Manson, and both are quite distinct from the followers of religious, spiritual, and political leaders who have left a positive imprint in the world.

A person naturally endowed with personal magnetism uses this attribute differently according to who he is and what he stands for. It is not conceivable that a Martin Luther King would ever have become a DeFreeze and in the disguise of social concern lead a band of destructive people. Yet some people may argue that Jim Jones started as a social reformer before ending up as a murderer and a suicide. And as for that guitar player and composer, fun-loving Charles

126

Manson, he was a small-time con who became the head of a gang of murderers. Only in exploring the life pattern of these individuals can one understand why they are so different from each other; and also in carefully analyzing, as I said before, what they really stood for.

A major leader, no matter of what persuasion, must have as a central concern the attainment of a power base since such a person, be he the true or the deviant, speaks for the disadvantaged. Nixon's nonappeal was reinforced because he addressed himself to the great majority; no matter its problems, the large American middle class is pretty well off and well protected by the law and other social institutions. The leaders I am referring to clearly state their intention to give power to the powerless. The acquisition of power is the essence of any movement on behalf of the destitute. Just to belong to an advocate group, to be spoken for by a forceful, persuasive voice, ameliorates the feelings of helplessness of its members and serves to channel anger and despair into action, productive or other, and even when adverse circumstances present problems that seem unsolvable, individuals can thus experience a spiritual lift. In the past the American black got this lift from religion. During the dark days of the Depression Roosevelt was able to inspire those living in fear, and it is possible that because of his influence a major political and social upset was averted. King was the first to give the blacks a sense of their own rights on a grand scale since television coverage was already available. When a southern black woman sat in a bus on a seat of her choice, an enormous block built by years of humiliation started to disintegrate.

These two leaders had a deep understanding of the powerful effect of their personalities and their message: that the dispossessed count and can take action. This type of leader is also seen as heroic not only by contemporary followers but by future generations. Even most people whose convictions are different from those represented by these leaders recognize their worth.

Hitler was a hero to his people and others during his time but today only a sick minority sees him as a hero. The difference is that the constructive leader does not seek power for power's sake or for self-aggrandizement. Hitler was insatiable; he was not just after a

127

more powerful Germany which could thus secure a better life for her people than that accorded to her by the treaty of Versailles. He envisioned Germany as the ruler of the world and the Germans as having the right to decide who should live and who should perish.

Manson is frequently compared with Hitler. According to popular lore he was able, like Hitler, to persuade his followers to kill for a cause, to provoke an Armageddon, to create a *wehrmacht* that would ultimately put the mansonites in power. John Toland, one of Hitler's historians, has said that the problem with the German dictator was that he took himself seriously; he truly believed his grandiose schemes and had a whole country to back him up. This we still don't understand: why such a large number of people would share such destructive beliefs and put them into action. The German people participated in and acted out a well-organized paranoid system. I doubt very much that Manson believed that he and his group were going to provoke a race war and then, joined by thousands, wait for glory and power in a mythical spot in the California desert. Although his harangues are full of lies and half-truths it is interesting that he referred to many of his group's happenings as just play and make-believe. The truly paranoid does not switch or deny his "convictions." When Manson had to defend himself, faced with a possible death penalty, he had this to say during his trial:

> There's been a lot of talk about a bottomless pit. I found a hole in the desert that goes down to a river that runs north underground, and I call it a bottomless pit, because Where could a river be going north underground? You could even put a boat on it. So I covered it up and I hid it and called it the Devil's Hole and we all laugh and we joke about it. You could call it a family joke about the bottomless pit. How many people could you hide down in this hole?

Manson must be rather pleased to be compared with Hitler but I doubt that Hitler would have compared himself with lowly Manson. I don't doubt, however, that he had many mansonite-like Germans among his followers. Hitler and Manson preached to their followers that they were deserving of a great destiny because they were

128

superior. At the time Hitler rose to power the Germans had lived for years in despair; defeated after World War I, their morale was at an abysmal low when their destructive leader appeared on the political scene.

Today we are witnessing a different phenomenon. The dispossessed are no longer just those who are politically, socially, and/or economically deprived (the highest suicide rate in the Los Angeles area occurs not among the people in poor East Los Angeles but among those living in wealthy, gorgeous Bel Air). The alienated are the new dispossessed, no matter what their economic or social status. Alienation, we know by now, is one of the most serious human problems of our time. In industrialized societies *angst* has replaced hunger as a painful reality. And people are ashamed of their loneliness. To feel that one is cut off from others, that one doesn't belong, means that one is a failure as a person. To be powerful, on the other hand, is to be sought after and is the key that opens the door to feeling wanted, to belonging. The young who have serious problems about leaving childhood are joining exotic philosophical or religious groups in their anxious search to belong. Never has the truism "Man would rather die in company than live alone" been more applicable.

There was a time when people had an automatic membership in their family network and in small working communities. But living within extended families is unusual today or else ties continue but have become impersonal; and the place where one works is no longer the setting where one has friends and old acquaintances but has become a competitive arena. Yet people continue to long to be a part of a clan, of a family, of a group where others care in a personal way. To a great extent the influence of the thinking of family psychiatrist Dr. Murray Bowen is due to his emphasis on the need not only to relate maturely to one's relatives and thus achieve one's self-potential, but also to satisfy basic emotional needs. Getting to know oneself by exploring relationships with one's family of origin and learning about one's roots was central to Dr. Bowen's work before author Alex Haley made it fashionable. The trend that Haley started deserves to graduate into permanency to counterbalance the tendency that many young people have today to retreat emotionally by pretending that

129

one can totally leave home and throw away his past into a sea of anonymity. To adopt a life-style completely different from the one a person grows up with—and to cast aspersions or try to bury his background—to embrace exotic philosophies or religions only makes a person a foreigner everywhere and a citizen of nowhere. It indicates that he must delude himself into believing that he is markedly different from where he comes from in order to reassure himself of having an identity. But to live a provisional life, to dress in the cultural garb of someone else while pretending that it fits is to have a fragmentary existence.

The female mansonites declared that their lives started—and all their problems ended—when they met Manson. They chose to be cut-offs from their own families; they had refused or avoided negotiating their differences with their parents and with society. But all the same they needed to belong and this they accomplished for a while; but they carried with them their non-negotiable conditions wrapped in their arrogance and endorsed by a guru. Where does this guru, Manson. belong? What is his true identity? What can we learn about this kind of individual by learning more about one of them?

A Visit with Manson

I visited Manson in the summer of 1977. I wanted to meet Manson in part to answer these questions but also to ask him about his women followers. And not only to hear what he had to say—all of which I was prepared to take cautiously—but to reflect on what I heard between the lines. I was confused by the picture of him that I was getting from others and from reading about him. He was, I heard repeatedly, mentally ill and deteriorating. Or still endowed with evil powers, ready to find ways to influence his alleged followers; or a sociopath, the natural product of early deprivation. These generalizations did not satisfy my curiosity because they did not explain anything. Hearing and reading about Manson, at times I got the impression that as a person he was either taken far too seriously or canceled out with artificial neatness, by referring to him as "sick." I wanted to know him as a person, not as a myth or as a pathological specimen.

130

I contacted Manson first by writing to him and we exchanged a few letters. I asked him to be my consultant on the subject of his women followers since I believe he knows a great deal about them. In one of my letters I asked him to grant me an interview, but even when I arrived at the California Medical Facility where he resides I wasn't at all sure that he would see me since just prior to my visit he had written to me:

If the different aspects of your self are difficult to grasp you should not of (sic) have convicted your selves in your court room of law run by the money crooks. You hide the truths & play act like your looking for it. No, woman you don't wish to visit me this summer or any other summer. 30 years in this cage leaves you with nothing . . . I say to you dont (sic) come to visit me cause I want nothing to do with you, your books or money . . . I told you in your last letter not to write to me.

I want to add that in his letters Manson made clear that he regarded me as part of the world that unjustly had convicted him. In his letters he lectured me and also tried to enlighten me with his insights about my motivations for writing this book:

C G L
You must first understand you befor you even try to understand someone else. Most people who are judging & trying to understand someone els is because they run from them selves in the name of looking for them selves—when you find your self then you'll understand the family women.

The California Medical Facility is part of the Department of Corrections. Its primary function is to provide psychiatric diagnosis and treatment for adult male prisoners who are mentally ill, grossly mentally defective, or suffering from serious emotional or character disorders. Inmates who for a variety of reasons, including their own safety, cannot be housed in a regular prison can also be imprisoned in this facility. The institution, which has a capacity of almost a

131

thousand beds, was opened in 1955; it is located between San Francisco and Sacramento adjacent to Vacaville, a small, charming town sparkling in the midst of orchards, its sky punctuated by soft hills.

The institution offers the inmates opportunities for high school instruction, college courses, and trade training; they can participate in the handicraft program and sell their creations which are displayed in the entrance hall.

The superintendent, Dr. Thomas Clanon, a psychiatrist, has been a staff member since 1961. Dr. Clanon introduced me to Ed George, a warden who has known Manson for years, ever since he was in Death Row in San Quentin. Warm, lively Ed defies all the stereotypes of a prison guard.

I was told that Manson is capricious, that he might decide not to see me or else he might just walk out on me after a few minutes. I was also warned that he manages to frighten some people. To my surprise (and I think theirs), Manson, anticipating my visit, had shaved and bathed. I was amazed to learn that many people unsuccessfully seek interviews with Manson. I guess that until that time I really didn't realize that Manson and his acolytes were celebrities. During our conversation, Manson, too, commented that I was lucky to be able to talk with him.

As I walked the long corridors and passed through locked doors accompanied by Ed, I had a sense of unreality because of the contrast with the more open areas of the institution, that were full of activity surrounded by nicely kept grounds where some of the inmates chatted with family and friends. Maximum security wards probably have more personnel and yet they give an impression of forlorn loneliness. Not even the loveliness of California can penetrate these locked doors. The corridors were lined by men standing alone or in pairs, talking quietly or just marking time.

We arrived at last at an area used for different purposes. Its walls were adorned by a large mural painted by a convict. The artist's intention was to depict all the famous and the infamous in world history, the virtuous next to the evil. Everybody seemed to be there, Hitler, Lucille Ball, Kissinger, Sonny and Cher, Golda Meir, and, of course, Manson, a marijuana branch above his head.

132

I was invited to a small side room where Manson joined us shortly after our arrival. Dressed in blue jeans and a T-shirt, his hair in a ponytail, Manson faced me with his well-advertised beautiful eyes and promptly proceeded to try to put me on the defensive. At the same time he tested me to see if I was frightened or awed by him. I wasn't so I passed the test. The first games over, Manson attempted to make me feel guilty in the best "Jewish mother" tradition. Here he was, through no fault of his own (maybe it was my fault?) but would I do something for him? Could I, for example, set him free? Could I see to it that he be allowed to go out in the sun he loved and needed so much? He asserted that I was of no use to him to which I agreed. Furthermore I brought up the matter of paying him. I stated that it would be against my convictions to do so, which he readily accepted.

Manson was hyperactive throughout the interview, but I know that when he is in his cell he can get involved in repetitive manual activities such as making dolls or playing his guitar and be calm and quiet. For me, he moved, gesticulated, mimicked, acted. I guess he has a well-rehearsed performance that he puts up for visitors. In a social context he regards any stranger as an audience, but this is not to say that he is not at all times sizing up the company. I felt comfortable with Manson and I don't think that the reason was that Ed was with us. Manson is not the type of person I would fear to encounter in a dark alley. I noticed that my Spanish accent was a point in my favor. For Manson "Spanish" is interchangeable with "Chicano." He reminisced about his stays in Mexico, telling me how once he gave a ring to an Indian. "Can you imagine," he said to me, "that now the Indian owns a ring that belonged to Manson!" He told me about the time in Mexico City when his landlady, a "big mother," took all his clothing because he was unable to pay his rent.

Manson the storyteller then gave way to Manson the socially concerned as he talked about the Indians and the poor Mexicans who "have nothing to eat while big corporations get bigger." He talked at length about air pollution and the contamination of water and pointing at me remarked: "Your children may not have any water left to drink." I must say that I don't know if these concerns were originally his or if he was championing Lyn's and Sandra's cause that made big news about two years before our meeting.

133

I expressed my agreement with his concern about the environment but asked him (as I am sure many did before me) how keeping the air pure and the water clear was related to killing people. He tried to avoid answering me by embarking on a monologue about his "philosophy" until I had to interrupt him and firmly remind him that I was not interested, that I was seeking concrete answers. After this he took some dominoes that were spread on the table, made a circle, and called it a star. Pointing at different pieces he stated: "This here is the Chinese, this is the Russian, this is the black. At the center there is an integrating force." When I asked about this force, he replied: "It is you." He meant the individual, who has it in his power to determine who should stay (in the circle of life, I presume) and who should be eliminated if the world is to be "pure." "For instance," he said, "this one has Negro blood, it has to go."

He had given me his version of the worn-out superior-race philosophy which has been around probably since the beginning of history and which blossomed in Nazi Germany.

I asked Manson how did he go about accepting people into his group. He said that when people came to him, he would ask: "Are you for clear water and clean air?" If the answer was affirmative (and what else could it be?!) he accepted them and gave them colors, "I name you Blue, or I name you Gold." And he asked another question, "Do you have your self?"

As I said earlier, I doubt that Manson was obsessed with the problems of pollution in the late sixties; what he wants to present as a consuming interest in the environment is a more recent development suggested by Lyn and Sandra that he uses as his "angle." His emphasis on the necessity that his followers be self-determined, that they had their "self," may have been prompted by the Van Houten retrial that was taking place at the time of my visit. Van Houten claimed that her criminal actions were the result of Manson power over her. In any case, however, Manson does not impress me as a person who would go for people who would cling emotionally to him. He certainly is not a giver by temperament. Young Dianne Lake, his most frequent sexual partner, irritated him because of her dependency on him. Manson illustrated to me some of the Family transactions with anecdotes:

"One of my men asked me: 'Someone owes me money. What do I do?' I says to him, 'Are you willing to die to get your money? Otherwise you may have to accept you aren't going to get paid. Just accept it.' "

He added, "I don't tell anyone what to do." When I asked him how did he go about "not telling" anyone what to do, he stood next to me and, looking at me sideways, said: "I am your father or your brother or your friend. You tell me what you want to do. I relieve you of guilt. Don't be sorry for anything you do."

Manson proved to be more interested in talking about himself than about his women. If time had permitted I am sure that he would have talked a great deal about his life's experiences; he seemed to derive a lot of pleasure relating to me what he regarded as humorous anecdotes from his unusual life. About the women murderers he had this to say: "Susan Atkins is a bitch. I should have slapped her ass real good many times. But . . . what the hell . . . I didn't do it." He told me of a time when a Mexican wanted Susan and asked his permission, which he gave. "But after a short while he came complaining to me . . . that Susan wanted to be on top . . . that's it with Susan. She wants to be the man!" About Leslie Van Houten, "I didn't have anything to do with her. She was Tex's girl."

He refused to discuss the other women, the ones who are still close to him. I got the impression that although he has feelings of loyalty towards them he is far less involved with them than they are with him. Another topic that he did not want to discuss was that of his sons. His son by Mary Brunner was cared for by her relatives while she was in prison and on parole in Los Angeles.

Manson, however, was eager to discuss his convictions about child rearing. He talked at length and with pleasure about his version of "the natural child" and described to me—and reenacted—the birth of a child in the Family. "The child is born free, he should develop without restrictions." He contrasted his views with that of the relatives with whom he lived during his childhood. Asked to elaborate, he assumed a dejected position, shoulders hunched, eyes lowered, a sad expression on his face, and said that all he heard as a child from them was, "Do this!" "Don't do that!" Thus he expressed verbally and nonverbally how overwhelmed by the adults in his life he felt as a child. Manson did not discuss his mother; in a letter he wrote me a few months after our interview he made a brief but revealing comment about her:

My mom was a runaway in 1933. 15 years old. Few run away in '33 and few babys were born. I am a speck. A little spot to what's coming.

I asked Manson if his group was really a family. His answer was oblique, perhaps because I asked him also to give me his definition of family. At various times Manson implied that I was expecting too much from him and remarked that he was not a book person who used difficult book-words, like me. According to him, "The family is going down, down, it will disappear." When I argued that many have said so and yet the family continues to last, he gave me his version of what a family should be: a free-for-all group, with no strong or possessive ties among adults and no identifiable parents of the children. As he was talking I thought of how frequently these days I hear from people whose conception of family is identical to that of Manson.

Manson has frequently referred to his group as being his family. To give just one example, in a letter written to me after our interview, he said:

In reality I had no reality for years before I met the family. I gave to their reality and hold (sic) them to their own word and reflected their love. They had the only love I ever knew outside the love of prison I thought it was love.

Manson keeps pointing his accusing finger at society, blaming it for his problems that have kept him in prison most of his life. He repeated his complaints during our interview with a tone that was as much self-righteous as it was charged with self-pity. We didn't go into what experiences affected him the most while he lived in institutions but he had this to say (letter to me, cited before):

In a reform school they trained the kids to be truthful. It

136

was run by catholic brothers who would beat you with paddles as big as ball bats. Next reform school used big leathers straps and kids with moms and dads never got beat, but they would beat me to show them what they could get.

Manson was never to forget the value of instilling fear in others, and this he taught his followers. To be afraid, constantly on guard, and to instill fear in others became one of his survival techniques. He told me of another. When things get tough he can build a wall around himself and be in a world of his own, oblivious of reality. In his universe he is the master and what happens is under his control; this is very helpful to him. To do so, I guess, comes in handy now since for years he has been walking on a tightrope. Within the prison he has no status as a big criminal; on the contrary, his crimes are regarded as despicable by most of the convicts. Some envy the success he had with women and his notoriety. It is conceivable that someone may try to kill him to attain fame, and most probably he is kept under tight security for his own protection. And in spite of his periodic attempts at getting paroled, Manson knows that he cannot live on the outside. Before I left, I asked him, "What would you do if you were set free?" With a mischievous expression and a wink, he answered: "Hide."

I was not to see Manson again. In a letter I received months after our visit, he was willing to help me in my project—on his own terms:

> You're 8 years with the divel (sic) loose and if you want to lock him back while there is some pussie left for the marriage best move to California. But only if you're over it and can do with me what I say in regards to your book. I must say you got a lot of guts and about the bravest person I've met in a long time. Ther (sic) is a lot we could do for the good of it but the question is first what can we do and then we can make up our minds about how to git on with it.

I revisited the California Medical Facility in the winter of 1978. Manson was permitted to see me but only during regular visiting hours which he refused to do. I was told that perhaps he refused because according to regulations he would have to be manacled which is unacceptable to him. Maybe he refused because I did not answer his letter offering me his collaboration. After I left the institution, disappointed at not being able to talk with him, I had lunch at a small restaurant in Vacaville, The Library, thus named because it used to be a library. The menus are written in the first blank pages of old books. After I made my selection I turned over the cover to read the title of the menu-book. It was *The Man Who Wanted to Be God.*

Dr. Joel Fort, testifying in the Van Houten retrial, stated that at the California Medical Facility Manson had been diagnosed as a latent schizophrenic. This diagnosis refers to individuals who have a marginal adjustment, who function in a limited way, and who off and on have one or more typical symptoms of schizophrenia such as poor contact with reality, overwhelming anxiety, chaotic sexuality, hallucinations, delusions, whose mood and behavior are influenced by their distorted thinking, and who have serious difficulties in forming relationships. Some of these characteristics could be applied to Manson. One can say, for example, that his thinking is impaired. It is, however, selectively impaired in that he wants to present himself as a victim of society. During our interview, for all his showmanship, he was cautious in what he said. He was in control of himself and most careful about not incriminating himself. He had refused a request by Leslie Van Houten to allow a psychiatrist chosen by her attorney to examine him. He is up to date about events and people who interest him. He was able to relate to me within the context of our contact and responded adequately to my no-nonsense approach.

During Van Houten's second retrial, defense asked Dr. Jesse S. Miller, a psychologist who specializes in psycholinguistics (the study of factors that affect communication and general understanding of verbal information) to report on his findings, which were based on his examination of a few of Manson's letters. (Dr. Miller's testimony was not accepted because he had not examined Manson or read documents pertaining to him.) He found evidence of a thought disorder manifested, according to him, by clang associations (words similar in sound but not in meaning call up new thoughts and lead to senseless rhyme, ex, "the air is thin I have a pin."), grandiose delusional ideas, incoherence, confusion, and the use of neologisms (new words, usually the condensation of several others, that have a special meaning to a person; frequent use of neologisms is characteristic of the speech of some schizophrenics).

One of the prosecutors, Dino Fulgoni, while cross-examining Dr. Miller, noted that some people, particularly writers, use words that are not understood by the majority but are either metaphors or terms that are known by those familiar with the writer. He stated that the mansonites actually used a private language as part of their everyday communications. Mr. Fulgoni remarked that Sartre's *Being and Nothingness* contains many neologisms. And Judge Gordon Ringer asked Dr. Miller, "What do you do with James Joyce's *Finnegan's Wake?*"

Manson's reading and writing difficulties puzzle me. He and his friends refer to his third-grade education as the cause. Manson obviously has an above-average intelligence. Why didn't he correct his deficits? During his long years of incarceration he had plenty of opportunity to upgrade his education or at least to learn how to improve his spelling and how to write with more ease. I speculate that Manson may have some form of learning disability. I was unable to get his records, so I don't know firsthand if he was tested for minimal brain dysfunction, which is an umbrella diagnosis for a group of characteristics that include the inability to learn properly how to read and write and in some cases hyperactivity and behavior problems, as well as a low tolerance for frustration and a poor attention span. I was told by people who have read his juvenile records that no such tests were ever performed, probably because only in the last twenty years has there been an increasing interest in this type of disability which to be corrected requires highly specialized teaching techniques. A bright child who has an unrecognized learning problem is under a great deal of stress because he feels frustrated and doesn't know that there is a reason for his difficulties. If one adds to this family and social deprivation, a lack of a consistent and nurturant environment, this individual's emotional development is seriously handicapped. Resentment builds up and shows in his unmanageable behavior. Children living under these negative sets of circumstances are frequently depressed but they don't show their depression in the usual way, by slow motions, poor sleep, poor appetite, and a sad mood. Instead they become "bad" and elicit rejection and punishment—which fits their low self-esteem—which in turn increases their anger towards others and further lowers their morale.

If the above description fits Manson as he was during his childhood, he might have learned to cope with his feelings of inadequacy by projection, by thinking "there is nothing wrong with me, but with the others," and by cultivating an active fantasy life colored by megalomania to compensate.

Manson has been in correctional institutions since the age of thirteen and in prison since he was seventeen. A psychiatrist who examined him in 1944 was of the opinion that Manson was then already "institutionalized," meaning that he had adjusted to prison life at the expense of his adjustment on the outside—for which he is still totally unprepared. And this he knows.

The Making of a Guru

His inability to adjust, his personal deficits, his socioeconomic background, all these factors played a role in shaping Manson's personality and marked him with antisocial traits. But we must probe further if we are to understand the Manson we all know. We must examine the interchanges in his family and his relationship with his mother.

Manson was born on November 12, 1934, in Cincinnati, Ohio, the illegitimate child of a loose sixteen-year-old. According to his popular historians, Manson never knew his father who his mother, Kathleen, said was a Colonel Scott. The young girl was sent by her strict parents to Cincinnati from her native Ashland, Kentucky, to have the baby. By the time the child, "no-name Madox," was born, his mother had married young William Manson who shortly thereafter gave Charles his name. Charles Manson's birth was not just one in a series of illegitimate kids produced by a totally deprived mother; Kathleen was to have only one other child, a girl, (now in her twenties) by her third husband.

Manson's early years were spent in Ohio, Kentucky, and West

140

Virginia, at times cared for by his young mother who by all accounts continued her reckless behavior, at times by her relatives. When he was five his mother and her brother were convicted of armed robbery and sentenced; she was paroled after three years. During her imprisonment Manson stayed with an aunt and uncle who were rather strict, the ones he portrayed for me during our visit. After being paroled, Kathleen took her son back and remarried. In 1947 at the request of his mother Charles was court-committed to the Gibault School for Boys in Terre Haute, Indiana, a semicorrectional institution operated by the Holy Cross Brothers. Only a few years earlier that institution had as a resident a model student, Bill Heirens, who in later years was to commit three horrible crimes in Chicago and whose story, *Catch Me before I Kill More* by Lucy Freeman, was one of the first psychological portraits of a real murderer. Manson ran away to his mother and from then on, and up to when he was imprisoned in McNeil—when his mother requested that he be released in her care—he kept in contact or lived with her. Charles Manson married, had a child, his wife left him and divorced him, he married or lived in common law with another woman who also left him, all during the brief interludes outside prison. During these years his only consistent relationship was with his mother.

We know what the prison records tell us about Charles Manson, his constant search for attention, his clowning, his manipulatory and seductive behavior. Next to nothing has been reported about the mother-son relationship and the "family" context of this relationship, which I believe left a most important mark on Manson's character. Kathleen's own version gives clues to a better understanding of her son. On January 26, 1971, the Los Angeles *Times* headlined in bold type MOTHER TELLS LIFE OF MANSON AS A BOY in which reporter Dave Smith presented his interview with Manson's mother. Smith wrote:

> Since his arrest on 11/69 for the slayings of actress Sharon Tate and six others, she has heard herself described as the worst kind of tramp and bad mother, whose son went wrong because he was so cruelly deprived.

Indeed one has to wonder about the mysterious ways in which the

laws that protect privacy are applied! In this interview the then Mrs.
C. agreed with some of the known facts about her son but denied the
veracity of others. She stated that she was the child of very strict,
religious parents and that to rebel against them she and her sisters
turned into wild teen-agers; then she became pregnant with Charles.
She repeated that Colonel Scott was Manson's father whom he knew
as his father since "Scott used to come and pick up Charles and take
him home for weekends with his own child. He just loved him." I
wonder how Charles felt about this poor-relative-son contact. Scott
died of cancer in 1954 but Kathleen and Charles had not seen him
since she went to prison and Charles was sent to McMechen, West
Virginia, to live with his relatives.

According to Mother, during her absence Charles was not
neglected; on the contrary, he was surrounded by relatives who really
cared for him. Their ideas of how to raise children, however, were
vastly different from hers. Kathleen had this to say in this respect:

> Maybe it was because my own mother had been so strict,
> but if Charles wanted anything, I'd give it to him. My
> mother did too; she eased up a bit as she got older. He never
> had to do a thing to earn what he wanted. Charles had a
> wonderful personality and always charmed people at first
> meeting. He was real musical and had a real nice voice, so I
> gave him singing lessons. But then he got so conceited
> about his music that I made him stop the lessons. He never
> had to take a fall, not till he was a grown man. Everything
> was just handed to him, I admit.

In 1944, when Charles was ten, his mother married a troubled man,
an alcoholic, with whom she stayed married for twenty-one years.
One can imagine this ten year old child's reaction at having
permanent competition, particularly from an unstable adult male. He
became more and more unmanageable and finally had to be committed by age thirteen. By the time he was twenty-one he had served
time in reformatories and already had a prison term for car theft.
Paroled, he came home to Mother; he took menial jobs that he always
lost "through lateness, absence or general neglect." His mother and

142

grandmother or his aunt always came through with the money he needed.

This published interview provoked an angry reaction from Paul Fitzgerald and prompted him to write the following letter to Mrs. C.:

January 27, 1971

Dear Mrs.

As you probably know, I represent Patricia Krenwinkel who is charged along with your son, Charles Manson, Susan Atkins, and Leslie Van Houten with murder. This case is, of course, on trial in the Los Angeles Superior Court and we are now entering the penalty phase of the trial to determine whether, among others, your son should live or die. While I technically am the attorney only for Patricia Krenwinkel, I have throughout this case acted as an attorney for all the defendants in an attempt to coordinate and facilitate the defense. It is in that capacity that I am writing you. I have also spoken with your son, Charles, and he asked me to communicate with you.

We were all shocked at the story that appeared in the Los Angeles Times on Tuesday, January 26, 1971. It amounted to an unprovoked vicious attack on your son. The Los Angeles Times is not exactly in your son's corner. The Los Angeles Times has printed unquestionably the most prejudicial, inflammatory, derogatory information concerning your son. The timing of the article was such as to obviously prejudice and hamper your son's chances of receiving a sentence of life in prison. The article, as far as I am concerned, was designed to see that your son loses his life. Assuming that you had been accurately quoted in the article, some of your statements, to say the least, need some interpretation.

I am in possession of a letter you wrote in December of 1963 to Judge William Mathes of the United States District Court, in which you pleaded for your son and indicated, among other things: "Judge Mathes, for the first time in my life, I'm able to give Charles a nice home and help him

143

to make a good life." Apparently, your present positon is that your son led a pampered existence and that you did in fact offer him throughout his life a "nice" home and surroundings.

The fact that you have abandoned your son is, I suppose, in the course of human existence understandable. However, your advocacy in terms of having him executed is not.

Furthermore, your secrecy is perplexing. If in fact you are telling the truth, why not tell it openly or publicly or better yet, why not come to Los Angeles and tell it in a court of law. Why not face your son and make the allegations you have made? As you well know, your son is being held incommunicado in the Los Angeles County Jail and is unable to respond to your remarks. One would also expect that you would engage in the common decency of communicating with your son prior to your interview with the Los Angeles Times.

To my knowledge, you have made no attempt to contact him nor have you made any attempt to contact anybody connected with his defense.

I deeply hope that you have been misquoted or your remarks have been taken out of context or in some other respect are inaccurate and do not reflect your personal opinion. If the article is not reflective of your point of view, please contact me as soon as possible by phone (collect) or by wire or letter. Early in the case, we tried very hard to locate you. Apparently the Los Angeles Times, with the assistance of law enforcement, did not face similar problems. Contact me soon so that I may set up some visitation with Charles and/or some method or manner by which you can be of assistance to him in this time of most grievous need. His life could in many respects depend upon you.

Very truly yours,

I do not dismiss Mrs. C.'s story even though I am sure that she may have twisted the truth here and there for self-serving reasons. Severe

144

deprivation alone does not explain Charles Manson. If such were the case we would live surrounded by Mansons! Lack of consistent nurturing and consistent discipline, plus poor socioeconomic conditions make a person vulnerable, but it doesn't follow that all people who grow under trying conditions become sociopaths. As I said earlier and will expand on here, the family transactions, in which he played a part, are at the basis in the formation of Manson's character.

Many researchers and psychotherapists, particularly those who work with families, have learned that antisocial traits can be transmitted from parent to child and not just by the process of identification with an antisocial parent. I have observed many children and adolescents who act out a parent's impulses. This significant figure in a child's life may be, but usually is not, aware of his own antisocial tendencies. A parent may, for example, show pleasure when his child misbehaves; or he may project the blame for his child's actions onto others, peers, teachers, a sibling. This parent, with whom the child has an intense and anxious relationship, consistently sends him messages that either give him an antisocial alternative such as "Go to the shopping center but don't steal anything!" or the wrong reason for avoiding antisocial acts: "Don't steal, you may be caught and you'll end up with a record." Or he may rationalize away any attempt from anyone to discipline his child.

Psychiatrist Adelaide Johnson was among the first to call attention to this type of interaction. While studying juvenile delinquency she discussed the transmission of what she called "a superego defect" from parent to child:

> It has become increasingly clear that many parents, particularly those with poorly integrated impulses, have become uneasy about setting limits, even concerning matters which are specifically destructive to society, such as stealing, pathologic sexuality, or even murderous intent. . . . The entranced parental facial expression apparent to the child describing a stealing episode, a sexual misdemeanor, or a hostile attitude towards a teacher conveys to the child that the parent is achieving some pleasurable gratification. No amount of subsequent punishment will act as a

145

deterrent against the recurrences of the acting out. A child wishes to do the thing which he senses gives the parent pleasure, even though he may be punished.

Manson's mother was, at least in 1971, aware of how she influenced her son, how her own resentment towards her rigid, puritanical parents affected her own behavior and in turn made her "mold" her son's, who promptly internalized his mother's feelings and attitudes and made them his own. I want to add that people who are excessively moralistic and judgmental are themselves warding off impulses which they are unable to integrate into their personality.

Another characteristic of this mother-son relationship was its intensity. Her illegitimate son represented to this mother her way to get at her forbidding parents, but also her guilt; her child was an emotionally loaded object to her; their strong tie was a part of them, whether they were together or separated. From five to eight while Charles lived with his strict relatives, having to be dependent on them, he was not relating or responding to them. He acquiesced and repressed his anger, waiting for the day when Mother would come back and unlock the door of his cage so he could fly into the dislocated paths of total freedom.

It is likely that other family members had negative expectations from this child whose illegitimate birth and whose mother had so embarrassed them. And Kathleen may well have had other yearnings that she instilled in her son. I think that Manson's megalomania did not start when he formed his family but has its roots in the interchanges with his mother. She probably invested her son with a sense of importance she was unable to attain for herself; she did so because of her low self-esteem, because the immature person she was encouraged grandiose fantasies but never taught him to realize them. For this young "bad" girl her son probably became the sun and the stars of her sordid life. Thus from the start Manson was ill equipped to compete with real people in the real world. It became easier for him to feel omnipotent in his daydreams than to fight the daily occurrences of life.

With his women, his bad girls, he was able to reproduce his early, most significant relationship. In a letter thanking me for presents I

146

bought for her at Manson's request—which he selected from a catalogue—Lyn wrote:

> We like the Owls and the Sun too . . . The sun I didn't like as it was, so I put Manson's face on it and now I am satisfied with it.

This piece of verbal felicity symbolizes how she feels towards Manson and explains why Manson felt close to her.

Manson and His Women

I believe that Manson's positive feelings towards his women are related to his feelings towards his mother. Many will challenge my assertion that he had (has) good feelings towards them. After all he had been a small-time pimp, on at least one occasion he was accused of rape, and he has come to represent a most exaggerated version of machismo. But I am talking here about his relationship with his women in the context of these people's beliefs. No doubt his female followers saw him as a loving figure because their views in regard to males and females were highly distorted. None of the members of the Family had a civilized view of male-female relationships; they were amoral in every respect. Manson tried to attract members of motorcycle gangs, notoriously chauvinistic, and he used the women for this purpose with no objections on their part.

The view that Manson had control—mind control—over his followers has been presented in the popular literature dealing with this case; during court proceedings Paul Fitzgerald described the women as "mindless robots." As I said earlier, these women joined Manson and his family voluntarily and stayed in the group of their own free will and not out of fear or because they were brainwashed by Manson. It is likely that at times they had to do things against their wishes or do without experiences they wanted to pursue. For instance, Barbara Hoyt testified that on one occasion Manson forced her to perform fellatio on Juan Flynn, and Leslie Van Houten had to be restrained from her involvement with bikers. But Hoyt also testified that she hardly used any drugs and was never forced to do so; and

Mary Brunner had arguments and fistfights with Manson, usually about their son. It is simply untrue that the women were afraid of Manson (and neither were the men).

George Bishop, author of *Witness To Evil,* had many conversations with the women who waited outside during the trial. He has this to say:

> Repeated talks with the female members, in addition to the tenacity implicit in their vigil and their frequent jail visits to see Charlie, leave me with the strong impression that, with Sandy and Gypsy especially, motivation is communicated in at least equal measure from the women to Charlie.

The fact is that he felt secure with his women who were not competitive towards him. It is possible that without meaning to he became quite dependent on them. In a letter to me he had this to say:

> They said them women were mine. Huh. They had me more than I had them. I would have got lost and starved to death if it weren't for someone holding my hand.

Manson's first encounters with women always involved sexual intercourse, which seemed to establish the bond between them and the women's attraction to him. One must keep in mind how central their sexuality was in these people's lives. Manson, in this respect, reminds me of Havelock Ellis's view of Casanova:

> He sought his pleasure in the pleasure, and not in the complaisance of the women he loved and they seemed to have gratefully and tenderly recognized his skill in the art of love making. Casanova loved many women, but broke few hearts.

Interestingly, Manson has other similarities with the Venetian lover who thought of himself as a philosopher and who was also obsessed by his sexuality. Like him he is a phallic man. His penis is his most precious possession. Both men were exhibitionistic and had a great facility to attain erections. Casanova's sexual feasts were depicted by

148

Italian filmmaker Federico Fellini for what they were: perform-ances. For the two, Manson and Casanova, the erect phallus symbol-ized manliness and all the attributes that put man on top—which is just an exaggeration of the way many men feel.

Manson's sexuality was not chaotic or even disorganized. He is bisexual and probably less successful with men. He accurately sized up girls who were ready to be seduced and he seduced them by a combination of his sensuality and his talk, a powerful aphrodisiac geared at pampering their narcissism. To a certain extent he supervised the sexual activities of his women—strangers had to ask his permission—but he was not possessive. He used the women to attract other men but also to elicit the admiration and envy of men. As is most frequently the case, his machismo was addressed more to the males than to the females. But machismo makes men vulnerable, not strong. More than anything it was the threat to his macho image that ultimately made Manson turn to violence. For him to fail once he had envisioned the possibility of great success probably meant to be castrated, and thus totally dispossessed.

The Other Charles

Little Jack Horner
Sat in the corner,
    Eating of Christmas pie:
He put in his thumb,
And pulled out a plum,
    And said, "What a good boy
        am I!"

Sometime in 1978 I learned about a book on the life of Charles "Tex" Watson. Not knowing the title or the name of the author I was unable to find the book in Baltimore so I wrote Charles Watson for information. In a few days I received a postcard from him with a picture of a stuffed animal, a baby monkey. Written above it were the words Thinking Of You. Printed inside was the following:

God made
Little monkeys
For children
And He made
You for me.

In Watson's own handwriting, addressing me as "Dear Clara," was

150

the information I had requested. It was signed, "In Christ, Charles."

I was vexed at the childishly bizarre format of his answer, more so after learning by reading his book *Would You Die For Me?* that at the California Colony for Men, where Watson is an inmate, he is a deacon, an associate administrator for the Protestant chapel—where he has his own office—that he preaches several times a month, celebrates communion, baptizes, and leads Bible study groups.

Why would this thirty-two-year-old man send me, a stranger asking for information, such a "cute" infantile card? The answer, I believe, is that Charles Watson *is* still the ingratiating little boy, playing at being big man on campus, this time a prison campus. His wish to feel big in macho fashion was his central motivation as the action man on the nights of August 9 and 10, 1969. It was then that he became a central figure in the Family as the only man of the criminal expedition that resulted in the Tate-LaBianca murders. According to Paul Watkins, who was second in command in the Manson ménage, after he left the group (at the time when it was becoming violent), Watson changed. He became more self-assured, gave orders, showed himself more able to assume authority, acted macho.

Watson's own account conveys the impression that he was a good, obedient boy who just carried out Manson's orders. Today he is the good kid carrying out God's orders. After all, during his childhood he was also just a nice little boy and as he recounts, "next to my stuffed panda bear and my older brother God was probably one of my favorite people." I fantasize that if God could talk in human terms his response to this would be "Why pick on me?"

Interestingly, Watson was the head executioner of the Tate-LaBianca murders, but within the Family he was a peripheral figure and after the murders, when he realized that he could be arrested at any moment, he fled to his hometown. Eventually he was tried separately. From the moment he left the Manson group, unlike the others, his only concern was to save himself. His claim was and still is that he was not himself during his Manson period because Manson completely controlled his mind, which was also shattered by the abuse of hallucinogenic and other drugs. Watson states that in effect he did not flee the desert just to save himself from being arrested, but

151

to avoid murdering for Manson. Again, "Manson made me do it."

Watson met Manson and his girls at Dennis Wilson's home on Sunset Boulevard. He got acquainted with Wilson, the Beach Boys' drummer, when he picked him up on a road and gave him a ride home. According to Watson, Wilson explained to him that "he'd wrecked his Ferrari and his Rolls-Royce so was having to use his thumb." Shortly thereafter he moved in with Wilson at his invitation and partook of the luxurious surroundings, the drugs, and the company of an assortment of people, flower children, the children of the rich and famous, dope dealers, in a continuous party that never seemed to be over. At Wilson's home he met the resident guru, Dean Moorehouse, the LSD self-appointed preacher who became his mentor. Through him, he first heard of "ego death" and all the other pseudophilosophical, pseudomystical babbling he was to hear more of later from Manson and his acolytes. When Wilson heard that Moorehouse was trying to seduce his female guests, he asked him and Watson too to leave the premises (Watson was Moorehouse's protégé). One of Wilson's friends, Terry Melcher, continued his friendship with Moorehouse, who with Watson visited him several times at his Cielo Drive residence. Once Melcher lent his Jaguar and his credit cards to his friend Moorehouse when he had to drive up north to face a drug charge. He took Watson with him.

When Watson found himself with no money and no roof over his head he asked Manson if he could stay at Spahn Ranch. Manson allowed him to live on the premises in a tent but did not accept him as a group member in the beginning. In describing this period Watson presents himself as a Cinderella, all hard work and no fun. He was asked to fix dilapidated trucks, to repair an old shack, to mend fences. But finally his day came, after he had proven his usefulness—he is a skilled mechanic—and Manson assigned him a "special love," Mary Brunner. He was in.

Shortly after the murders, Manson for some reason (maybe he wanted to scatter the murderers) ordered Watson to go to Olancha, a place at the foot of the Sierra Nevada where at one point he was questioned by the police in reference to a series of car thefts that had been reported in the vicinity. Frantic trips to and from the Spahn Ranch followed, as well as expeditions with Bruce Davis, to steal dune buggies. Contrary to his assertion that at that time his mind was clouded by drugs and possessed by Manson, Watson took careful "unclouded" precautions to cover his tracks after the murders (one of his fingerprints, however, was found in the Cielo Drive residence).

Finally, early in October 1969, Watson called his parents and asked for money to go back home to Copeville, Texas, where he stayed for a few days and then left for Mexico, then went back to Los Angeles. And then to Hawaii where he went to look up some people he knew. Eventually, after stealing the money to buy a ticket, he flew back to Los Angeles and called his distressed parents who again dutifully wired him money to return home. Watson's version of this period— and that of his supporters—is that he was a confused, disturbed young man; according to him, "I still was living in my own peculiar world, caught between Charlie and my past." Watson is careful to mention in his book that at that time he was going out with a girl he had initially met at college, since this young woman testified at his trial. But she presented quite a different picture as she told a story of fun days, the two of them driving back and forth from Copeville to Dallas. According to her, Watson "looked great, just thinner but was vigorous sexually, the same old Tex" she had known in college.

On November 30, 1969, while he was in Copeville, Watson was arrested and taken to the McKinney County Jail where he was to remain for nine months while his attorney, William Boyd, fought extradition. Mr. Boyd felt that sending Tex Watson to California to be tried, "would not serve justice" because of the publicity of the case. Mr. Boyd was, of course, talking from a legal point of view. A defendant's right to a fair trial is part of our system of justice. In this case, however, I can't help but wonder (I really can't!) how the law can be invoked to protect a criminal. Many people questioned then what right Tex Watson had to try to avoid extradition.

Sheriff Montgomery of McKinney was Tex Watson's second cousin and at the jail he was allowed to have a television set, his record player, a styrofoam icebox, and home-cooked meals prepared by his mother who visited him twice weekly. But finally, on September 11, 1970, Watson was returned to California where he promptly started to exhibit bizarre behavior. He refused to talk except with his attorney Sam Bubrick, did not eat, and as a result his weight went

153

down to 110 pounds. He was ruled incompetent to stand trial and was sent to Atascadero State Hospital for observation and treatment. According to Watson, at the hospital he was beaten up by attendants and exposed to "psychiatric" games. Following his attorney's orders he refused to talk about the murders. Bubrick told him, in Watson's words, "Don't say anything to anyone. You have the right to remain silent." His ability to follow these suggestions carefully indicates, in my judgment, that his "mental breakdown" was rather selective.

He was in Atascadero for nearly four months. Psychiatrists at the institution were of the opinion that Watson was not psychotic. It became obvious that whenever he was about to stand trial, he acted "crazy" which was understandable since his attorneys Sam Bubrick and Maxwell Keith pleaded that he was non-guilty by reason of insanity. No effort was spared to avoid for him a conviction of first-degree murder. Eight psychiatrists were called by the defense, testifying that his mental capacity was greatly impaired at the time he committed his crimes. And Judge Alexander, who presided, did not hide that he was biased in the defendant's favor; besides, he was a personal friend of attorney Bubrick. Vincent Bugliosi and Steve Kay, the prosecutors, of course attacked the validity of the psychiatrists' testimony. Bugliosi, at one point, had this to say:

> I got the impression, ladies and gentlemen, that they [the defense psychiatrists] looked upon Tex Watson as a patient of theirs, that they would have gladly wrapped up their collective bosoms and take him home with them to nurse him. The poor guy. All he did was murder seven people and anyone who murders seven people deserves a lot of sympathy.

The defense presented Watson as an all-American boy, a small-town kid who had the bad luck to run into drugs and Charles Manson and as a result had become psychotic. Watson told how Manson worked on people to make them follow his orders. In spite of the impressive legal and psychiatric support that Watson received, it took the jury two hours of deliberation to find him legally sane at the time he committed the murders and six hours to determine that he deserved the death penalty.

154

In November of 1971 Watson arrived on Death Row at San Quentin. Now he was in the same place, in the same situation, as Manson. One of the Charleses had arrived at Death Row after a lifelong experience of being in prison; he was born out of wedlock and raised by a troubled, sociopathic mother and was shifted among relatives as a young child. The other was the product of a decent, intact family, raised in a strictly religious environment, given the opportunity of a higher education. Yet both ended up together, waiting to finish their lives in the gas chamber.

After the death penalty was abolished in California in 1972, Watson was transferred to a model prison, the Men's Colony in San Luis Obispo, where he promptly adjusted, was satisfied—all things considered—had a good job, dabbled in religion, and received frequent visits from a German girl who had fallen in love with him during his trial. But by 1974, according to his account, he was bored. It was in that year like his friend Susan Atkins, that he "truly" converted and devoted his life to Christ. I wonder if these two conversions are somehow related to the publication of the book *Helter Skelter* that same year. Surely the two knew of prosecutor Bugliosi's book even before it was in the bookstores!

Charles Watson was born on December 2, 1945, the youngest child of a lower middle-class family. He has a sister ten years older and a brother five years older. He grew up in Copeville, a small Texas town, population two hundred. His home was a religious one—his parents are Methodist—and from early life he participated in church activities. His mother, the only member of his family who testified, had this to say about his religious upbringing,

> I have gone to church all my life and when Charles was three months old I took him to church and he had to be sick to miss church and he was very active in church. . . . Many times he was up in the pulpit leading the services for the preacher to take over and Charles would sing and he worked in Sunday School and he went to vacation Bible school every summer.

Charles was industrious; being mechanically inclined he helped his father who operated a gas station and general store. According to his mother and others who knew him, he developed a great interest in sports, and excelled. Mother remembered the exact details of her son's accomplishments.

> . . . He was a class yell leader and he raised beautiful calves, and in his track he won in everything that he run in, 220, 100 yard dash and 440 relay; and he played basketball. In the sophomore year he was an usher for the senior play and he sang between acts and he had track . . . he won everything he went in that, second place in low hurdles, first in high hurdles. Third, he led in the 440 relay and he was in football and he was all district that year; and in basketball he was also all district.
> In '63 he won several basketball trophies and he went to regional in track. He was first place in everything he ran in track, 220 dash; he won first in broad jump, first in high hurdles and he led the 440 relays, and he was a leader in American history and he was halfback football, all district. He was in the Spanish Club; he was the class favorite; he was the sports editor . . . he was a Boy Scout . . . he belonged to 4-H Club . . .

And so on, and so on.

According to Mother Charles had lots of friends. She fondly remembered the following among her son's "social" activities:

> One of the things that I remember most, a lot of his friends came back home on Sunday afternoon with a lot of frogs and they took off all the skins and all of the meat off these frogs and they put the frog bones on a picture-like thing, a frame, and then they named it after the boys and they just had a lot of fun.

Mother "never knew of him having a fight." "He was our pride and joy"—she said—"because he was ten years younger than his sister and we all loved him very much."

The intense emotional involvement of this mother with her son, her great expectations, came alive through her own words. She stood

156

by him all the way during his trial and thereafter. Reports present her as a strong woman who overprotected Charles and who was the dominant influence in her son's life as he was growing up. She was, out of love, completely unaware that her darling, the son whose life she followed step by step, was hiding a growing monster inside his soft skin. He was also mothered by his sister and it is not surprising that psychiatrists' reports describe him as a child as "an extremely immature and infantile boy."

Charles graduated with honors from high school in nearby Farmersville. The small-town high-school world in which he had excelled was actually a narrow one, but he had by then high expectations of what life had in store for him. Charles yearned for excitement, a life of thrills he knew he could attain only away from home. College—North Texas State University—offered that opportunity. For him college life meant parties, beer drinking, women, and sporting the Ivy League look. For his fraternity initiation—or so he says, the robbery being now a matter of record—he stole four typewriters from Farmersville High School. However, he was not booked. By then Charles was leading a dissolute life, interested only in what girl he would make next, what tavern he would be drinking in. Away from Mother's control, he broke loose. He had several car accidents because of drunken driving. But he continued to have his own apartment, a new car, a boat, and what he saw as a great life. His marks went down, and tired of listening to his parents' reproaches he started to think of golden California. He made up his mind to move west after he had totaled his car as he was leaving a nightclub. At that time he had a part-time job with Braniff Airlines that afforded him the opportunity to fly to California where he bought marijuana for himself and his acquaintances a few times.

In 1967, with the reluctant approval of his parents, he moved to Los Angeles, ostensibly to enroll in California State. There he stayed with a former classmate whose brother was an aspiring actor. The two started to make good money as wig salesmen so Charles quit college. During this period, by his account, he was elated by his new life, by the Los Angeles scene that fitted his yearnings so well with its sexual freedom, drugs, lack of conventions. He made his the uniform of "love," longer hair, beads, frayed jeans. Life became a

157

banquet for his senses and his appetites turned to gluttony. To earn more money he and his friend went into the wig business for themselves but this venture failed. He then tried to make it as a dealer in marijuana but was unable to make a go of it.

Like all the mansonites who claim that Manson made them get rid of their inhibitions, Charles Watson had little left in the way of inhibitions by the time he met Manson. He realized even before he left home for college that he was bored sick with his "good kid" facade.

Today Charles Watson, the kid preacher, has a ready explanation for what happened to him during the years of his contented sinful life: He was possessed, and Manson was the dark demon who found him and made him act as other than his real self which is all good. God has forgiven him because God is forgiving. His demons have been eradicated like bacteria with the antibiotic of religion, which he now is eager to administer to other sinners. To feel comfortable with his fraudulent life, he has enough supporters who agree with his version that his dissolution was "injected" into him temporarily by the forces of evil.

Dr. Joel Fort, a psychiatrist appointed by the court to examine Watson before his trial, had a different opinion:

> I would say that years of relationships with a mother or a father or both is bound to have more of an impact on a person than some months of a relationship with somebody else, even under the circumstances that we are talking about. It is not an all or none kind of thing . . . you don't completely replace past values; you are at any given moment in time a combination of what you grew up to be through the influences of your family life, your school, your religion, other institutions or forces that help people or sometimes fail to help them as they develop; and then a significant event or influence at some later stage in life operates on that foundation and certainly may influence it, but it does not in any way totally replace it or supplant it.

Charles Manson always knew all there was to know about who he was and so did everyone around him. Charles Watson probably perceived something about himself he knew his family could never accept, and consequently he could only express a fragment of his identity and never had the chance for a harmonious, healthy integration of his feelings. But Charles Watson could not ignore what he tried hard to repress and the time came when he didn't want to, so he dislodged his imprisoned "evils." When he did, the two Charleses, Manson and Watson, became equals as they have become equals in the eyes of the law.

III

The Women: Introduction

"Sugar and spice,
and all
that's nice . . ."

I see no way you can touch the women of the Family. She's
as vast as the universe & the world & all his colors. I took
her & showed her the earth balance & she picked it up
behond words. There is no doubt in her mind. I seen her
deliver her own babys and put babys on her back & walk
acrost the desert in heat without water & 2/3 dead smile
with an endless love for her own—I could spend years
explainin her but only she understand my words motions
and my ways.

Thus spoke Manson in a letter to me. I had asked him to tell me
about the Manson women. It came as no surprise to me that he would
express such high views about those who had put him on a pedestal.
For the mansonites, mutual support and absolute acceptance of each
other were the central motivations that kept them together. Within
their group the women felt secure and free to be themselves. As I
have reported earlier there was an amazing lack of friction among

them and even now they are seldom if at all critical of each other. During the Tex Watson trial his attorney, Maxwell Keith, asked Dianne Lake, a young mansonite who was testifying for the prosecution:

> What was it about him [Manson] that caused you to want to live with him and the other members of his family and stay away from home?

She answered:

> Cooperation among the girls and the happiness and the music.

Insofar as the women's feelings towards Manson are concerned, however, it has been widely reported that their support of him was based on fear and that Manson despised them and harbored intense anger towards women, which he expressed towards his female followers. Witnesses testified that at various times he slapped Dianne Lake, annoyed by her attention-getting disruptions. Ed Sanders in his book *The Family* quotes Manson as saying, "We live in a woman's thought, this world is hers. But men were meant to be above, on top of women." According to the author this is an illustration of Manson's resentment and distrust of women. I don't agree with Sanders' interpretation. Knowing Manson's baroque style of speech and his uncanny ability to convey paradoxical ideas, one realizes that the first sentence of his quote does not necessarily contradict the second; the latter also has a sexual connotation. Sanders also states that Manson hated women and that "Charlie's greatest hold on the girls was fear." This was the prevailing opinion at the time he wrote his book and it still persists. It is because of this view of the women that they are still perceived by a great many people as having acted under Manson's control, in spite of the court decisions to the contrary; these people also regard them as having been totally dependent on Manson. Thus, Bugliosi comments in his book that "Manson had severed their [the women to their parents] umbilical cord while fastening one of his own." The Redwood City (Ca.) *Tribune* echoes other recent newspaper reports in stating (November 18, 1978):

164

At his highly publicized trial in 1970, Manson followers told how Manson programmed their thoughts with the use of LSD and other drugs. Manson "family" members said that they vowed to follow Manson's orders even when they involved murder.

These opinions present a one-sided view of the mansonites' relationship. The women are regarded by many to this day as young, confused girls who were drugged and bewitched by Manson into complete submission. As I said earlier, these people ignore that these women chose to join Manson because they felt highly valued by him. From the start they were fascinated by him, by his cultish delivery, by his obvious sexual response to them, all of which implied that he found them attractive on all counts. They were accepted by him in a grand manner befitting their own sense of importance. They simply adored what they heard from him and that's why they stayed with him, of their own free will and not out of fear.

Why, then, are these women still perceived as robots who were manipulated by Manson?

There is little doubt in my mind that most people I talked with have a protective attitude towards them because they are women. Even those who recognize that these women are guilty have benign sentiments towards them, particularly for those who have repudiated their former liaison with Manson. This attitude is not atypical in that it reflects the way in which most people feel about the woman criminal. The assumption is that women cannot be markedly deviant and cannot commit major crimes unless they are laboring under extreme emotions or unless they are forced to do so by the men on whom they are dependent or whom they fear. In the case of the Manson women, many do not think of them as criminals but as special cases, as people who were caught in a unique situation, who freaked out, but who otherwise cannot be considered sociopaths. If they are to be considered criminals, as I believe, where do they fit?

To answer this question I must comment on women's criminality in general. Dr. Rita James Simon in her monograph *The Contemporary Woman and Crime* notes that the crime rate for women has greatly increased while recognition of the woman as criminal is not proportional to the extent of her criminal behavior. Chivalry from law enforcement agents and from the men who commit crimes in conjunction with women—she thinks—are factors that prevent detection of the woman or reduce her penalty if she is arrested. Dr. Otto Pollak, a sociologist, published in 1950 a small volume *The Criminality of Women*, a book that is important not only because there are so few studies of women's criminality but because Dr. Pollak's thesis was also that many crimes committed by women go undetected and that when she is convicted a patronizing attitude from the jury works in her favor:

> One of the outstanding concomitants of the existing inequality between the sexes is chivalry and the general protective attitude of man towards woman. This attitude exists on the part of the male victim of crime as well as on the part of the officers of the law, who are still largely male in our society. Men hate to arrest women and thus indirectly to lead them to their punishment; police officers dislike to arrest them, district attorneys to prosecute them, judges and juries to find them guilty, and so on.

Traditionally women have been involved in criminal activities typical of their gender such as infanticide, murder against a husband or a lover, and also in criminal activities as a result of opportunity, such as domestic theft, shoplifting. Or else they have "worked" under their men. It has been argued that after all many women commit crimes because their men put pressure on them to do so. This kind of reasoning ignores that it is up to a woman to get or not to get involved with a lawless man and when she does, to yield or not to his demands. Women, like men, have a choice.

Dr. Pollak believes that the need to maintain the myth of male superiority, ironically, is responsible for our attitude towards female criminality. It is noteworthy that the following was written by him in 1950, years away from the women's movement:

> Basically they [the men] have attempted to deny women the ability to do things men do and have either idealized them into a sweetness and purity which made them appear docile and harmless, or they have maligned them in order to be able to condemn them. Both types of behavior help

166

men to feel better about their denial of equality to women. Thus, many male attempts to understand women have actually been attempts to rationalize men's treatment of the other sex and have frequently been nothing but self-deception. With regards to crime this male self-deception about women seems to have been excessive. It has been the traditional opinion of criminologists that women commit relatively few crimes and that when they do so they somehow betray their womanhood by venturing out into the reserve of men.

In his book, Dr. Pollak expressed that in our society man is the oppressor and that many are afraid of women's rebellion and eager to rely on any "evidence" which presents women as less likely to participate of their own free will in crime.

Was Leslie Van Houten's attorney trying to capitalize on this attitude as he consistently tried to present his client as a model of graciousness? Or does he himself have the same bias, and is he totally unable to perceive his client's dark side?

Some criminologists think that there is a correlation between the increase of female criminality and women's strides towards liberation. The types of crimes that women commit are changing, becoming more serious. Dr. Simon speculates that crimes of violence by women will decrease (some such as abortion are no longer on the books in many countries) because women are less frustrated, more independent of men, and less tied down by children from unwanted pregnancies. The role that women play in violent groups, however, is becoming more prominent. Patricia Soltysik is said to have trained Donald DeFreeze; Diane Oughton, Emily Harris, and Camilla Hall are other examples of violent, dangerous women. Priscilla Cooper and Nancy Pitman—former Manson followers—have continued their careers in crime; they pleaded guilty to the murders of James and Lauren Willett, committed in Stockton, California, in 1972. Mary Brunner and Catherine Share, also mansonites, participated and organized a robbery of weapons to be used to free Manson after he was convicted. While serving time at the California Institution for Women they staged two unsuccessful escape attempts. They were planning to join Share's "revolutionary" boyfriend.

In regard to violent behavior, the same controversies that permeate

167

the subject of male-female differences and similarities exist about men and women criminals. These differences—biological, genetic, physical, social—how real are they? At this point we don't know for sure and when we know we can arrive at different conclusions according to other factors involved. Men, for example, are by and large physically stronger than women. Firing a gun, however, requires the same strength from a man as from a woman. What it requires from a woman is a different attitude, the acceptance that if she is criminally inclined she can buy a gun and learn how to use it. The female mansonites eagerly learned from Manson how to use a knife to kill and when the occasion arose they put their training to use. In the macho world they lived in, firearms were reserved as the males' precious possessions. Squeaky Fromme, however, managed to obtain a gun and used it in her attempt against the life of President Ford. Some people think that she didn't intend to kill him. This may be so. Or maybe it is difficult for us to accept that a woman can commit a crime that until then has been committed solely by males.

Since women are perpetrating more serious crimes, particularly against property, one may conclude that women can possess the same criminal drives as their male counterparts and if they do they are more free today to act out their tendencies. Criminologist Freda Adler in her book *Sisters in Crime* has this to say about the subject:

> The increasing similarities of social attitudes towards and activities by both men and women in areas as diverse as politics, liquor consumption, smoking habits, industry choice of profession and sexual proclivities will eventually enable us to delineate how the biological (as distinct from the cultural) differences between the sexes will be manifested. Until there is complete social equality it will not be possible to tell with any certainty which of the demonstrated differences between the sexes are biological and which are cultural. But what is clear is that as the position of women approximates the position of men, so does the frequency and type of their criminal activity. It would therefore seem justified to predict that if present social trends continue women will be sharing with men not only ulcers, coronaries, hypertension and lung cancer (until

recently considered almost exclusively masculine diseases) but will also compete increasingly in such traditionally male criminal activities as crimes against the person, more aggressive property offenses, and especially white collar crime.

Women, however, by virtue of their gender and their social learning do not have machismo as one of their problems and consequently do not suffer from its results. When apprehended, when tried, when convicted, women feel free to cry, to show their helpless side, and thus can be appealing to other women and to men. Women can be aggressive in crime and submissive in prison without losing face. Conversely, for many their "little, helpless girl" stance takes over and is a great obstacle to their rehabilitation since such process involves the development of responsibility, greater frustration tolerance, and self-assertiveness at the service of emotional growth.

The way in which the new woman criminal operates—the experts are saying—mirrors that of her law-abiding sister. Today women in the working force, for example, are learning the rules of the game from men. They accept that they cannot be loners or submissive if they have job or career aspirations and that like men they must form or become part of a network. Career women today more deliberately search for and use mentors—who still are mostly men. The Manson women understood this. They became part of a sociopathic network. They joined and used a mentor who instructed them on how to survive as outlaws. Manson, who had a great deal of respect for the police, trained them in many aspects of criminal life. He insisted, for example, that they should always be afraid in order to be on the alert; he also talked repeatedly about the usefulness of promoting fear in others to have power over them. The so-called paranoid attitude of the mansonites is a misnomer. These people were not paranoid. They were, they had reason to be, suspicious and careful. Any person who chooses or who must live with danger is better off if he has fear as his constant companion.

The Manson women were at a crossroad in their time; their life-style and their "careers" can be said to have some of the characteristics of a period of confusion for women that is still with us.

Those who investigate female criminality, as I said earlier, think of this problem within the framework of our times. Women are changing in the way they think about themselves, in their wish for self-realization, in their eagerness to compete. Faster than men, they are escaping the narrow niche assigned to them since the beginning of history. The mansonites did not repress their inclinations; instead they found a niche that accommodated them and the group they formed reinforced their tendencies.

To "locate" these women I want to comment on where women and women criminals are today by using a simplified spectrum to illustrate my views. I want to clarify that some women are in between the groupings I present and I will start with women in general:

The liberated-traditional woman. She has a diversified life. She is married and has or plans to have children. Or she is divorced but plans to remarry. She may or may not work while her children are preschoolers. When she does she tries to be partially employed. This woman prepares herself before marriage and while the children are young for work outside the home. An increasing number are career-oriented rather than job-oriented. Their husbands, to varied degrees, share household chores and the care of the children, two areas that continue to be a source of friction; but more women freely express—that is without guilt and without feeling inadequate as females—a dislike for home-related activities. This group is increasing in numbers not only because of social change but because of economic reasons.

Women whose main priority is their career. These women make an important investment in their work and postpone marriage. Or else they are able to do so after their children are grown. When these women marry they and their husbands carefully time the arrival of children or decide against having children. These women frequently feel conflicted as they approach their thirtieth birthdate when they feel they must make a choice between raising a family, which today still demands a great deal from a woman, or continuing a serious career commitment.

Working women who are not career-oriented but who remain single. There is no stigma attached today to being single and these women

170

find it difficult to give up their independent, "no-ties" life-style. More women today are part of this group, at least for a good portion of their adult lives.

Women who are against any changes in the traditional female-male roles. When these women work they do so because of financial pressure or to fill time after their children are grown.

Women who are conflicted about choices. These women feel themselves trapped in their roles of wives and mothers but are unable to take a stand and have a more diversified life. These women, of course, have always existed; probably their numbers were larger in the past. Today they are particularly vulnerable because rigid stereotypes are disappearing and do not offer them a way to rationalize their problems. They are confused and struggle with their infantile dependency on their husbands and their wish to cut loose. Some of them act impulsively, for example, embarking in pursuit of a career but unable to cope with its responsibilities; some get a divorce before they are ready, others drop out into a markedly different life-style from their own. Some of these women are single and keep searching for continuous excitement and "love" which they expect to acquire or obtain from outside sources only.

I speculate that the Manson women could have ended as part of this latter group if they had remained in the mainstream.

More pathways are open to the woman sociopath today than in the past. Lest misunderstandings arise from my comparisons, I want to emphasize that typically the antisocial woman, the repeater, is not a feminist. On the contrary, she either has no interest in women's issues or is against the woman's liberation movement. And yet this is not to say that the woman criminal is not becoming increasingly liberated. As I see it, here is where she is today:

The liberated woman criminal. She is determined to get more for her travails. She wants more money and more of what money buys. She may work with men but refuses to be exploited by men. She abandons or initially does not get involved in petty crime such as shoplifting. Some of these women, because today they have better opportunities for advancement in their jobs, commit serious crimes against property such as larceny and embezzlement; some are members of violent gangs. (I doubt, however, that women have become part of the power

171

structure of organized crime, the counterpart of big business, where women have yet to have a big impact.) Prostitutes of this group no longer pay heavily for protection and some do without pimps altogether. They have learned how to take care of themselves and work as independents; some of them have formed protest groups to gain acceptance as part of the working force.

The infantile dependent antisocial woman. She continues to resort to petty crime only since she does not dare to commit serious crimes. Many in this group are dependent on their men for their criminal activities. If she is a prostitute she operates under a pimp who she perceives as a nurturant parent figure or she may be involved with a homosexual "strong" figure. These women do not regard themselves as exploited by their partners.

The multiproblem and highly conflicted criminal. Her criminal activities are the result of a different set (for each one) of causes such as serious socioeconomic and/or emotional deprivation since early life, mental retardation, severe emotional problems, mental disease at times of organic origin. Most of these women's acting out is the result of intense anger at authority and unfulfilled dependency needs. In this category also belongs the extremely narcissistic woman whose parents were unable to set rules or who themselves projected into their children their own unresolved problems towards authority and conventional morality.

The woman criminal of any of these groups, like the man, frequently abuses alcohol and other drugs.

I place the Manson women somewhere in groups 2 and 3. They yearned to be more aggressive but felt incapable of doing so on their own. They opted for a compromise, the Family, that allowed them to act out their tendencies without having to assume responsibility for their actions. The group provided them with emotional and actual security and satisfied their distorted needs. These women do not have a history of severe socioeconomic deprivation. The emotional climate of their families, however, was one that promoted serious deficits in their characters. They are similar to each other in their antisocial tendencies and other traits but they are also different from each other. Susan, Leslie, and Sandra (and probably Pat) were thrill-seekers. Lyn and Sandra are the closest to terrorist types and continue

172

to have dreams of power; they had a seniority position within the Family and no matter how it was disguised, their positions were symmetrical to that of Manson. These two women's megalomania matches that of Susan Atkins, who, however, stands alone in her blatant exhibitionism; she is devoid of the paranoid tendencies of the other two. Socially, Susan was a few notches below the others and she is also less intelligent than the other women. Leslie and Pat have a remarkably similar background which may account for the friendship they developed.

The women's relationship with Manson was also different. Although he was most sexually involved with young Dianne Lake, he was closest to Lyn and Sandra and probably Pat. It seems that his big romance was with Lyn which continues on her part to this day. Susan tried to compete with Manson and felt that she could also be a leader of the group.

The Manson women shared another trait that I have referred to before: a need to belong to a cultish, semireligious, semiphilosophical grouping. They needed to feel special (they still do). To experience thrills via sex, drugs, and lawbreaking, to be able to lead an irresponsible, hedonistic life was not enough for them. They had a self-righteous, snubbing attitude towards the world outside their own, a world they despised and grew to hate. Such was the stuff that cemented their relationship. They denounced the society in which they grew up but took no positive action to change it. They felt nothing but contempt and anger towards their liberated sisters and made the point of playing a subservient role as cooks, embroiderers, and sex objects for the men. Like many of their generation during the sixties they professed to be on a love trip. But their very lives were a statement of hate.

At the time of the original trial the women were described as robotlike, having the same facial expression, the same manner of speech, expressing the same ideas and feelings. It is true that they shared the same concerns and the same ideas and feelings. But the rest of their "sameness" was an agreed-upon posture. To understand their real sameness, one must look into their background. Before I portray each woman individually I want to say that for three of them their serious behavior problems started after their families broke up.

Patricia Krenwinkel's and Leslie Van Houten's parents had separated; Susan Atkins' mother had died. In the case of Lyn, her serious disagreements with her father amounted to a breakup of their relationship. Sandra and her family seemed to have given up on each other after she went to college.

The time comes, in any person's life, when the young must leave the parental nest; increasingly couples with children break up their marriages. Separation—breaking up of family relationships for a number of reasons—is a fact of life that most people wrestle with and learn to live with even at the time it is occurring. The Manson women didn't.

Susan Atkins

My first contact with Susan Atkins was by letter. I asked her for an interview or at least for information about her family background, explaining to her the kind of book I was about to write. At that time Susan's book, *Child of Satan, Child of God,* was being distributed to bookstores and promoted, or to be accurate, Susan was being promoted. I got a prompt reply from her; in her letter Susan stated that not only would she not see me but she opposed the idea of a book about the Manson women. If I went ahead with my project, she demanded I exclude her. She wrote me that in 1974 she had had a personal encounter with the "Living Son of God, Jesus Christ" and had become a Born Again Christian:

> Since then, many doors have opened up to me, and this year a book about my own life, with all its sordid details and my Christian experience is going to be on the market.
> . . . Enough people have written about me who knew nothing of my heart or mind and gave a lot of erroneous ideas to the public. I am not saying any book you might write would be of the same category, but I am at this time informing you I do not approve of or desire anymore books written about me unless I personally write them myself.

Susan suggested that I read her book if I wanted to know about her and that I abandon my idea of writing the book I had in mind. I have read her book. Carefully. I learned about Susan from various sources but also from having read what she wrote. My interpretation of the material *she* presented, however, may not meet with Susan's approval.

My last contact with Susan was personal. I met her while touring the California Institution for Women in September 1978. I chatted with her for a short time, during a tour of CIW, in her small room where her walls are covered by pictures of friends, relatives, acquaintances. She proudly showed me the picture of her grandmother with whom she corresponds; she told me that her father is very sick and that she talks with him on the telephone. She and Mike, her oldest brother, had then started to communicate after years of silence. About her younger brother she only said that he is very badly off; she didn't even know where he was at the time.

Susan was calm and seemed eager to talk with me. But I had not requested permission to interview her so I did not consider the possibility of prolonging our conversation. At the prison Susan has an office where she does clerical work and her own writing. I have samples of the latter because after I first contacted her I was put on her mailing list by Prison Outreach, a religious group that works on behalf of inmates, and receive her newsletter. In them Susan reports her achievements, the results of her ministrations, and appeals to the readers for prayers.

Susan became a Born Again Christian in a grand manner. She is not one of thousands who quietly have converted and lead lives guided by the Bible's Christian principles. Instead she made it clear from the moment she suddenly embraced Christ that she regards herself as a leader, a person endowed with great spiritual qualities who is to preach the Word and minister to others. She does not hesitate to compare herself with great biblical figures:

> Lately the Lord has been leading me in a very quiet walk with Him. I am reminded of how He led Moses into the wilderness for many years before He was able to use Moses; He did the same thing with Paul before Paul was placed once again before the people of God to minister unto them. (Newsletter, April '78).

176

In the September 1978 newsletter, Susan informed her readers that she no longer will be able to write her newsletters and she has this to say:

> . . . for I believe up until now these letters they have not been Susan's letters to you, but Words of encouragement and strength from God through the Holy Spirit through this vessel. . . . I feel maybe in some small way, the way Paul the Apostle must of felt when he got on board the ship in the book of Acts, bound for Jerusalem.

There can be no doubt of Susan's aggrandized view of herself. She is still the same Susan who once said, "To be big, that's the only thing that counts." As one reads between her lines and her biblical quotations one gets the clear impression that Susan does not worship God, but herself. She believes that today she is up front where she always wanted to be, where the action is, leading, and that is the reason, I would judge, why she feels at peace. Obviously she has decided that in her circumstances she can feel better and live better by relating to people who have a modicum of power and who admire and support her. One must keep in mind that after all many of her fellow residents including Leslie and Pat still regard her as a snitch. She has been able to form her own network which gives her a feeling of belonging and of importance. Just to belong would not be enough for Susan.

At the institution Susan resides in the psychiatric unit which is located within the maximum security area. This is not because she is under psychiatric care but because she has not as yet been released into the campus with the general population. According to Susan the administrators still regard her as a risk. According to others there is concern that someone may attack her. As of November 1977 Susan had lost her privilege of walking on the campus grounds because of her determination to minister which prompted another of her megalomaniac statements:

> . . . I was reminded of Paul when he was imprisoned for sharing the Gospel of Jesus Christ amongst the Gentiles.

At CIW opinions are divided about Susan's conversion; some believe

177

in it, others think of her as a fake, and still others are unable to make up their minds about this woman.

In her book Susan talks candidly and with gusto about her former depraved life. What else could she do, since she can't deny what is on the record? Yet one frequently gets the impression that her writing is addressed to the Parole Board. For example, she, like her friend Tex Watson, "discloses" that the two were sniffing methadrine at the time of the Tate murders (she also says she took speed before and during the Hinman murder). Pity nobody else knew about this or can substantiate it since the two, according to Susan, had a secret cache of the drug!

Some of the comments and the statements that Susan makes in her book would be hilarious if it weren't for the brutal realities she is writing about. For instance, after telling of her gross promiscuity, her abuse of drugs, her disavowal of any decent conventions before she met Manson, Susan states that Manson "worked on ridding us of our inhibitions." What inhibitions, one wonders, did she have left before she met him? After describing the cruel murder of Gary Hinman and their zeal (hers, Beausoleil's, and Mary Brunner's) to clean up any prints, she writes.

> Then, fighting desperately to control ourselves, we went into a restaurant and ordered coffee and pie.

Susan Atkins was born in May 1948 in a small California town. She was the middle child and only girl in this lower middle-class family. Although her parents were alcoholics the family had stability up to the time of her mother's death from cancer when Susan was fifteen. According to the report of one psychiatrist who examined Susan before her trial, on at least one occasion the police attempted to take the children away from the parents. All the same Susan attended church, participated in the Girl Scout program, and was a good student in grammar school.

Susan reports that she felt a strong resentment against her parents as she was growing up because they favored her brothers; father was close to the oldest, Mike, while mother gave her attention to the baby, Steve, and was indifferent to Susan. Susan perceived that there were two groupings in her family and that she was out of both. In part to compensate for this she became an accomplished thief and soon discovered that stealing gave her thrills and also a feeling of being important, big. By the time she was in third grade she had become "the best shoplifter" in her neighborhood, sought out and even admired by some of the kids who knew that through her they could get candy, toys, and eventually clothing and accessories.

By the time she was in high school all that Susan wanted out of life was to have fun; by then she had become thirsty for excitement, continuous excitement. Her grades deteriorated in spite of her attempts to manipulate her teachers.

The family moved a few times, probably because of the father's inability to hold a job. An early move, to San Jose, was particularly traumatic to Susan because shortly thereafter her younger brother was born and her mother's attention focused on the baby. When she was twelve the family moved to another section of town, a move that Susan found painful because she had to be separated from her friends and her familiar grounds. In her new neighborhood she regularly attended the Cambrian Park Baptist Church and frequently stood up asking for forgiveness of her sins, another of her ways to be in the limelight since she had no intention of modifying her behavior. Susan reports that it was at that time that she had a religious experience, a vision of a large burning cross. But nobody believed her story.

Susan was fourteen when her father told her that her mother had leukemia. After nine months and several hospitalizations her mother died. Susan found herself with an ineffectual father devastated by his wife's death and a younger brother to care for since shortly thereafter her older brother Mike joined the Navy. Susan was overwhelmed by responsibilities which she resented. The coffers of nurturance for the family were now depleted and she was expected to replenish them for the others. The family had to move again. At Los Banos Susan's behavior became reckless; she frequented bars her father was not likely to visit. For a while she lived with an aunt and uncle who were very kind but Susan was unmanageable and had to move back with her father. She worked part-time besides going to school and dreamed of the day when she would be eighteen and free

179

of any restraint, free from home responsibilities and from school pressures.

When her time came she moved to San Francisco and got a job but soon realized that she was getting nowhere. One night, influenced by a movie she had seen, *The Slender Thread,* she faked a suicide attempt by swallowing some codeine, immediately calling the emergency room of a hospital. She enjoyed the drama that followed but refused psychiatric help.

Eventually she got a better job, as a waitress. Her older brother through a detective had found her, but she refused his help. It was around this time that Susan was first arrested. She fell in love with a handsome "fascinating" young man immediately after meeting him. He and a friend were on the run and preparing a heist. Susan traveled with them, had a few days of fun and excitement, and learned how to use firearms. The trio was caught and as a result Susan spent three months in the Rock Butte County Jail in Oregon.

Back in San Francisco Susan became more and more attracted by the drug scene and particularly interested in hallucinogenics. She was sleeping "with one guy after another," always searching with enthusiasm for the next high. At a certain point she worked as a go-go girl on the strip and participated in Anton LaVey's satanic show. Susan had become interested in show business but she describes her reluctance to be a part of the LaVey troupe and her fear of LaVey's "piercing" eyes. One wonders about her reservations because in her book she actually brags about her success, which suggests to me that she enjoyed her work:

> I had shaken several people with the reality of my performance. The audience went wild over the perform-ance.

LaVey remembers Susan as an irresponsible worker, who lied constantly mostly to cover up her drug use.

Life for Susan was now at a whirlwind pace; in spite of the insecurity of her circumstances and her bouts with venereal disease, she felt comfortable in the Haight-Ashbury. She liked the scene, she felt that she was in her element. Everything related to the straight

180

life was for her "a drag." Nevertheless she started to realize that her yearnings for excitement were no longer satisfied, that she was too weird even for the Haight-Ashbury residents. It was at this point in her life that she met Manson and his women followers and decided to join them, feeling, I think, that within the group she could be herself and be protected.

Susan sensed that Manson would not let a family fall apart (like her father did?), that he would know how to keep it together. "He could make one for all and all for one work. He not only preached love, he had power." The group gave complete approval to her depravity and afforded her opportunities for more thrills. Burglarizing homes provided her with emotional peaks, "the fear and thrills were exhilarating," and reinforced her "taker" attitude:

Everything in the world is ours—the homes, the cars, the credit cards. People only *think* these things are theirs.

This was, of course, the attitude of all the members of the gang.

Cautious to serve her own present interest, in her book Susan frequently mentions her fear of Charlie. But her actions and most of her own statements, as well as those from others, tell a different story. Susan was regarded and saw herself as quite independent. She could come and go as she wished and a few times moved out in search of new experiences that were, however, in line with the group's mores. She was competitive towards Manson and felt that she, too, could lead the group. Referring to herself she often uses the words "soft" and "softly" but about the existence of this aspect of herself we have only her word. The name she used in the Family was Sadie Glutz and in her book she reproduces the complete lyrics of the Beatles' song "Sexy Sadie," giving the impression that she felt it was written in homage to her. The lyrics describe Sadie as thinking of herself as "big," "the greatest," one who fools everyone.

Susan's personality is a patchwork rather than an integrated whole. It is as though some areas of her early development have remained rigidly fixated and were and are still acted out. Primitive yearnings and experiences appear in her next to the tough resilience

181

that makes Susan a survivor and a fighter on behalf of being herself, of achieving what she perceives is right for her, to be "big," to get a great deal of attention.

The very young child goes through a period when he harbors fantasies of being all-powerful. Young children crave attention in the most obvious ways. Many of the human's early yearnings are repressed or greatly toned down or sublimated. There are, of course, many civilized ways to get a great deal of attention. Susan has not repressed, toned down, or sublimated her primitive tendencies. And where does her thirst for thrills come from? How did she "learn" it?

It is likely that Susan's family atmosphere was at times chaotic. She may have witnessed her parents' drinking and perceived it as a thrilling experience, much more exciting than it actually was. She may have also witnessed sexual intercourse. In both situations she probably had a strong wish to be a participant rather than an observer, eager not to miss anything.

Susan was never psychotic. Predictions that she would be the one among the mansonites who would break down proved unfounded. She is highly narcissistic but she knows who she is. People, the world at large, exist to serve her, to be manipulated by her for gain or to be grabbed, incorporated. Her relationships with men, particularly, are colored by her wish to incorporate what they have. Because of her pattern of trying to acquire what she perceives as power from men, her promiscuous behavior for the sake of searching for that elusive big "something" she was and is after, her exhibitionistic behavior which amounts to a demand, "Look at me!" (what does she really want people to see?), because of all of this, thinking of Susan my mind kept turning to Freud.

In 1908 Sigmund Freud published a paper which shocked many, including most of his medical colleagues. In recent years some of the conclusions he put forth then have again become controversial. In this article, *On the Sexual Theories of Children,* Freud wrote:

> It is my conviction that no child—none, at least, who is mentally normal and still less one who is intellectually gifted—can avoid being occupied with the problems of sex in the years *before* puberty.

182

In his paper Freud elaborated on the dynamics and consequences of children's sexuality. According to him all young children assume that everybody, boys and girls, are born with a penis and that the clitoris—the small penis—is the source of excitement that gives little girls' sexual activity a masculine character. He speculated that repression during the years of puberty is needed in order for this masculine sexuality to be discarded and "the woman to emerge." He thought that for this reason little girls become envious of boys, penis-envious, and feel unfairly treated.

We are unable to this day to confirm or dispose of the idea that children's discovery of their anatomical differences is of great importance to them. There are so many variables in the way a child is brought up that such may be the case for some and not for others. I have little doubt that Freud and other clinicians had and do treat women who are envious of men; I myself have been consulted by some of these women. It is likely that some women as children tied up anatomy with other lacks in their experience. Certainly Freud must have seen women who felt powerless because of their gender. And we can't dismiss that even today in some families and for a variety of reasons women are devalued. Some of these women grow up with a distorted view of the sexual act. For some of them being promiscuous means to be reassured that they can get a penis; others with that life-style are expressing their serious doubts about their femininity. And some women even today grow up in situations similar to that of the women Freud heard from long ago in his office in Vienna.

I don't want to imply that Susan's only conflict was due to her wish to possess a penis; she obviously had others, more primitive in origin. But in her family she was the only girl. She was strongly resentful of the closeness that existed between each parent and one of her brothers. The problem may have started or become more intense when her younger brother was born. In his paper Freud referred to the traumatic effect of sibling rivalry:

The loss of his parents' care which he actually experiences or justly fears, and the presentiment that from now on he must for evermore share all his possessions with the

183

newcomer, have the effect of awakening his emotions and sharpening his capacity for thought.

Susan, indeed, developed her own thinking on how to cope, which was based on her distorted perceptions, that of a child, uncorrected by mature reality since her parents were neither stable nor nurturant towards her. Most likely her parents' drinking was their way to deal with anxiety, depression, maybe boredom and emptiness. This was a low-self-esteem family and Susan was at the bottom of it. Within her family she felt insecure and "out," a point of two triangles the existence of which the others didn't even recognize. Susan obviously did not give up. She attempted to feel important by becoming a thief and it worked. I wonder, what did she fantasize she was appropriating that belonged to others? The thrill, the excitement she felt when she shoplifted and later on when she became a burglar has a sexual quality and is colored by doing that which is forbidden, the taking away of other's possessions but with a secret agenda, "I am actually taking what is mine." Maybe Susan felt that by robbery she could change her situation and have everything she wanted; maybe she wants to be a woman but also wants to be a man. She knows who she is but she identifies with men. Whether the man was/is Tom or Cliff or John or Manson or Christ, she suddenly becomes bonded to him and feels that then she has what they have. And she wants to show it. Her murderous spree was for her an ultimate thrilling experience, a big high, as she made clear when, unable to contain her exhibitionistic pleasures, she told all to two cellmates at Sybil Brand. Susan gave vent to her need to brag probably because she felt invulnerable, intoxicated with self-admiration and feelings of power after having made the big time by becoming a murderess.

I don't think it is likely that Susan, in spite of her hopes, will be released in the near future. I doubt that she can live in the world outside unless in a situation of close supervision. Susan has completely avoided real change by suddenly shifting from being, to use her words, a child of Satan to being a child of God. I am afraid she hasn't changed at all.

Susan Atkins' assertion that she was a child of Satan, possessed up to the time of her conversion in 1974, made me wonder whether had

184

she not met Manson she would have joined a satanic group. Since I know nothing about these groups or about diabolical possession, I consulted Reverend John Joseph Nicola, a Jesuit priest who has been studying these matters since 1953. Father Nicola was the consultant for the film *The Exorcist.* (He was, in fact, offered the role, but declined.) According to him cases of diabolical possession are extremely rare. His description of people who are allegedly possessed does not fit Susan Atkins. The possessed are nice people, rather naive, who are subject to bizarre and at times violent fits. Father Nicola knows of two types of satanic groups, the innocuous and the dangerous. The participants in the first are people who think that Christian religions greatly inhibit a person's capacity to enjoy life if his pleasures are in any way out of the ordinary. Satan for them is the antithesis of God who is regarded as depriving. They worship Satan to give free expression to their quirks, particularly the sexual ones. One of these groups is The Very Alternative Church of Satan, located in San Francisco. It was created by Anton Szandor LaVey who is most of all a talented showman. LaVey told me that many years ago he realized that some people are attracted by the bizarre and want to express their own unusual tendencies, which harm no one, without guilt. Since he himself is attracted by the unusual and has a hedonistic philosophy, he decided to provide for their needs. Thus his satanic shows were created, performed in his strange-looking house in San Francisco (known as the Black House). Susan Atkins, as I mentioned earlier, was at one time employed by him.

The harmful satanic groups are quite different. Their members take their beliefs and their marked depraved tendencies seriously. According to Father Nicola they hold "witch covenants," practice the so-called Black Arts, and believe in malignant occult forces by which they abide. Their conception of the universe is pantheist but also violent. Their members engage in orgies that include chaotic group sexual experiences, violence, and at times the spilling of blood, all of which they regard as the way to release power and to acquire it. Sex, violence, and blood—the symbol of life—are allegedly harnessed during these orgies.

One need not subscribe to a religious point of view to accept that these people exist. They seem to need a satanic religion and ritual to

185

carry out their sickening tendencies. In his book *The Family,* Ed Sanders wrote about these dangerous groups but only in reference to Manson's alleged acquaintance with them. In my view Manson is, among the mansonites, the least likely candidate to become part of a satanic group. But as I was listening to Father Nicola, I asked myself, are the members of these groups similar to Susan Atkins, Patricia Krenwinkel, Leslie Van Houten, and Tex Watson as they were in the summer of 1969?

Lynette Fromme and Sandra Good

My first contact with these two women who still keep the Family fire burning was not personal. They, however, became real to me in the summer of 1977 when I spent a couple of days in Sacramento where they had lived for more than three years before their anger exploded into action. I was to visit Sacramento again in March of 1978. Both times I stayed at the old Senator Hotel from where on a lovely morning, September 5, 1975, President Ford walked towards the Capitol across the street and on his way met Lynette Fromme, robed in her red cape, a gun in her hand, ready to shoot him dead.

The Senator is a dowager, its glitter long gone. Maybe time has not passed it by because of its location just across the enchanting park that leads to the Capitol. I sat in the dark rundown lobby to plan my daily work. I ate at the all-plastic cafeteria, the tasteless food enhanced by the warmth of the waitresses, the anonymous decor forgiven by the presence of a bunch of red roses or a giant pink camellia.

Sacramento has a dream quality. It is hard for me to accept that this city is the bureaucratic seat of the wealthy state of California; the shining government buildings do not detract from its atmosphere. I marveled at the trees and the flowers. Up there in the north,

Sacramento, with its embarrassment of greenery and blossoms, is redolent of the tropics. Roses, gardenias, pansies everywhere in the summer. Camellias and orange blossoms splashing the city with color and fragrance even before spring arrives. Some of the city's unreal feeling is suggested when one walks around the new malls and sparkling streets of downtown and sees the skid-row characters that populate them. The old Victorian homes, now divided into apartments, speak of another era. In one of them, on a street lined by orange trees, Lyn and Sandy led their forlorn lives, chugging along their anger, oblivious of the beauty that surrounded them while they claimed their devotion to protecting it.

I met Lyn and Sandy at the Federal Institution for Women in Alderson, West Virginia, in December 1977, shortly after they had been transferred from prisons in California. They were now together again after being separated for almost two years. This transfer was temporary until the Federal Institution at Pleasanton, California, completed its change from a youth center to an adult facility for women.

Lyn called me at home two or three times before my visit and I was surprised at her silver-bell voice, and at her refined and articulate speech. I think she wanted reassurance that I was going to visit them; she also wanted to ask me in advance if I would pay for copies of pictures taken of her and Sandra. I had no idea then whether the long drive from Baltimore to Alderson would be worth my time since I was familiar with these women's proselytizing and one-track minds. I remember thinking as I got in my car, my God, what am I going to find?

The institution is located next to the humble town of Alderson and less than half an hour from the Greenbriar, one of America's finest traditional resort hotels. It looks and "feels" more like an old state hospital than a prison. I talked first with then warden Carlson Markley who informed me that the women would not see me individually. He also told me about the institution which at the time housed about 625 inmates of which 265 were serving from ten years to life. In his comfortable office we talked about matters pertaining to women's criminality. The bookshelves that lined one of its walls

188

contained volumes on penology, sociology, psychiatry and, to my delighted surprise, a couple of books from *Alfred Hitchcock Presents.* In talking with the staff I learned that Sandy and Lyn presented no problem; they stayed together all the time and were polite and cooperative. They lived in the maximum security hall that also housed Sara Moore, the woman who, wanting the attention that Lyn got, was caught while attempting to point a gun at President Ford, shortly after Lyn's attempt.

I was taken to a small office for our interview, the room furnished with odds and ends, a butterfly print on a wall, a desk, a few chairs, shelves with worn-out books, maybe all discards from other rooms, other homes, that ended up in this office, the same as the inmates who also once belonged somewhere else. I was surprised at how lovely Sandra and Lyn looked, one dressed in blue, the other red, honoring the names given them by Manson. Thus, by the way they dress they make a statement. They were healthy looking, poised most of the time, and very distrustful of me. It was obvious that they had prepared carefully for this interview. As we went on talking I realized that they wanted to impress me and they also were bent on controlling the interview. They wanted as well to ascertain whether they could use me for their purpose, to be a courier between them and Manson with whom for many years they have not been allowed to communicate in any way. Both were well informed about my work because Warden Mackley had talked with them about it.

The two refused to discuss their families; when one was tempted to answer some of my questions the other interrupted the exchange. Nevertheless they freely expressed their contempt and anger towards parental figures. Sandra for example:

"Television is the parent now. Parents put on a facade, show off their children, but then, behind closed doors, slap them in the face.

"Do you know real upper-class families? Ah, the little woman behind, who demands a fur coat, jewels, a better home! Man should be the leader."

And Lyn:

"The worst problem is the lying, the way parents lie to their children, their lack of honesty."

189

Lyn corroborated that her father kicked her out of her home. "It was fate. The same day I found Manson." When I asked her if she ever had tried to relate better to her parents, her response was, "I wanted my mother to come my way, to be the child and to let me be the parent. She didn't understand me, she didn't want to accept my way, so I left her. I have been on my own since I was fifteen. I worked my way through high school."

I have learned that in reality Lyn's mother has tried through the years to help her daughter, always meeting with a blank wall since Lyn accepts only those who totally agree with her.

Both women explained their lack of interest in discussing their families by saying that their family is the Family; according to them life was meaningless until they met Manson. Sandra, however, took the initiative in telling me about her former glamorous life, her traveling in Europe, visiting museums, going to concerts. As I said, she wanted at once to impress me and to convey that she had given up a great deal for her convictions. They were not reluctant to talk about their violent yearnings nor did they make apologies for the Family's murderous deeds. As they talked I found myself upset and overwhelmed by the waves of rage coming from them as they calmly expressed their feelings. Lyn insisted that she is reacting only because her life is endangered by those who poison our air and our waters. According to them the only thing that will work to stop this is killing the culprits since everything else that they have tried has failed to produce results. Sandra insisted that people who pollute the environment should be "butchered." Lyn stated, "I must attack back to defend myself."

These women have strong feelings against "mixing the races" which they see as a way of polluting the human environment. About the time of my visit I received three virulent hate periodicals—without a sender's address—with extensive editorials against Jews and blacks. At one point during our conversation Sandra went into a tirade against Maureen Stapleton for her support of publisher Larry Flynt who according to her—and I very much agree—pollutes our life with his publications. I remembered her hateful words a few months later when Flynt was shot. These two women, however, had no words of disapproval for any members of the Family. According to

190

Lyn, Susan Atkins was a troublemaker. "She brought undesirables to the group but she provided us with a great deal of energy." Both admire Leslie Van Houten whom they consider a strong person. They love Pat Krenwinkel and insisted that "she is still with us."

Sandra and Lyn both completely lack any sense of humor. Above all, they take themselves seriously always and convey the impression that they think of themselves as important personages. Their megalomania, in effect, colored all their statements. For example, I learned through Sandra that they were reluctant to present to me their ideas for fear that I—like others, according to them—could rob them and write about them as mine. By the end of our interview Sandra got carried away and expressed her desire that my book be written as a vehicle for their and Manson's ideas. About the latter, they hope that eventually Manson will send them the Word that will guide them, so they can save the world.

Just before the end of our three-hour talk Lyn taped a message to Manson (Sandra refused on the grounds that she doesn't talk to machines). I made it clear that I might not be permitted to send the tape to Manson and that I wouldn't even try if it contained any remarks of violence against others. As it turned out Manson was not allowed to receive it. I promised Lyn not to make public her message which she dictated as tears filled her eyes. By then Sandra had become rather depressed and we parted company on that note of sadness. As we exchanged goodbyes, they expressed satisfaction with the conditions at Alderson and tried to convey to me that their imprisonment was of their choice and so were their quarters.

We exchanged a few letters thereafter until they realized that there was no chance that they could use me. Then one day I received a change of address card, to the Federal Institution at Pleasanton, from Lyn. No words, just the remittent and inside a large picture of a spider. So much for Lyn's ambivalent feelings towards me, her intense anger and yet her wish that I learn where she was. Her mixed feelings towards me or towards talking with me were again manifest when I visited the Federal Correctional Institution at Pleasanton, California. Warden Charles Turnbo talked with Lyn and Sandra beforehand about my request to see them. They responded that not only would they not meet with me but that they would hide to avoid any chance meeting while I was touring the facility. After the tour was finished and I returned with the warden to his office, there in the lobby was Lyn waiting for me. Surprisingly she was without her companion. Soon after, however, Sandra started to walk near us and finally she joined us.

Still dressed in their colors they proceeded to give me another dose of their philosophy and made no comment about their new surroundings.

At Pleasanton the inmates have a great deal of freedom on the inside because of the architecture of this modern facility that relies on peripheral security. The institution really looks like a modern college campus; it has private rooms for the inmates and large common areas which afford them privacy; staff and inmates share the same cafeteria. Because of the small number of residents, 250—who stay from 30 days to life—there is a great deal of interaction between staff and inmates and Warden Turnbo seemed to know everybody by name. But even in this atmosphere Lyn and Sandra remain isolated. Not only have they no following but most of the others regard them as crazy.

Lyn and Sandy, however, are not psychotic; that is, they have good reality contact, in concrete terms. Many people who harbor distorted beliefs they live by, such as members of the Ku Klux Klan and other hate groups, are not psychotic and yet like these women they cling to their bizarre beliefs.

Sandra and Lyn rigidly focus their limited existence on their "cause," that pollutants are slowly killing our environment and that they could save it if they were allowed to communicate with Manson, spread his Word, and exterminate the offenders. It is the latter component of their beliefs that marks them as disturbed persons since no serious person would disagree with their concerns for the environment. Their fixed ideas on how to accomplish their purpose are totally irrational: Not only should the polluters be killed but random murders are justified to call attention to their plea so people will become terrified and forced to correct the situation. They regard themselves as the high priestesses of terror who can thus save the world. Their megalomania is fed by their ruminations which also serve to justify their rage against a world that does not recognize

192

their worth. For them there is no middle ground, no possibility of dialogue; people are either their friends—if they totally agree with them and obey them—or enemies, the rest of us. They have no support network, they belong nowhere. I sent them periodicals and magazines devoted to environmental problems but, as I expected, they showed no interest. Unlike other persons who hold bizarre beliefs, these two are isolated even from people who in some measure share their paranoia.

Because of this combination of their fantasies, their strong bond and their alienation from others, except Manson, who, however, they have not seen for nine years, the two could be thought of as suffering from a rare psychiatric syndrome, *folie à deux*.

During the Manson trial, psychiatrist Joel Simon Hochman expressed the opinion that the Manson group represented a case of *folie en famille*. Leslie Van Houten's plea when she was retried also was based on the alleged existence of such group pathology; her attorney argued that Leslie acted under the command of Manson who was mentally ill.

Two French psychiatrists, Fabret and Lasegue, are credited with describing a process they called *folie à deux* in which mental illness is communicated by one person to another or to more than one, all of whom have a close relationship and are emotionally isolated from others. According to the French psychiatrists and others before them and some present-day clinicians, in these cases a passive, naive person(s) is influenced by a strong and sick paranoid partner who imposes his delusions on him; when separated, the passive one recovers while the other does not. This is the traditional view of this process but the picture is not that clear. In some cases reports present the partners as equally and simultaneously suffering from the same delusions; furthermore the so-called passive does not always recover after separation. Besides, after some exploration clinicians have found it difficult in some cases to determine who initiates the pathology.

Most of the cases reported occur between two women, sisters or inmates in institutions. These women isolate themselves and usually build up an elaborate persecutory system from which they feel they have to defend themselves. Their alienation exacerbates their delu-

193

sions because their mutual dependency is thus increased; the more bizarre they become the more others avoid them which in turn stimulates the vicious circle they live in.

I have trouble accepting the classic view of this type of relationship because I can't accept the simplified view it presents, the idea that one person can totally control another. After all, there are reasons why people form close relationships and stay together. Any systematic observer of intimate relationships would find it impossible to verify who influences whom consistently. We are all familiar with how active a passive person can really be in maintaining his passivity and stimulating others to be controlling and vice versa.

Lyn and Sandy's relationship is cemented by their shared distortions and by their strong interdependency which protects them from having to interact with others who would not cater to their narcissism. They make each other feel irrationally important. As long as they maintain each other's illusions of grandeur they can tell each other that they are right and the world is wrong. I don't know that one is stronger than the other, that is, that one is the "transmissor" and the other the recipient. At Pleasanton some people think that Lyn dominates Sandra but I was unable to make such distinction. Among other reasons, they might "fit" comfortably because one, Lyn, is the oldest sibling in her family and the other, Sandra, is the youngest.

I asked Warden Turnbo why these women are kept together. The reason is that the facility at Pleasanton is the only federal prison for women west of the Mississippi. If they were one day to be separated, both would need considerable support to cope with their separation, unless they could retain the hope that they would be reunited. One must remember that they were separated for about four months when Sandra was jailed in 1971 and again for almost two years after their conviction. Yet neither changed nor was their intense bond diminished.

What are the life experiences that have brought these women to where they are now?

Lynette Alice Fromme was born on October 22, 1948, in a hospital in Santa Monica, California. She is the oldest of three, with a brother two years younger and a sister eight years her junior, and comes from a middle-class family. Her mother, originally from Minnesota, was twenty-five when Lyn was born; her father, a New Yorker, was twenty-eight. Her father is an engineer and it is said that he was disappointed at his wife's lack of college education and that at least early in the marriage felt that she was beneath him. Lyn was a healthy and bright child. She was artistic and trained in ballet; for several summers during her childhood she traveled with a small ensemble that gave performances in colleges in other states. Mother made her costumes for these trips. At one point she refused to do so because she felt that the child should no longer participate in these trips. Lyn appealed to her father who, as usual, gave in and ignored his wife's wishes. The relationship between father and daughter was intense, while mother, in this triangle, was odd man out. The parents' marriage was not a happy one and husband and wife were emotionally distant. Mrs. Fromme's attempts to correct the situation both in her marriage and with her daughter were feeble and ineffectual. Lyn's father was described to me as a strong-willed, rigid man who, however, deeply loved Lyn and catered to her wishes. Even when the next child, a boy, was born his intense involvement with Lyn was not affected.

When Lyn reached puberty she had also become strong-willed and refused to accept any restrictions. Her father tried to discipline her, to no avail. Now the two were at loggerheads, constantly involved in a power struggle. Father and daughter became competitors, at times for the mother who found herself in the middle but sided with her husband. Lyn's anger and frustration mounted as she realized that she no longer was Father's special child, that he would not give a blanket approval to her opinions, her ways, her behavior. She probably interpreted her father's attempts to impose rules as rejection. She felt dethroned, a queen without a queendom, without support within her family circle since she failed to convince her mother to form a coalition with her against the father. Thus during Lyn's adolescent years the home atmosphere become so tense that finally she had to move out. Her mother contributed to her support and the youngster still kept contact with her family.

On two occasions, after arguments with her father, Lyn made

195

suicide attempts. Once she cut her wrists; later on she took barbiturates. After her last attempt her parents considered psychiatric hospitalization for her. At least Mother and Lyn had counseling but after a few sessions both felt that the meetings were not useful. It was after another serious argument with her father that Lyn and Manson found each other.

Lyn, who is quick to dismiss her life before she met Manson, in fact replicated with him the relationship she had with her father as a child. She was admired and respected by Manson, unconditionally. As earlier with her father, she felt that according to Manson she could do no wrong. Furthermore, he, like her, was dead set against any conventions, any restrictions. His adulation protected Lyn from facing any criticism and any mature responsibilities. He helped her to encase her infantile yearnings in the gilded and fashionable frame of antiestablishment "convictions" and catered to her increasing megalomania, and for these reasons she regarded him as a sage, great human being and stayed with him. Repeating the model of her parents' marriage she chose to be subservient to the male and thus also avoided responsibility for herself.

From then on and to this day Lyn's life is a reenactment of the family drama that she has internalized. She is the powerful aggressor and the powerless partner, father, mother, and daughter. She has become, through a glass darkly, a combination of all three, still trapped in the conflicts of her past.

And how do these conflicts fit the Lyn who attempted to assassinate a president?

Psychiatrist Edwin A. Weinstein in a paper he published in 1969 reported his findings about people who have killed or attempted to kill a president. He notes that in the United States such acts have been committed by disturbed individuals who acted alone, rather than by political groups. The only exception was the assault on President Truman by Puerto Rican nationalists in 1950. Dr. Weinstein regards this act as highly symbolic and remarks on a common characteristic of these individuals: their isolation that they try to deny by their delusions or by professing that they belong to groups that have a cause with which they identify. Richard Lawrence, who attempted to kill President Andrew Jackson, claimed that he was the

196

king of England and that the President had dethroned him. His mythical England became his pseudo-community. John Wilkes Booth regarded himself as a proud Southerner but he never fought in the Confederate Army or gave support to the Southern cause. At the time of Lincoln's assassination a throat ailment had ended his theatrical career. Charles Guiteau who assassinated President Garfield in 1881 was at that time destitute, a fanatic of eccentric cults who claimed he had to kill the President to save the Republican party. Leon Czolgosz who shot President McKinley professed to be an anarchist but he was never a member of an anarchist group. Lee Harvey Oswald, in spite of his claims on behalf of Marxism, was never a member of a Marxist or any other political group.

Lyn fits the model. The Family, during its short existence, was the only group she ever belonged to. She has never been a member of any political group or pro-environment organization. As I discussed in another chapter, her letters giving instructions on how to threaten people to correspondents she had never met were not just the result of her naiveté but of her need to pretend that she has a following, a group she belongs to.

Her attempt to assassinate President Ford symbolically represents her wish to do away with the "bad" and powerful father who she felt rendered her powerless, while keeping alive the illusion of the "good" father, Manson, who eventually, in her fantasies, will be powerful again and put her back in the position of child-queen that she had as a child.

Sandra Collins Good was born on February 20, 1944, the youngest of three daughters by her parents' first marriage. When she was born her mother was twenty-nine and her father thirty-eight and their marriage was already in serious trouble. The Goods had married in 1934 and separated in 1947; Sandra's sisters are three and eight years older than she. After her parents' divorce the children remained in the custody of their mother but her father had liberal visiting privileges. Both parents eventually remarried and had children by their second marriages.

Mr. Good was a mild-mannered man who was quite involved with Sandra. All her relatives, in effect, were concerned about her during

197

her childhood, in one way or another because of Sandra's serious health problems. By the time she was one year old she had been pronounced dead twice and she had two tracheotomies before she was nine months old. She continued to have bronchial and pulmonary problems for years. Between the ages of six and eight (I don't know for sure when) she had a lung lobectomy (removal of a portion of the lung) which at that time was a very serious operation. Thus Sandra was born of an unhappy liaison and from early life became a source of anxiety for her parents. Her father grew to be extremely indulgent with her and while this lasted Sandra was close to him. Mother, who had to care for her and watch her child during many sleepless nights, probably developed mixed feelings about her. She wouldn't be human if she didn't. Her sisters resented this baby who ever since her arrival had demanded so much attention.

As a child Sandra was reticent and withdrawn. She was also difficult, sullen, always dissatisfied. She remembers her mother as rejecting, as being interested only in her social life and not at all in her role as mother and housewife. By now Sandra has generalized her anger to include women who have interests outside the home, particularly liberated women who, according to her, "compete with the men for power" or else put great demands on men.

Contrary to the information she gave me and others, Sandra does not come from a family of socialites nor were her parents moneyed people, although both her father and stepfather were comfortably well off. She wants, however, to present an image of herself as a former society girl who enjoyed all the privileges of her class, who partook of the best things in life, who traveled through Europe. In actuality she went to Europe for a few months at the time when her stepfather was located in Brussels. While in Europe she promptly became bored and dissatisfied.

It is likely that Sandra was traumatized by the birth of her two half-siblings, a brother and a sister (her father also had children by his second marriage). Sandra's mother, naturally, became increasingly involved with these children of her new family. At a certain point she started to discipline Sandra firmly not only because the child was difficult but also to counteract Mr. Good's indulgence. Sandra herself and others told me that she was considered a spoiled brat. So

198

accustomed was she to being so regarded that she asked me if that was the way I saw her. She did act out her anger on her half-siblings; she constantly frightened them and threatened them not to tell on her so effectively that for years they didn't. It was then that Sandra first applied terrorist techniques. It was then that she learned she could attain revenge and at the same time a feeling of power by making others powerless through fear. Manson taught his followers the value of instilling fear in others but I am sure he learned a thing or two from Sandra Good who today is in prison on a federal charge for trying to repeat what she succeeded in doing as a child.

After graduating from high school at seventeen, Sandra attended the University of Oregon at Eugene. According to her she was a student there for three years and then transferred to San Francisco State where she had two years of college education, all with no trouble. The truth is that from the very beginning she had difficulty in adjusting. She could not make friends because of her personality and her expectations and because, as is mostly the case with those who are not happy at home, she had trouble separating from her family. College was her first experience away from home which she regarded as the cutoff point. She continued to be in contact with her father but her relationship with her mother was strained and she saw little of her. In San Francisco she lived with a sister and transferred her major from English and Spanish to Marine Ecology. There her academic difficulties became more apparent; she was a slow reader and needed tutoring, which her father paid for.

For a while, in 1965, she lived in Minnesota with the family of a boyfriend. Her life had become aimless and her father was always ready to help her financially. In 1968, while she was living in San Francisco, an artist of her acquaintance who was also a pilot flew her to Los Angeles for some scuba diving and introduced her to Manson and to the Family. Sandra felt that at last she had found her place under the sun. She became instantly "bonded" to Manson and to the group because of her realization that they accepted her as she was, and more, they admired her as they did each other. She visited them frequently, gave them money that she obtained from her father, and finally moved in with them permanently. I wonder if her awe of Manson was stimulated by her belief that he could resuscitate the dead. She has told of how, one one occasion, she saw him "breathe" life into a dead bird.

Sandra denied to me that her health problems were of importance in her life. When I asked her when she finally became healthy, not surprisingly she responded, "When I met Manson." According to her, all her problems were resolved once she found her family. Yet a former member of the group told me that she used to carry a "suicide box" containing razor blades and pills. This same person told me that Sandra was not promiscuous and that her use of drugs was minimal.

In September 1970 Sandra gave birth to a son whom she placed with friends after her arrest. The child's father was Joel Dean Pugh with whom she lived for a while. Pugh, a disturbed man, was found dead in a London hotel room on December 1, 1969, at the age of twenty-nine, on the day members of the Family were arrested on suspicion of murder. There has been speculation that his death was the result of foul play (Bruce Davis, a member of the Family, allegedly was in London at that time), but the London police ruled his death a suicide. Sandra's father stood by her when she had her baby and she lived in his home for a while; but she did not get along with her stepmother, and she refused help from her mother. Eventually her father's patience was exhausted by her life-style and her demands for money, and their relationship also broke down, greatly angering Sandra, who applied her terrorist methods to him so the man became extremely afraid of her, according to many newspaper reports published at the time of the original Manson trial. Mr. Good died in 1973. Of her two sisters one is married, on her third marriage; the other is single. One of them has become a Born Again Christian and is trying to reach Sandra. Interestingly, it was this sister who resented her the most as they were growing up.

These two women continue to be bonded and keep the illusion that they still have Manson as the all-approving, all-nurturant parent. Both have identified with the aggressor, a parent who in their view betrayed them by attempting to puncture the feeling of omnipotence and power they had as children. They cannot let go of their anger.

Patricia Krenwinkel

In a letter postmarked September 25, 1967, Patricia Krenwinkel wrote to her father:

> For the very first time in my life, I've found contentment and inner peace.

Patricia, however, did not convey in her letter any rebelliousness or any feelings of anger towards her father; on the contrary, her letter ends, "I love you very much, take good care of yourself."

Pat, known as Katie during her Manson days, has kept a low profile since her incarceration. Even during the notorious trial she was less talked about, less flamboyant than her companions in crime. Now a resident of the California Institution for Women, she answers letters only of those close to her and has refused to give interviews. Like the others, she hopes to be paroled but has not made any spectacular comeback either religious à la Atkins or Watson, or legal à la Van Houten.

I met Patricia in September 1978, shortly after she had been denied parole (the mansonites were eligible for parole in 1978). At that time she was in the maximum security unit, the usual location for inmates after a parole hearing. Before that time and for some years she lived on campus among the general population because she did not present any disciplinary problems. She is a homely young woman and when I talked with her briefly her facial expression was serious and preoccupied, which under the circumstances was appropriate. Pat has no reason to be happy and it shows.

Pat refused to testify on behalf of her close friend Leslie Van Houten. I have heard different reasons to account for her refusal, that she did not want to come out and face the public, that she did not want to jeopardize her own chances for parole, that she is still emotionally involved with Manson and consequently resented Leslie's defense plea which incriminated him. Manson, Lyn, and Sandra in their conversations with me declared that Pat is still one of them, a part of the Family.

In September of 1967 Pat abruptly cut her ties with her family, abandoned her job, and joined the Manson group. At that time she was living with her half-sister Charlene. She left immediately after she had called her father to inform him that she was leaving for a vacation with two girl friends. Her car was found in a service station across the street from the apartment she shared with her sister. She didn't even get her paycheck from the Insurance Company of North America where she worked as a secretary. Mr. Krenwinkel would later speculate that she was hypnotized by Manson. She just disappeared and her father was not to hear from her until October 1969, when suspicions arose about the Manson group. At that time he arranged for his daughter to go to Mobile, Alabama, where his ex-wife lived with a sister. It was in Mobile that Pat was arrested while she and a boyfriend were driving a sports car near her aunt's home; she tried to conceal her face to avoid identification and when stopped by the police gave her name as Montgomery. Mr. Krenwinkel retained an attorney in Mobile to represent her in resisting extradition, but after a while Pat decided to go back to California. While still in Mobile her attorney arranged for a psychiatric examination. The psychiatrist who interviewed her reported that Pat was acutely psychotic, suffering from hallucinations, extremely anxious, confused, and altogether inappropriate in her affect and her behavior. This report was discredited during the trial on the grounds that

202

Patricia faked her mental state at that time. Referring to that interview, Pat was to say later on, "Well, certainly, that is one way to fool the law, to fool them all."

During her Family days Pat was among those in the inner circle. She had standing within the group where most regarded her as a mother figure. She and Leslie Van Houten became close friends which is not surprising in view of their remarkably similar backgrounds and what appears even to be similar family atmospheres. Both have been described as perfect children who grew up within perfectly well-adjusted families. Both are the younger of two children, both were very close to their fathers. Both families were broken up by their parents' divorces when they were adolescents, and both seemed totally unable to cope with the demands of adolescence.

This woman, who at age twenty-three went on a savage rampage, who participated in both the Tate and the LaBianca murders, who carved the word "war" with a fork on Mr. LaBianca's abdomen, was a beloved figure within her adoptive group, a person who could do no wrong. When questioned about the contradiction between her claims of love and her murderous behavior, she "explained":

> People put the word "wrong" upon things because they are playing games, very strange games, beginning with each other . . . If you fail to stay away from where God is or where love is to begin with, as far as destruction, that is all that has ever been done, the only thing people listen to is destruction.

Patricia Krenwinkel was born on December 3, 1947, in Los Angeles, the only child of Dorothy and Joe Krenwinkel who had married in 1944. Her mother was a young widow when she met Mr. Krenwinkel and had a daughter, Charlene, by her previous marriage; Charlene was seven when Patricia was born. Charlene was later to become addicted to heroin and died at the age of twenty-nine by drowning. The Krenwinkels divorced in 1964 when Pat was seventeen and for a while she moved back and forth between mother, who had moved back to Alabama, and father. Eventually she moved to Manhattan Beach, near Los Angeles, with her sister.

Her father is an insurance agent and Patricia's family was comfortably off financially; Mother stayed home but participated in civic and religious work. She was active in the World Church Women's Council and was on several committees of organizations such as the March of Dimes and the Campfire Girls. Pat did relatively well in school, graduated from University High School in West Los Angeles, and attended one semester in a Jesuit institution, Springfield College in Mobile, Alabama. The description given by Pat's parents of her as she was growing up is so revealing that I think it is better to let them speak. According to her father,

I would say she was an exceedingly [sic] normal child, surprising in comparison to some children to the degree that when Pat was tired, as most children will fight going to bed, Pat would go get her pajamas on and say "I am going to bed" and that was the end of that deal. I'd say, other than that, she was a very [sic] normal child. She liked to play, she could entertain herself . . . she liked to go to the beach, liked to swim . . . She belonged to the normal childhood organizations . . . She liked animals . . . we had dogs, hamsters, goldfish, parakeets, canary birds . . . She was very gentle with animals . . . She presented no disciplinary problems at any time to her parents . . . Got along very well with classmates and playmates at school . . . got along with other people very well . . . very much so . . . The teachers said they enjoyed having Pat in their classes . . . She got good grades . . . took school seriously . . . she worked hard to obtain the grades that she obtained . . . Patricia was baptized in the Presbyterian Church . . . was enthusiastic about her religious training . . . instructed or assisted or helped in the church school program all churches have in summer for children . . . Pat was very enthusiastic about reading the Bible . . . When she was a young child she would spend hours in a swing, thoroughly enjoying it. We could put her in a swing even as a young child . . . We bought one of the kind that you slip through and bounce on a spring. And you put her on that swing, and that was it . . . Never saw her hostile or

204

angry . . . never saw her fight . . . never saw her cruel
to animals . . . never saw her cruel to other children . . . never saw her physically violent . . . not a
person with a quick temper . . . not a person with a
violent temper . . . She was a model child . . . never in
trouble with the police . . . never received a traffic ticket . . .

Mother confirmed the picture of Patricia that father presented and
portrayed an idealized image of the family where the parents' major
involvement was with the children. It seems, indeed, that once the
children were out of the nest there was nothing left between the two,
so they separated. There is no way to know at the present time how
these people's frustration and disappointment in their marriage
manifested itself.

Mother had this to say.

Like most children, we started both of the girls on Easter
egg hunts and all the neighborhood children would
come . . . on Halloween we made all sorts of costumes and
we always went out with them . . . All of her activities as
a child, her father and I both went along with
them . . . He sponsored some things and I sponsored and
worked with the Bluebirds and Campfire Girls. We taught
Bible school which Pat helped me with . . . Her sister
was married at a very young age. They [Charlene and Pat]
really didn't have a great deal of time together. But what
time they did have together, they were friendly. As a small
child, she looked up to her sister, her older sister, you know,
like most children do, and they want to do what their sister
does . . . Pat was a very gentle person and just her love of
animals and causes . . . she liked belonging to the Little
Wildlife Society and getting the magazine . . . She would
rather hurt herself than harm any living thing.

Pat dated boys but at that time Pat was still quite
studious and she read a great deal . . . She liked music . . .

If she awakened first in the morning, when she was still
in her crib, she was doing little drawings or playing with

205

little things . . . she would play with them and not create a disturbance. She would not cry for anyone to get her up or to do anything for her . . . I never had any trouble with her . . . Patricia was never hostile or angry . . . never disrespectul . . . had minor disagreements, but that was all . . .

I have thought much and with compassion about these parents' reports. They present such an unreal picture of Patricia and of their family by omission of any problems that I had to wonder whether their statements were carefully planned to convey that everything was all right with their daughter, that she was "brainwashed" by Manson since there was no other explanation for her deviant behavior. But it is their version of what is "normal" that I find disturbing since it provides such an example of the psychological castration of a human being. How did Pat learn never to cry for attention, never to disagree, never to protest? It seems to me that during her childhood Pat invested all of her emotional energy in warding off any authentic feelings of her own and adopted a facade of "supergood," "supernice," "supernormal." But Patricia was aware of that other aspect of herself, of her anger, her wish to protest, all of the feelings that she had to keep under surveillance because they were "bad." All the time while she was living with an image fabricated to please others, she had the internal realization that there was another Pat who was a "no-good." Her parents, probably with good intentions, tried to mold their daughter into, to use her father's words, an "exceedingly normal" child. They obviously had severe problems at least in parenting, judging by the tragic destiny met by their two daughters. They took all the "right" steps in raising Patricia. But it is likely that she felt that the religious education, the civic responsibilities she engaged in, were instilled by her parents and remained as foreign bodies within herself and were acted out only because she felt she had to comply.

The Krenwinkels separated in 1964. Characteristically they described even this event rosily:

. . . It did not involve the children. It was a very quiet

something—very personal, and it was nothing that one would—that the children would have any part in it or be hurt by it.

The way they presented the breakup of the family after twenty years of marriage is as unreal as the rest of their statements about their family life.

Pat's perception of herself as she was growing up is markedly different from that of her parents. She told a psychiatrist that she always felt unwanted and unloved and perceived herself as ugly. At times she felt that her feelings of self-rejection were due to her physical appearance which she tried to correct. At fourteen, being overweight, she went on a forty-day crash diet and reduced her size from fourteen to eight. She was always conscious of a feeling of physical and internal ugliness. She was plain looking, hairy, and totally unable to relate to people spontaneously, in any way that would gratify her. Not even after her arrest did Patricia express any feelings of anger towards her parents. She continued to be considerate towards them because she accepted that the way they acted as parents was based on their ideas, not on bad intentions towards her. A psychiatrist who interviewed her had this to say:

> . . . she went into details to explain to me that she did things in their [the parents'] way, that they were right in what they thought . . . She described it that they had programmed her, they projected certain things into her head and had programmed her into their way of thinking.

While she was under her parents' control, Patricia continued her totally inhibited behavior. According to her she found her own "truth" only when she met Manson. It was then that for the first time she was able to unveil that other side of her self without shame, without self-condemnation. The aspects of her that she had chastised so much now became free and took over. Pat now felt she had found her real self, forceful, uninhibited, alive! She promptly and totally discarded the goody-goody image that she felt had kept her imprisoned. She was unable to integrate the two extremes of her personality; one had to be obliterated to let the other free.

When Pat met Manson he asked her permission to stay at her place for a few days with two of his girls. He began their encounter by telling her what she was hungry to hear:

> Everything is all right—he would tell me. I felt ugly; I always had too much hair on my body; all things that people tell you, that make you feel these things, everything about you is awful, they seem to tell you . . . My sister was shooting stiff [sic], and I was dragged into that by her. She was going from man to man, all kinds, Chinese, etc., etc. I would always make love in the dark before that, but with him [Manson] it was all in the open instead. I was crying; I didn't want to look at myself. I cried that first night with my head in his lap. He was like my dad. It got pure, it was so good . . . I told him, I've got to go wherever you go. He said if I wanted, okay. I got into the VW and we left, and I said to myself, "It has to be right because I feel so good."

From the rigidly sheltered world of her parents Patricia had drifted into the devastating world of her sister in which she simply could not cope. Manson and his girls provided the shelter she desperately needed, a real refuge where she felt truly accepted for the first time in her life. In joining the group Pat, like the others, was attracted by the quasi-religious mysticism that was a part of it and that resembled in its "goodness" her previous life. It is interesting that the description of her by the mansonites parallels the description of her by her parents. Her strong attachment to Manson resembles the strong bond that exists between her and her father who to this day is devoted to her. She has said of Manson that "he was always underneath something pushing him down." It is likely that she identified with him. Her two nights of murderous carnage served to express all the rage she had accumulated under a facade of bland, perfect behavior.

Leslie Van Houten

According to Greek mythology, Persephone, the daughter of Ceres, goddess of agriculture, was carried off to the underworld by Pluto while she was gathering flowers. Zeus persuaded Pluto to let her go. But she had eaten in the underworld the seed of a pomegranate and thus could not stay away from him forever. So she was allowed to spend half of her time with her mother to allow for the growth of vegetation and the other half as the wife of Pluto for whom she sent specters, ruled the ghosts, and carried into effect the curses of men.

After I sent my editor this manuscript I read that Joan Didion herself felt like Persephone after visiting Linda Kasabian at the Sybil Brand Institute:

> Each of the half-dozen doors that locked behind us as we entered Sybil Brand was a little death, and I would emerge after the interview like Persephone from the underworld, euphoric, elated.*

Myths being what they are there is no way to know how Persephone felt each time she came up from the underworld to visit her mother.

*The White Album, Simon and Schuster, 1979, p. 43.

209

At any rate I found it unsettling that another author would use the same mythical figure in relation to the same case. Perhaps it was the "we-ness," Joan Didion, Linda Kasabian, "us," that took me by surprise. The two, it seems, evolved a friendship and visited each other. Once they took their children on the Staten Island Ferry to see the Statue of Liberty. The gifted reporter-writer-celebrity, the quasi-murderer-celebrity. What did they talk about? I wonder. Did they finally get to discuss Cielo Drive and LaBianca? Did they exchange tips on how to bring up their daughters? Where would Didion's daughter "locate" Kasabian in relation to the many celebrities she had the privilege to meet through her mother?

The fantasy of the young innocent girl who is seduced into wrongdoing and carried off by a sinister male is a universal one. According to Leslie Van Houten, her attorney, her relatives, her friends and acquaintances, Manson attracted Leslie and took her to his underworld of depravity and murder. They all agree, however, that she is not returning to that world, that she has been rescued forever and can go about safely gathering the flowers of the good life. The fact that twelve people, the jurors, have again found her guilty of first-degree murder does not alter the beliefs of her many supporters. During her retrials Mr. Keith focused so intently on Manson's guilt that at one point prosecutor Steve Kay had to remind the jurors:

> One thing I want you to remember in this trial: Miss Van Houten is on trial, not Charles Manson. Charles Manson has already been convicted. It is Miss Van Houten's guilt or innocence of first degree murder that we are deciding in this case, not Mr. Manson's. That's already been decided.

I attended part of Leslie Van Houten's second retrial and met her; I chatted briefly with her two or three times. Leslie has a face full of shadows that breaks into an ingratiating smile the moment anyone talks to her. She tries to establish instant rapport and I got the impression that she assumes that any person who approaches her is on her side. I talked with her (under the stern gaze of Mr. Keith, her attorney) only about a project I had in mind dealing with women's

210

criminality. She spontaneously offered me her help "when this is all over." Naturally we did not discuss her or her case. To do so would have been impossible in our brief conversations during recess. Most of all I would not approach the subject because in my view doing so then would have been unethical. At that time I met other former members of the Manson group who were testifying and made a point not to discuss Leslie Van Houten with them. I assumed that Leslie knew about the book I was writing since I had written to her attorney and explained the subject in some detail.

At the time of the interchanges I have just described I did not know that I would be asked by the prosecutors to testify as an expert witness. As it turned out I didn't, because my testimony was to be a partial one to complement that of two other forensic psychiatrists (which I am not) who were unable to testify. I acted as consultant to the prosecutors in the area of my expertise, the family dynamics of the so-called Family.

I had previously read the transcripts of the Van Houten first retrial that resulted in the jury being deadlocked, with seven finding the defendant guilty of first-degree murder and five finding her guilty of voluntary manslaughter. On reading these transcripts I was at first pleasantly surprised by the decorum of this trial as compared with the original Manson trial. But as I went along with my reading I became increasingly uncomfortable with the court procedure. The whole atmosphere did not seem to be that in which a defendant was being tried for the deliberate and premeditated killing of human beings but of a sedated, even gracious gathering that the defendant was patiently attending, she and her attorney cozily exchanging comments and everybody behaving so nicely to each other. At first I attributed my reactions to not being accustomed to the informal light ways of Californians. Nevertheless I remained uncomfortable and my uneasiness only increased when I attended the trial. Actually I was present before, during a few sessions of the jury selection phase. I remember the people smiling at each other, the purpose for their congregation, a murder trial, all but buried under the mantle of politeness. The only one who looked overwrought or tense was Mr. Keith. Otherwise, at the early phase there was an air of jubilation in the sparkling corridors adjacent to Room 126, most of the prospective

211

jurors exchanging greetings. Everybody, defendant, attorneys, sheriff, clerk, were nice in the extreme, in some cases, I am sure, because to be so is the right legal strategy. The expression of anger, unless as a deliberate ploy, is in poor taste and at cross-purposes in a court of law. I was reminded of some wakes I have attended. I guess because in both situations people act as though they experience a feeling of relief as they think "Thank God, it is not happening to me!" "I am not on trial!"

I guess that once the jurors are selected and get to work, these pleasant feelings, including those of anticipatory excitement, tend to disappear, especially if the trial is long and demands much of them. That's the good thing about wakes. They last only a few hours.

The jury selection is an important phase in the view of the attorneys, who ask probing questions before deciding to accept or to reject a juror. In this case at times it seemed to me that psychiatric testimony in court was also about to go on trial.

"Do you think that psychiatrists rather than the jury should decide her state of mind at the time of the murders?"

"Do you have any adverse feelings about psychiatrists?"

"Do you believe that psychiatrists have no business in a courtroom?"

"Do you believe that free will can be subjugated?"

"Can you consider the intent as separated from motive?"

"Do you understand that you must decide on intent?"

My hopes for the human capacity for impartiality kept going up as I heard that most of the jurors felt that they could be fair and devoid of any biases that could cloud their minds and their hearts. With a few exceptions those called to serve were eager to become jurors in this case.

The jury selection phase reminded me of a wake; the trial reminded me of a baseball game where some action and excitement punctuated periods of seeming inactivity. Presiding in this court was a much admired judge, Gordon Ringer. The defense attorney, Maxwell Keith, was an experienced and respected trial lawyer; his slow style and soft voice contrasted with the active, lively manner of prosecutor Steve

Kay and with the Byzantine presence and baritone of scholarly Dino John Fulgoni, head prosecutor.

All accounts I had read and heard depicted the Leslie of today as a very different person from the almost twenty-year-old who, on the night of August 10, 1969, with her close friends Patricia Krenwinkel and Tex Watson eagerly participated in the LaBianca murders, after hearing of the Tate debauchery. Dr. Joel Fort, who testified for the prosecution in the Van Houten first retrial and who had examined her in 1971, "did not feel that her mental state now is the same as that at the time of the crime." Dr. Seymour Pollak, director of USC Institute of Psychiatry and Law, in a letter written to give his opinion about Leslie's suitability for probation—in 1978 after she had been convicted—had this to say:

> She has matured emotionally . . . Should the court wish to consider probation for her following her most recent conviction, in my opinion, from a psychiatric point of view, she would be a suitable candidate and can be returned to live in the open community with minimal risk . . . In my clinical opinion her personality change is genuine and she will probably remain prosocial and non-violent and non-dangerous in the foreseeable future.

Dr. Pollak had examined Leslie in 1977 at the request of her attorney who, however, decided not to call him to testify as to her mental capacity at the time she committed the murders. His opinion in the letter above does not refer to that issue.

Probably I myself doubt that if released, Leslie Van Houten would commit violent or antisocial acts. I don't, however, share the other views expressed verbally and in writing about the present-day Leslie. These reports are unnecessarily glowing and I become suspicious of their veracity. From beginning to end her attorney insisted in presenting her image as that of a "young gracious lady," nothing less, nothing more. Leslie, according to him and to others, is a perfect being. All the years of highly deviant behavior since age fourteen, all the years in prison, have not touched her; instead they have produced a model of emotional stability, including high moral values, warmth, and such an enchanting personality that people instantly relate

213

positively towards her. I really don't understand this; it seems to me to be going overboard to present such an unreal picture of Leslie. I hardly think that it was necessary to do so. As I read and heard these accounts I remembered that Leslie was described as having been a perfect child. It seemed to me that once again she was giving the same messages, or even if she didn't quite, to everyone, others were motivated by her or manipulated by her into giving such opinions.

In reading the transcripts I was particularly puzzled about the testimony of psychiatrist Leigh Roberts who testified for the defense. Dr. Roberts is a highly qualified forensic psychiatrist. He interviewed Leslie for many hours and wrote a 390-page report based on the tapes of his conversations with her—only 13 of them dealing with the murders. His description of Leslie's emotional health today perplexed me. It was too good to be true. Such a person as this psychiatrist was describing simply does not exist. I don't know what prompted this experienced professional to portray such an unrealistic picture, for certainly the jurors would have understood that a woman with Leslie's history would have problems. Worse, Dr. Roberts did not disclose that Leslie Van Houten is presently a lesbian who has a relationship with a woman she met in prison. This is surprising because he and Mr. Keith knew that the prosecutors would read the report. When one of them, Dino Fulgoni, as was to be expected, brought up this matter, Mr. Keith objected. Approaching the bench, out of the jurors' hearing, Mr. Keith said that he based his objection on "the prejudicial effect of her sex life in prison, which is obviously homosexual in nature, it is degrading, it is demeaning, it really doesn't bear on the issues of this case." Mr. Fulgoni expressed the view that Leslie's homosexuality was not situational, that it is not the result of being institutionalized, since according to Dr. Roberts' report "she was freaked out by men" and turned around and left a room where other inmates put up photographs of nude males. Mr. Fulgoni added, "To me this is not the picture that Mr. Keith portrayed in his opening statement, let alone the picture that this witness (Dr. Roberts) has painted during the time he has been on the stand."

Judge Gordon Ringer agreed that the witness's credibility was at issue and overruled the defense attorney's objection.

From the start Mr. Keith made a point of presenting his client as a confused girl who had the misfortune to meet Manson and fall under his spell; according to Keith, at a certain point during her imprisonment she rid herself of Manson's influence and reverted to her real self. He did not deny that Leslie had some responsibility for her criminal actions but, according to him, these actions were the result of a marked change in her personality due to, besides Manson's influence, the chronic use of drugs. To that effect he showed pictures of Leslie as a child and as an adolescent taken at parties, picnics, and other social occasions, as though people would take pictures of their children to portray unhappy times or deviant behavior! I don't pretend to know what an experienced trial lawyer knows about how to impress jurors. All the same, the sugary, flawless picture he insisted on portraying of his client struck a false note. I understand that jurors are human and that some of them, even in California, could be prejudiced against homosexuals. I think, however, that a psychiatrist and a lawyer could have presented Leslie as homosexual or as having conflicts with her sexual identity in a realistic, humane way. The relentless effort to present Leslie Van Houten as an idealized human specimen before and after her Manson liaison couldn't but discredit the reporters and the subject.

Since Leslie's defense—diminished capacity because of being under the influence of manson who was mentally ill—was based on psychiatric reports, she was extensively examined by at least five psychiatrists. Those who testified for the defense stated that her mental capacity at the time of the murders was diminished owing to different causes or a mixture of causes, mainly Manson's influence and the use of drugs. Dr. Joel Markman, one of these psychiatrists, made clear that he did not regard the Manson group as experiencing a case of *folie en famille*:

I would say that the whole constellation of thinking that involved the Helter Skelter phenomenon was not in my opinion what I would label psychotic or group psychotic in quality.

According to him the mansonites were an example of gang mentality. Dr. Markman had interviewed Leslie in 1970 for a limited purpose, to determine if she had the capacity to change her counsel. At that time:

> I found her to be rather superficial, somewhat frivolous
> and flighty, non-psychotic . . . by that I mean she did not
> suffer from what I saw, a clinical psychosis at the
> time . . . no significant evidence of major symptomatolo-
> gy.

Reports about one aspect of Leslie's personality are contradictory. I am referring to her dependency traits and to her capacity to act independently. During her adolescent years, including her Manson period, some people saw her as utterly dependent, easily influenced by others and having to cling emotionally to another person. Others describe her as independent, strong, aloof, her own person. Some saw her as the controlling one in a relationship, others as the submissive, compliant partner.

Tex Watson: "Leslie was like a little girl . . . There was no question that she would do anything he [Manson] told her to, just as she obeyed Susan. I was the only one she'd talk back to." Bobby Mackey, her boyfriend before her Manson days: "A beautiful human being, outgoing, great self-image, socially active. She was aggressive. She knew what she wanted, and she got it." Paul Watkins, former mansonite: "She appeared to be less of a problem case, more able to cope . . . She seemed more level-headed to me than the average person there."

As I will discuss later on, there are reasons for these inconsistencies. There can be no doubt, however, that Leslie stayed with the Manson group by choice and that she was not afraid of Manson or anybody else. She had in fact little to do with Manson. Furthermore there is no question that she willingly participated in the LaBianca murders. In her defense she has said that she stabbed Mrs. LaBianca when the victim was already dead. Asked how did she know that Mrs. LaBianca was dead, did she for instance take her pulse? she responded that she didn't. On various occasions Leslie stated that she just held Mrs. LaBianca down so Pat could stab her!

Leslie not only knew the details of the Tate murders but, even before, she knew of the Gary Hinman murder, as she testified in 1977 under questioning by Mr. Fulgoni:

Sadie [Susan Atkins] come in grinny, said "We killed him" and then I asked her "What it was like," you know. And she just said, "It was real weird and he made funny noises."

Leslie went on to say that she was curious and was weighing whether she "could kill for her brother" and decided that she could. According to Dr. Markman, her question was not "Should I or shouldn't I?" but "Can I?" She was not wrestling with her conscience; what she asked herself had to do "with reality testing, with 'What will happen if I do this, is it worth the risk?' "

Like any other defendant, Leslie was determined to avoid incrimination. It was Leslie who carefully cleaned the LaBianca home to erase any evidence, any prints. But according to her she did so to have "something to do" and at the request of Pat. Later on back at the Spahn Ranch she burned clothes and other articles that could incriminate her and hid when a man who had given her a ride after the murders came looking for her. According to her she had to be careful because of her fear of Tex Watson who, she said, threatened to kill her if she talked about the murders. All the same some of her statements for that purpose—to appear innocent by incriminating others—are surprising. To a psychiatrist who interviewed her in 1977 before her trial, Dr. Keith S. Ditman, she stated that "she did not kill anybody, the actual slayings were done by Tex and Katie [Patricia Krenwinkel]." This doctor's impression was that "she assisted, but was in a partial dissociative state, apparently. She speaks of being 'fogged' and also of fearing that she would have been killed if she had not participated." Katie and Tex were Leslie's closest friends, and she most certainly did not fear them. Leslie also lied in telling another psychiatrist, Dr. Markman, that she didn't know of the Tate murders before she went on her own murdering trip.

Why did she tell such gross lies? Was it a calculated risk, to make a favorable impression on these psychiatrists? Did she hope that she could "put something over" on them (which in fact she did!) and that they could in turn influence others on her behalf?

Her lying gives credence to reports that Leslie has a tendency as well as the ability to con people. She also can play con games; this became evident when in 1970 she was interviewed by Sergeant

217

Michael McGann, before she was a suspect. She was questioned only because she was a member of the Family and the police wanted to get information from her, hoping that she would know something about the murders. But she turned the tables with experienced Sergeant McGann as she cleverly toyed with him and played the cat in a game of cat and mouse. According to Dr. Markman who heard the tape of that interview, she was "leading him to the brink of the cliff, and then back, so to speak."

According to Leslie it was a fellow inmate (a murder convict) at the California Institution for Women with whom she became friends who made her "aware" of con games. Carefully wording what she had to say she testified that this woman "taught me not to believe everything that everybody tells me . . . I was very gullible and naive when I first met Jean." But to a psychiatrist who interviewed her she had this to say (in 1977):

> I don't lie, and I don't con others unless when it's to make something more comfortable for myself. If I would need to have a phone call made, and an officer said no right away, well, then, I'd begin, you know, I don't do it—I am not the kind that nags and whines and stuff. Usually the way I would do it is just crack a couple of jokes and get them laughing and then convince them that's really not that hard—for me . . . hard for them, to pick up the phone and dial it. And then pretty soon they are picking it up and dialing it. Or I involve them in my problems too, so they are just as interested in the end result as I am.

Why was Leslie Van Houten granted a new trial? During her original trial in 1970 Van Houten was first represented by attorney Marvin Part but before the trial began she replaced him with another lawyer, Ira Reiner, in February 1970. In July she dismissed Reiner and appointed Ronald Hughes who disappeared around November 30, 1970 (he was later found dead). On December 3, 1970, attorney Maxwell Keith was appointed by the court to represent her. After he became her lawyer Mr. Keith asked for a mistrial, saying that he was unable to assess the credibility of the witnesses against his client because he had not been present when they testified and consequently he had not been able to observe them firsthand and tailor his questions during cross-examination. He also stated that Van Houten's defense was handicapped by the disappearance of her attorney Hughes because there was no continuity of representation: When he came on board, he argued, the trial was in its final phase; after five months of testimony and eighty-eight witnesses he could not effectively defend his client and evolve an appropriate closing argument. He considered the unexplained disappearance of attorney Hughes an event of "legal necessity" (an event beyond the control of the court which requires the discharge of the jury and permits a new trial without the benefit of a double jeopardy plea) which should have resulted in the granting of a mistrial for his client. The court denied a motion for a mistrial in 1970. On appeal, however, Keith's arguments prevailed and Van Houten was granted a new trial in 1977.

Justice Wood of the Court of Appeals expressed a dissenting opinion that obviously did not prevail. His arguments, however, deserve to be presented here. He noted that when attorney Keith was appointed as counsel for Van Houten he was asked if he would accept the appointment and he agreed to represent her. He didn't say he could not represent her as things stood. He did not argue then that he would be ineffective because he had not personally observed and questioned the witnesses. During the trial he discredited, in front of the jury, the credibility of the principal witnesses for the prosecution, particularly Linda Kasabian. Furthermore the court had instructed the jury that Kasabian was an accomplice and her testimony "ought to be viewed with distrust." Keith also did his best to discredit another witness for the prosecution, Dianne Lake, stating that the seventeen-year-old was mentally disabled and had been confined to a mental hospital for a few months prior to testifying, and that consequently her statements were not reasonable and should have been distrusted. (Lake testified that Van Houten told her that she stabbed someone who was dead, that the more she did it, the more fun it was, that after the killings she wiped off fingerprints, that she, Krenwinkel, and Watson showered and ate at the LaBianca home before leaving it.) Attorney Keith, however, stated that his colleague Hughes had done an excellent job in cross-examining Dianne Lake.

In Justice Wood's opinion, the fact that Mr. Keith was unable to

219

observe the witnesses and assess their credibility was not a valid argument for granting a mistrial. Four other attorneys for the defense did observe the witnesses' demeanor. Furthermore the jurors, who were to decide the facts, observed the witnesses while they were examined and cross-examined, and they were instructed by the judge and told by attorneys that they were to observe their demeanor while they were testifying, to determine their credibility.

Justice Wood also argued that a great number of valid decisions have been rendered in cases where the evidence was based on former testimony of unavailable witnesses.

Leslie Van Houten was retried twice. Her first retrial in 1977 ended when the jurors declared themselves deadlocked, unable to reach the required unanimous decision. Five of them found her guilty of voluntary manslaughter and seven of murder in the first degree. She was tried again in 1978 and charged with murder in the first degree. Each of her two retrials lasted several months. The first alone cost the taxpayers more than $290,000.

Does a "common" criminal get a chance of such magnitude? The implication of allowing these retrials is that this individual, Leslie Van Houten, should have another chance to get away with murder because, after all, she used to be a real nice kid and she is now a young lady loved by her family and befriended by the "right" kind of people. Obviously there are some fine points of law that allowed these new trials to take place, but I wonder how many of the poor, the lobbyless, the obscure who have committed lesser crimes ever get that second chance.

Leslie Van Houten is now back at the California Institution for Women where she first arrived in April 1971 and where she, together with Patricia Krenwinkel and Susan Atkins, was on Death Row until 1972 when the death penalty was declared unconstitutional in the State of California. From the very beginning Leslie was cooperative and well adjusted at the institution. She looked happy, was friendly and "making the best of it." During the first two years she defended her "philosophy" and stated that she did not kill anybody but was sentenced because she refused to accuse Manson whom she spoke of as being a decent man. She insisted that the people living at the Spahn Ranch did not call themselves the Family, that that name was used by the news media and by the prosecution. To a prison psychiatrist, Dr. Michael Coburn, she admitted "that although she had no desire at the present to kill anyone that she would have no difficulty again doing so if she wanted to."

No one who examined Leslie thought that she was in need of psychotherapy or medication. In short, during her years in prison and from the start Leslie appeared to all to be normal, contented, friendly. Her antiestablishment statements decreased after a while. Leslie did crochet, needlepoint, cleaned her unit, watched television, eventually did secretarial work, took courses, at one time was editor of the prison's newspaper. All with a wide smile on her face, looking forward to being released to the general prison population, the campus, so she could make new friends besides Pat with whom she remained close. She maintained a correspondence with relatives, friends, and acquaintances. Her mother visited her once or twice weekly, her father rarely. She took a writing course and one of her short stories, *Ima Fibbin*, was published in a volume of short stories.

In spite of Leslie's claims to the contrary, she never showed signs of remorse. No breakdown, no severe depressions which necessitated medication or psychotherapy, no sleepless nights, no marked loss of weight—she was always slim—no severe somatic symptoms masking emotional pain. Her only admission of regret was for the effect that her crimes had on her life: "I blew my life in one night of senseless violence."

Leslie Van Houten was born on August 23, 1949, in Altadena, near Los Angeles. She spent her childhood in Monrovia, a small town humbled by its proximity to wealthy, beautiful San Marino and dwarfed by geography. The Sierra Madre (who thought, I wonder, to name it thus!) looms dark and menacing over the town. A neighbor and a close family friend described Leslie's childhood as "idyllic." One can understand why. She was well behaved and had caring parents. She was a Campfire Girl and earlier a Bluebird. She was a member of Job's Daughters (a religious group) and during high school held offices. She was elected Homecoming Princess and Homecoming Queen. She was raised in the Presbyterian faith,

221

attended church regularly with her parents, and had a religious education.

Leslie is the younger of two children; her brother Paul is four years older. When Leslie was seven, her parents adopted two Korean orphans. When she was fourteen her parents separated; her father left home and remarried immediately after the divorce was final. Mr. Van Houten is a recovered alcoholic who for many years was active in AA. He used to take Leslie to work—he is a car auctioneer—and unwittingly provided the first training Leslie had in the art of con as he thought he was teaching his daughter salesmanship skills. Otherwise these parents provided their daughter with every opportunity. How then did this perfect child of a perfect family become one of the notorious members of the Manson Family and a murderess?

All reports picture the Van Houten family as supernice, and as is the case with the portrayal of Leslie herself, that picture too tells us something. Although the Van Houtens divorced in 1963 they had had an unhappy relationship for many years. A few years after their marriage the husband left for the service; after his return the couple started to have problems that were never resolved. Mr. Van Houten had made a significant change: He stopped his drinking and started to attend and to work for AA. This type of change is highly dramatic and affects the balance of a relationship. I have no doubt that Mrs. Van Houten was happy about her husband's recovery. Yet she had married a troubled individual, an alcoholic, who was probably quite dependent on her. Leslie had said that her mother is the type of person "who needs to be wanted." To be wanted and to be needed. The time came when her husband no longer needed from her what he had sought in the past and the gap between the two grew wider with the years. Mrs. Van Houten, by her own account, knew that her husband was unhappy but she tried to keep the status quo, tried by herself to hold the family together. She had high moral standards and what appears to have been an idealized image of what a family should be like that she tried to instill in her own. Reading documents and reports about this family it is plain to see that the expression of anger towards each other was taboo, togetherness was emphasized as a major virtue, and individual expression of differences was reasoned away.

222

Throughout many years of practice, I have been consulted by this type of family in which an "as if" atmosphere of unreality prevails. Its members perceive themselves and each other as devoid of any negative feelings towards each other, spontaneous interchanges are avoided to keep the ideal image at the expense of emotional growth. The parents usually consulted me because of unexplained problems in one member, for example a severe depression in an adult, a child whose symptoms had become too dramatic to be ignored or who had come to the attention of a teacher or a pediatrician. The parents saw their problems or any member's symptoms as a foreign body that had no relation to the family life. They tended to describe their family as "average." When pressed for more information their comment was that they had "the usual problems every family has." These people were not liars; in most cases they were not aware of how stifling and rigid were their relationships. What they were, what they are, is afraid to rock the boat; and therefore, extremely cautious in exploring, testing relationships which they perceive as threatening to the family's fragile equilibrium. A child growing up in these families frequently becomes a repository of unexpressed feelings. From early life he may have to fill the emotional void of the parents' relationship for one of them or for both. He promptly realizes how important he is to his parents and becomes either unmanageable or extremely compliant. In the latter case he learns to express only "niceness" and to keep under control other feelings, other yearnings, particularly his anger.

A great deal of anger had to be repressed by the Van Houtens who for years had a troubled marriage while trying to present a facade of being an ideal family. Leslie was daddy's girl. Mother was the authoritarian. Leslie has said that she knew that her father wasn't happy and through the years she saw him becoming withdrawn and uptight. Of her relationship with her father she has this to say: "I think I always felt a close relationship to my father. And I think my mother was cautious that I didn't abuse it or flaunt it in front of the rest of the kids in our family. But it wasn't something that was like, you know, openly discussed."

The adoption of two orphans when Leslie was seven, while of benefit to these children, also afforded the mother a chance to fulfill her unmet need to be needed. This event probably also served to postpone the breakup of the marriage. Mother and Leslie, the only ones from the family who testified, deny to this day that Leslie had any feelings of rivalry towards the new arrivals. Yet she had been the baby, the white knighted princess for seven years in this child-centered family. Even today Leslie and her mother present a rosy picture of family life past and present.

No matter how much Mrs. Van Houten tried, her husband became increasingly dissatisfied and finally asked for a divorce. He told Leslie first of his decision, a decision that his wife had said she did not expect. *Do not see problems, pretend they do not exist*, and automatically they will not exist. According to Mrs. Van Houten the separation and ultimate divorce were friendly; there were no angry feelings. I speculate that in reality the family breakup was catastrophic for her and for Leslie. A beloved father with whom she was very involved leaves for another woman. At home the situation changes as mother who had been at home, always available and devoted to her children, now has to reshape her life. Everybody had to adjust to a new situation. Mother went back to school and took a heavy load of credit courses in special education, to prepare herself for employment; there were two younger children to care for. The hurt, the emotional storm caused by the need to adjust psychologically and practically, particularly when feelings had to be repressed, were obstacles that Leslie was unable to overcome. At fourteen her make-believe world was torn apart. Mother, who was able to adjust to her new situation, probably expected that her daughter would follow the excellent example she was providing. But Leslie had not been prepared to leave her golden childhood. Even under the best of circumstances she would have had difficulties during her adolescence. Many parents mistakenly expect that in the natural course of life their children can make the transition from an overprotected childhood to adolescence. Children whose relationship with one parent or both is too intense are at risk and so are children of child-focused families who find it extremely difficult to be other than young children no matter what facade they adopt to cover their infantilism.

Like others in her situation Leslie was angry at having her

sheltered, magic world ruptured and at realizing that her parents were involved in their own lives. I doubt that she allowed herself to express her feelings, particularly her anger, to her parents; it is likely that she regarded her mother with whom she lived as forbidding and demanding. She sought indirect ways to get at her parents, ways that also reassured her, gave her a sense of pseudomaturity and a sense of individuality as she started to act out against the conventions she had grown up with. It is likely that in doing so she unveiled aspects of herself that had been inhibited before.

At fourteen Leslie became sexually active and started to experiment with drugs, mainly marijuana which was still rarely used by middle-class kids. She actively sought the company of a new student, Bobby Mackey, once she learned that he was using LSD, and soon after they became lovers. It is noteworthy that Leslie was not a shy, lonely girl; on the contrary, she was popular and didn't lack male company and social opportunities as attested to by the fact that she was elected at various times to hold offices in her school. Her inclination was, however, "to fall in love" with a troubled young man who resorted to drugs. Pregnant by him at fifteen, she told her parents and had an abortion. Around that time her mother saw the need for counseling and she, Leslie, and the two youngest saw a psychologist for a few sessions that they interrupted because they felt that nothing was being accomplished.

Leslie and Bobby, probably seeking restraint from other than parental figures, joined the Self-Realization Fellowship, a semireligious, philosophical organization whose members acquire discipline through Yoga and meditation. Bobby decided to become a monk and Leslie a nun, which called for abstention from sex and drugs. Now Leslie had made a full turn from being wild to being a saint, her own version of her mother's identity. Her aim was to achieve nirvana, the total sense of contentment she probably perceived she had lost with her childhood, and to reach that state within a moralistic, holy framework. It was at this point that she became acquainted with concepts that would be a part of her future life with the mansonites, such as "karma," cleaning one's consciousness of moral limitations to attain perfection, and other mystical and philosophical ideas.

After nine months Leslie became dissatisfied with the extremes

225

she had imposed on herself and left the Fellowship although to do so meant to break up her relationship with Bobby. By then she had finished high school and had moved with her father and stepmother to a duplex where she had her own place. She attended business school to become a legal secretary and was among the top students. About her relationship with her father at that time, Leslie said:

> See, my father doesn't express affection that easily. He felt by me having an apartment and by him buying my business college, and I had a car, and he set up this checking account so I could get food . . . he felt that was what was required of taking care of me. So I just didn't see him that much.

She was by then leading a double life, acting out the two sides of her identity, going to school, preparing herself for work, for adult responsibilities, but at the same time using psychedelics and other drugs and striking up relationships which involved sex with unsavory characters and thrill-seekers. She simply was not attracted to straight people.

Among the letters that Judge Gordon Ringer received during the probation phase of Leslie's trial in 1978 was one written in her support and asking that she be granted parole. The writer wanted to illustrate how different the Leslie of today was from the way she was at eighteen, before, however, she met Manson. To illustrate how much Leslie had changed from the girl she was at eighteen, before she joined the Family, the writer refers to Leslie's actions at that time. The following fragment of that letter was read in court:

> My mistrust of her turned to outrage and hatred the day she told me blithely that she had given my 11 year old sister LSD about a month before, and that since that first time . . . they had taken other LSD trips together. She had also introduced her to other drugs.
>
> In early 1975, when my family committed Melissa to Synanon in Venice, California, in final desperation of her drug addiction, it was Leslie Van Houten that I cursed, not only for my little sister's addiction to hard drugs at the age

226

of 17—but also for the incalculable pain and trauma, and the constant trial the members of my family suffered trying to work with her those six years.

Leslie graduated from business school but never even tried to get a job. She joined a girl she had known for a few days and the two, in her friend's red Porsche, stayed a while with that girl's parents on a ranch in Victorville. Then she went to San Francisco where she met Bobby Beausoleil, then an aspiring musician and actor who was traveling around in his van with three girls. Leslie decided to join that ménage and called her worried mother to inform her that she was "dropping out." She did drop completely into the wild side of her self, drugs and group sex with her companions becoming central to her life as the group, for a month or two, traveled around the California coast. She fell in love with Beausoleil; she was in her element, contented, free to express her tendencies. "I didn't have any ambitions or goals," she has said of this period, "just to find the truth and try to live in tune with the earth was my main objective." She has to place even her lack of ambition and goals within a moralistic, grand design, "to find the truth."

Through Beausoleil who was an on-and-off member of the Family she met Manson and after a while decided to join his group, according to her because she was tired of traveling around. Actually she had found her heaven, a place to settle down, a group of people who fulfilled her needs for protection and belonging, who met her wants, a group of people who, above all, shared her proclivities. In them she found not just a collection of thrill-seekers, not just people acting out their anger at society, not just a gathering of kids giving vent to their narcissistic whims. It was that, too, of course, but it was more than that. It had a much-admired leader. It was a group united in the belief that its members were a superior breed, a group that had a philosophy, and even its own language to express it. Within this Family Leslie could be herself, she could use drugs, albeit now at prescribed times, she could be promiscuous, and most important to her, at the same time she could wear a halo. In her new family Leslie could live out the two aspects of her personality without having to integrate them. Wrong and right were one and the same because

227

every one of the group was assumed to be perfect. No need here for long hours of meditation or for controlling self-indulgence as in the Self-Realization Fellowship. This was instant nirvana. She could do as she pleased and, in a strange turn, feel arrogantly moral at once. Her murderous behavior expressed the many emotional elements that were a part of her. She wanted to kill to experience the ultimate high that LSD was no longer giving her, to feel different and important, to defy the conventions she had grown up with. And she could rationalize that her actions were the result of her high moral values. Leslie never lifted a finger to help any moral cause, but just by living the mansonites' version of the antiestablishment she could identify with those whose struggle was authentic.

In prison for a while she kept the remnants of the philosophy of her mansonite days and yet she reverted quite easily to her "good little girl" identity, was compliant, eager to please. In the wardrobe of her psyche Leslie seems to have only two dresses, although it is possible that she has added another, more wearable, in her present circumstances.

Her mother immediately came to her side and out of love reinforced Leslie's remorselessly contented attitude, her subtle form of arrogance, her feeling that persists today, in spite of lip service to the contrary, that she did no wrong.

Mother set herself to rescue her daughter from the demons she felt possessed her. She could not accept that the child she had raised with so much love and care was capable of committing murder. She immersed herself first in operation Save Leslie (from Manson's influence) and, that accomplished, with Get Leslie Free. Her persistence is credited by Leslie with persuading her to come back to her senses, to become, in Mrs. Van Houten's terms, "the Leslie she would have been" had she not met Manson. As a result Leslie developed a "prodigal daughter" attitude and after she was "saved" she was a source of gratification to her mother.

From the age of fourteen Leslie has been walking in and out of the two extreme opposites of her personality. She has been described as dependent and independent because in fact she acted both ways. She has been extremely pious and extremely sinful. Duplicity may be one of her character traits, developed by her to negotiate the two aspects

228

of herself. It is evident that she can relate warmly towards her mother at least, who by all accounts is a respectable and generous person. But after age fourteen she became close only with deviant people. She loved handsome Beausoleil, a cold-blooded murderer, she was not close to Manson but greatly admired him, she became Patricia Krenwinkel's closest friend. Her last love relationship during her Manson days was with Tex Watson.

Leslie had the advantage of a good upbringing. She was raised in a moral, religious home where she learned the difference between right and wrong. Her parents did not fail in *what* they taught her but in *how*. It was the internal atmosphere of her family, the unspoken messages, the covering up of the family schism that she internalized. Maybe someday Leslie, without the pressure of having to present a front, will be able to integrate the conflicting fragments of her self. People who love and support her think that she already has, and they may be right. During her recent trials she had to be concerned with presenting herself as a homogenized version of the girl next door. Paul Fitzgerald joined the defense team during the probation phase of her trial. He presented Leslie as a victim who had suffered far too much already. He emphasized that she should be freed, that she has a strong support network on the outside, and quoted his colleague Keith, saying, ". . . if released she isn't going to be put out on the street, a thought out of some 1939 movie, when the ex-convict gets a $10 suit and two dollar bills and has to go out and try to make his way."

No indeed, such a humble destiny would not be fitting for Leslie Van Houten.

In spite of good arguments in her favor, however, Leslie Van Houten was not granted parole. Probably prosecutor Steve Kay's argument weighed more heavily than the profuse list of supporters presented by the defense:

What confidence would society have in our system of criminal justice if Leslie Van Houten was released on probation? What deterrent effect would it have on future potential murderers to have Leslie Van Houten released on probation?

229

It would have none. They would say, "Well, Leslie Van Houten participated in one of the worst murders in the history of American crime, and she got probation. We have nothing to worry about."

Leslie Van Houten spent eight years in prison. Well, eight years in prison is just a year over the minimum. Any person for any murder has to spend at least seven . . .

I've heard a lot of tears shed in this courtroom today, verbal tears by Mr. Keith and Mr. Fitzgerald about Miss Van Houten.

What about the LaBiancas? Who is going to rehabilitate them? Who is going to resurrect them?

IV

Concluding Thoughts

It is significant that most of the Manson followers were women. Until recent years women have been "tabooed" out of many experiences, constructive and destructive. The female mansonites were able to express their destructive tendencies when they joined the Family. While thousands of other women were searching for ways to express themselves, to channel their yearnings for mature self-realization, the mansonites found their own "solution" to the limitations of being female: They "dropped out" from society, they used illicit drugs, they became sexually promiscuous, they broke the law, all actions that until their time had been mostly the province of the male. But at the same time they perceived themselves as being child-women, submissive to the males.

These women had serious problems before they joined Manson but they did not regard themselves as troubled and consequently were not motivated to change, to grow, to adjust. On the contrary they viewed society or their parents or both as deficient and as the cause of their dissatisfaction. They searched for and found a group that suited them and once they did their lives became meaningful and defined. They became Manson's children.

Charles Manson nurtured his women and supported their infantilism and their narcissistic stance. He praised them and gave full approval to their deviant tendencies and joined them in their anger at a society that could not possibly satisfy their irrational expectations. Regarded by his women as a guru, his unconditional approval gave them a sense of importance that reinforced their grandiosity. Manson himself, for the first time in his life other than in his fantasies, felt important because his women fed his megalomania as much as he fed theirs. Manson and his women were made for each other. Their relationship was not linear, "cause and effect," but like all relationships it was a process in which all had an equal input to make it what it was.

We all bring our assets and our debits to the families we form as adults. The mansonites had only minuses to contribute to their Family, the fragmented kaleidoscopes of their psyches, the ghosts of past unresolved relationships, their marked immaturity.

Manson's life was tainted from birth by the response of his mother's strict parents because he was illegitimate and by the conflicted relationship he and his mother had. She for years acted out her rebelliousness against her parents and against society, and her son identified with her to the point that by age thirteen he had to be institutionalized because he had become unmanageable. After that he was unable to make it on the outside. He learned how to adjust to prison life but not how to adjust and how to compete in the real world.

During her adolescent years Lynette Fromme became involved in a painful power struggle with her parents; she relentlessly sought to control them and reverse roles. Sandra Good had been unable to accept being other than the center of attention; her anger, her frustration grew to dominate all aspects of her personality. Leslie Van Houten since age fourteen had been actively searching for drug experiences to achieve nirvana, in her case a childhood experience of total comfort. Drugs also provided her with thrilling experiences and she experimented with sexual modalities also in search of thrills and to appease her doubts about her sexual identity. Patricia Krenwinkel during her adolescence tried to hold on to her "perfect child" image until she was thrown into the disturbing world of her sister and became aware of feelings and tendencies in herself that she had kept tightly under control to accommodate her parents' expectations.

234

Susan Atkins as a child had found devious ways to compensate for the feeling that she was an outsider in her family circle. Stealing reassured her by making her feel "big." Her search for thrills was to continue and by the time she joined Manson her life had become a chaotic search for peaks of excitement via drugs and sex.

Although there were differences among the women, there also were striking similarities. They were arrogant to the point of megalomania and had a need to cover their deviant tendencies with a cloak of virtue; their antisocial behavior, according to them, was due to their wish to challenge the wrongful established order and their destructiveness was an expression of love. In effect, they regarded themselves as a superior sort. It is likely that the murderers saw themselves as being the group's overachievers and that Lyn and Sandy in 1969 regarded themselves as the Family's gray eminences.

No doubts clouded these women's narrow minds, no mixed feelings disturbed their souls. Their selves were rigidly divided into "good" and "bad," and in themselves they perceived only goodness while projecting their badness onto those who did not totally agree with them.

As is usual in rigidly closed groupings, the mansonites' aggression was projected to the outside. In this type of group outsiders are suspect and perceived as a potential danger to the group's existence. The intense loyalty among its members is actually frail and cannot stand any critical opinion, no matter how constructive it could be. Loyalty crumbles when one or more members start questioning the group's basic tenets and when this happens each member of the group feels threatened, at times panicky. It is then that their aggression may become self-directed and directed towards comembers. Probably this was the situation in the suicide-murder of the Jim Jones group.

The Family is indelibly identified with the sixties. Thinking about that period moves me to paraphrase Dickens: It was the worst of times, it was the best of times, it was not the age of wisdom, it was the age of foolishness, it was the epoch of belief, it was not the epoch of incredulity.

Some may take issue with my view of that era, thinking that after all great strides were made then in civil rights and the emancipation

of women, for example. But I think that these and other developments would have occurred anyhow for myriad reasons, and that
their occurrence had nothing to do with and indeed were probably
handicapped by the childish anything-goes atmosphere of the sixties.
This climate was the result of a demographic accident, the baby
boom, and of other cultural factors: The generation of the young grew
up in a child-centered society in which the adults were confused
about *how* to be concerned about their children. I am referring to the
children of the middle classes. The lot of the poor didn't change much
during the sixties. Many ghetto mothers during that enlightened era
saw their children deteriorate at an early age; many children
continued to live under the most adverse conditions, all of which is
still the case. The problems of the children of poverty are too
complicated and too ugly to attract an interested and powerful lobby.

Many people worried, others were personally hurt by the young
people's use of freedom during the sixties. Yet others catered to the
adolescent's immaturity and regarded the young as sage, as the ones
who were "making a statement." (About what? I often wondered.)
This admiring attitude from juveniles of all ages increased the unrest
and the arrogance of the young and in many cases served to
perpetuate their irresponsible behavior well past their adolescent
years.

We know that as a group the young cause the largest number of
problems. It has been said that each generation is invaded by a horde
of barbarians, the young. This generalization is valid in regard to the
behavior of a segment of the young population, the destructive who
vandalize and violate, the ones who smash cars and have frequent
accidents because of their recklessness, the ones who totally defy
authority. Some of them have character problems, others are quite
disturbed. This type of behavior cannot be lumped together, as some
people seem to do, with characteristics that are typical of the
adolescent period, a certain degree of rebelliousness, adherence to
views different from that of their parents, shifts in mood, a wish to
experiment with relationships, with ideas, even temporarily with
drugs. All of this is part of growing up. The life-style of the
mansonites was not due to their striving towards maturity but to
their determination to hold on to childhood.

236

To be sure, in part the mansonites' behavior was facilitated by the negative aspects of the sixties. Their narcissism, for example, matched that of many others at that time. It seems as though narcissism as a cultural manifestation was invented in America during the sixties when for the first time such a trait came out into the open, acted out by large segments of our until then puritanical society. Self-indulgence, self-adoration, the constant pursuit of pleasurable sensations were encouraged by highly visible and audible groups. The culture of decadence in which narcissism flourished had been for centuries the ambiance of aristocrats of older nations but it had never before penetrated American society.

Sexual experimentation, and most of all its public (glamorous) disclosure, was another novelty of the sixties. People who experiment or enjoy only unusual sexual modalities, from group sex to sadomasochism, have always existed. For a number of them their sexuality is not an obsession, not their central concern; they function well and have other interests. Most of these people keep their sex life behind closed doors. But during the sixties the whole spectrum of sexual expression was made an open matter by those whose life revolved around their sexuality. The much-publicized sexual activities of the mansonites (they were eager to disclose their sex life to anyone who would hear them) were an important aspect of the Family's life. These rigidly stereotyped males and females were not only occupied with sex, but preoccupied by it. For them sex was a way to live on a wave of sensations—or to pretend they did—and to reassure themselves by dramatic orgasms and showy erections that they were superfemales and supermales.

The narcissism and the marked self-indulgence characteristic of the sixties are still with us as we enter the eighties. And so are the problems that a segment of the young pose to society. Because of this we frequently hear pronouncements today to the effect that we should revert to the past, to the time before the sixties that is, if we are to remediate the moral ills of our society. I think it is useless to try to compare human behavior at different periods because history does not repeat itself. Human life occurs within such a complex network, the variables are so numerous and so intricate that to ascertain whether one period was better or worse than another is an impossible task. One thing we all know: Jeremiahs about the state of the world may give some people relief but solve nothing. But we can and must aim at having a clearer, more specific understanding of the problems we face and try to resolve some of them and minimize the impact of others. To do so we must accept the fact that human problems are not the abstractions that we are led to believe they are by bureaucrats and by some social scientists. And we must get to the task. To expect that a shining white knight will appear on the horizon and resolve our present problems (as they are now) will only perpetuate the conditions we are complaining about.

I want to address myself here to two areas that concern us all and that were interrelated in the case of the mansonites: criminal behavior and "followers'" behavior even when it is not criminal.

Today people are disturbed about the extent to which charismatic leaders attract young followers to their esoteric or deviant movements. We hear a great deal about how we should instruct our young to be less naive, to avoid becoming the victims of those who could snap their minds with carefully packaged speeches and incantations. Followers have the sympathy and support of public opinion to a lesser or greater degree and are often considered to be the victims of the leaders they follow. The Nazis are an exception although in fact we know a great deal more about Hitler than we do about his followers. Other than in the case of political terrorists, followers are regarded as meek or basically insecure individuals who feel like outcasts and yet have a strong need to belong, to be accepted, and for these reasons they elicit sympathy. But, I ask, where do some of these followers want to belong, by whom do they want to be accepted?

To answer these questions we must cease to focus our entire interest on the leaders and start learning more about those who are so eager to become part of the entourage of devious or sick leaders. Only when we do this will we be able to answer a rather important question: What can we do to produce fewer of these followers?

Concerning criminal behavior and particularly that of young offenders who commit serious crimes, we seem to know next to nothing about how to reach them and do an effective job before they break the law or how to rehabilitate them after they do. People seem resigned to the idea that part of the youthful population will become

238

that "horde of barbarians" and there seems to be little interest in trying to answer some very urgent questions, such as how can we bring up children so that fewer will become criminals? Are we to struggle to preserve our pure water and our clean air but continue to pollute the world with destructive people?

I am well aware that it is not easy to answer these questions. Furthermore we are getting weary of answers that are "simple, neat and wrong." People, even when a problem touches them because it is one of their children who committed a crime, have a tendency to abide by generalizations and to find reasons that explain nothing or find culprits somewhere else, outside their own lives, for fear that otherwise they may have to find fault with themselves. The leader-mania of today is just one example of the massive denial of where problems really lie. People concerned about cults have become more interested in deprogramming than in the healthy aspects of "programming" their children so they can evolve their own blueprint for a rewarding life.

When people are shocked by sensational crimes there always follows a flurry of talk about the possible causes that motivate the criminals, and everybody wonders about what can be done to decrease violence. Not about what can we do to create fewer violent individuals. Most people, even the psychologically sophisticated, probably take more time in planning the purchase of a home than in planning the parenting of their children. But since obviously people-problems are human problems, we must look at families if we are to learn about them and about how to resolve them because families produce people. And some families pollute society with their debris and fill their own existence with sorrow and shame.

We know that our jails and prisons are mostly occupied by the poor. It is obvious that the highly disadvantaged are vulnerable because of the handicaps that are their lot. Bureaucratic attempts to deal with the troubled children of the poor have failed, yet we continue to ship these children to foster homes or to institutions or else we leave them unprotected, living in families that have severe deficits. For all practical purposes the families of the poor are invisible. We hear of their problems, disorganization, neglect of children and other mi-nuses but never of attempts to compensate for these serious deficiencies. But these families exist and these children may be better off if, with appropriate help, they can remain where they belong; these families must be studied with an eye to helping them keep and raise their children. Some of the mothers are, we must accept, children themselves. They may require a great deal of attention before they can be ready to assume their role; or they may have to be supervised by a network of people who can act as a healthy "family" network. To elaborate more about how to accomplish this would require another book. But it can be done. The financial cost would be high but far less than what it is now.

I don't want to imply that we know much about the family dynamics of the offender of middle-class background. In fact we know next to nothing except that he is much less deprived socially than his poor counterpart.

We must also keep in mind that the Family transactions that encourage antisocial behavior may be different in different families; they may so affect one or more individuals because of dissimilar circumstances and problems. For example, a person who is not conforming to the law may be a member of a family burdened by severe economic and social deficits and his behavior may be clearly related to these deficits. An equally deprived family may have individuals whose continuous social maladjustment, although worsened by their conditions, may be primarily due to other intrafamilial conflicts. A middle-class family that appears stable to an outsider may be abysmally disorganized in many important areas such as decision making, the ability to provide consistent nurturance and discipline, the style of coping with strains that specifically affect them; incest and other forms of sexual acting out may be contained within that family. Emotional absenteeism from parents can be present in families of all social levels.

It is important to study the families of criminals to obtain other than the usual evaluations of how these families affect their children. By this I mean that what the public learns about how parents influence children are usually worthless generalizations: for example, that divorce affects the children or that it doesn't; or that it is terrible to have a working mother unless it is wonderful! We should aim at getting something more than a resounding "maybe" for an

240

answer. To do this we must first evolve the kind of questions that would provide answers geared to action, answers that can help parents and parent surrogates to perceive danger signals and to modify their strategies accordingly.

A barrage of information about child rearing reaches the public continuously. And most of that information is valuable. Or should be if people would become educated, not just passively informed. To be educated one needs information, but one also needs to acquire the ability to put facts in perspective, to look into oneself as an active participant who can think of information as applied to himself and his or theirs (the parents') life situation. It is not enough for a parent to decide "what's good" for his children. Certainly the parents of the female mansonites provided them with care, saw to it that they attended school and participated in extracurricular activities, attended to their health, gave them religious training. In my discussion of each woman I elaborated on what I perceived were the trouble spots in their families. The mansonites are an extreme case but it is not surprising that many people were demoralized when they learned that these middle-class young women had turned into sinister criminals. When all is said and done, and much has, people today have no way to know why and how a person becomes antisocial and destructive other than in the case of people who grow up in grossly adverse circumstances.

We know that those who opt for a life of crime are irresponsible and immature no matter how careful they may be in planning their criminal actions (I am not talking here about the big crime entrepreneur, who of course is a different breed altogether). It is about time that people reevaluate the way in which they think about children to prevent these traits from developing in them. A child is not a container to be filled with care, information, confusion, conflicts. A child is an individual programmed naturally for growth; at each stage he has areas ready for mature functioning. But parenting is not a one-way street; it is a process in which parents and child have equal participation. At the start, however, the adults define the quality of this process by the way they are, by their own emotional maturity. Parents who understand at what level their child is and who focus on his already achieved masteries and encourage his further maturation

241

and independence promote emotional growth. Those for whom the word "child" immediately evokes—in the case of their child—an image of helplessness should question their feelings and their ideas. Furthermore people who are unhappy with themselves, highly dissatisfied with their marriages, should be alert to the possibility that their problems may contaminate the way in which they relate to their children.

It shouldn't be a utopian reverie to expect the people of today to attain better control of their lives and to attempt not to pass on the results of their conflicts to their children. People may not be able to resolve their own problems and yet they could by a deliberate effort bring up their children as "separate" individuals. Many parents who were abused children are doing it today.

Endless ruminations about what's wrong with human nature, how anyhow we have no control over our young who more and more are being badly influenced by others and by society, are futile and destructive. All prophecies of doom are.

We are beset by the problems of violence and we have become concerned about women's criminality. It is all well and good to keep creating programs to rehabilitate offenders and to fight for prison reform. As yet we don't seem to know much about rehabilitation, what works or what doesn't, what is just a waste of time and taxpayers' money. Why not put time and money in trying to find out why so many keep coming into prisons? What have we gained by repeating that they came from poverty, from institutions, from troubled families, "troubled" used as a generalization that covers everything and clarifies nothing?

In researching this book I became aware of how difficult it is to obtain information about convicted felons and about how the Privacy Act can be manipulated. Anyone can write about a public figure who has never committed a crime and reveal things about that person that he never intended to make public. A criminal can produce his own self-serving version of his life and of his crimes for public consumption, and he can choose those who support him to relay information about him and refuse to talk with impartial interviewers. I find it unacceptable that those convicted of serious crimes are entitled to total privacy or selective disclosure. And after they are convicted their relatives also should be persuaded to disclose certain facts that would be helpful for others to know.

If we are to understand criminal behavior and use that understanding to help others we must understand the transactions in their families. Even among the very poor many do not become criminals. What is the difference between those who in the same circumstances break the law and those who don't? Obviously the kind of data we are using is not productive. We explain nothing and gain nothing by saying of a defendant that he is a sociopath or mentally ill or alienated or a drug addict or that his father was an alcoholic or that his mother was overprotective or rejecting or both. Not because there might not be truth in these statements but because flat descriptions and labeling are of no help. And we have enough "information" coming from investigators who hide behind a collection of "facts" elegantly assembled in statistical tables and diagrams. Too many of these studies cannot be used by the public, which is bad enough, but cannot even be applied by professionals and only add to everybody's confusion in the name of the sacred cow, research.

Carefully done family studies can provide accurate and specific information if they are geared at illuminating specific areas, if they aim at providing the kind of understanding that can be used to educate people, to move public opinion into action. Anecdotal life stories, looked down on by behavioral scientists, are the richest source of information when they are obtained from a number of relatives. That these studies have to be retrospective does not detract from their value since not only the subject but others close to him can give data that can be systematically assembled. These types of studies can pose valid questions to evolve other studies in vulnerable populations and can give answers as to how these families of criminals function in different areas, to name a few; how and what they communicate to each other; whether they discourage emotional growth in each other or only in one member and why; whether they promote total submissiveness within the family but give conflicted messages about outsiders; whether they promote disregard for authority frankly or in veiled messages; whether they openly or in a disguised manner teach children the fine art of "putting one over" on others; how these families are structured as to power, coalitions, triangular entangle-

243

ments; how they "teach" their children sexual identity. And how and why some of the children of these families become persons who have a total disregard for human life.

Families can be investigated and at the same time protected from prying and from blaming. Furthermore, studying the family dynamics of a felon need not jeopardize his legal situation. For example, the fact that he was emotionally entangled with a parent, or knowledge of how specifically his parents' marriage or other family relationships affected his emotional development can hardly influence an appeal or the decision to parole him. Relatives of people who commit serious crimes should be educated to cooperate in the manner that parents who abused or killed their children have been persuaded to do. They know something that we all need to know.

As I come to the end of this book I want to say that the legal profession, prison administrators, and mental health professionals have an obligation to address themselves to this issue, to make this type of investigation and education possible and available. We must insist on knowing the real stories behind criminal behavior.